Hombres y Machos

HOMBRES Y MACHOS

MASCULINITY AND LATINO CULTURE

ALFREDO MIRANDÉ
University of California at Riverside

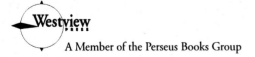
A Member of the Perseus Books Group

Unless otherwise noted, translations from the Spanish are by the author.

Copyright © 1997 by Westview Press, A Member of the Perseus Books Group

Published in 1997 in the United States of America by Westview Press, 5500 Central Avenue, Boulder, Colorado 80301-2877, and in the United Kingdom by Westview Press, 12 Hid's Copse Road, Cumnor Hill, Oxford OX2 9JJ

Library of Congress Cataloging-in-Publication Data
Mirandé, Alfredo.
   Hombres y machos : masculinity and Latino culture / Alfredo Mirandé.
      p.   cm.
   Includes bibliographical references and index.
   ISBN 0-8133-3196-X (hc.).—ISBN 0-8133-3197-8 (pbk.)
      1. Hispanic American men—Psychology.   2. Hispanic American men—
Social life and customs.   3. Masculinity (Psychology)—United
States.   4. Machismo—United States.   5. Sex role—United States.
I. Title.
E184.S75M59   1997
305.38'86073—dc21
                                                                                                    97-8980
                                                                                                        CIP

The paper used in this publication meets the requirements of the American National Standard for Permanence of Paper for Printed Library Materials Z39.48-1984.

PERSEUS
POD
ON DEMAND   10   9   8

To my Father,
Xavier Ándres Mirandé Salazar,
for giving the Mirandés a sense of
pride, dignity, and importance

Contents

List of Tables and Illustrations

Tables

Figures

Photographs

Acknowledgments

A number of people contributed directly and indirectly to the completion of this book. Special thanks to Enrique López for his substantive comments and his unwavering friendship and support. Gerald López has served as mentor, exemplar, and friend for many years. I would like to thank Jerry for believing in me and for always finding the time to listen. My former student and friend David López and my cousin Bill Neebe read the manuscript and provided valuable input.

Douglas Lyons and his wife, Stephanie Coleman-Lyons, deserve a very special thanks. Douglas read the entire manuscript and made excellent editorial suggestions. More importantly, Douglas pushed me to address the more difficult and sensitive issues and to make the manuscript more readily accessible to the general reader. Since our collaboration on *La Chicana*, Evangelina Enríquez has challenged many of my ideas about gender and masculinity and forced me to reevaluate my role as a man and a father.

Finally, *muchas gracias* to my family—*las tías*; Tía Margara; my paternal grandparents, Alfredo and Ana María Mirandé; and my mother, Rosa Maria Gonzáles Ochoa, for her intelligence, intuition, and insights. My sister Sylvia Léon and her son Carlos ("Carlitos") Ramírez read the manuscript and made important suggestions and corrections. Carlitos also accompanied me on a very special trip back to the old neighborhoods where I grew up, Tacuba and Tacubaya, and to *el árbol de la noche triste*. Even in the most difficult of times, my nephew Armando Mirandé has always been a source of encouragement and affection. Finally, and most importantly, I thank my children, Michele, Lucía, and Alejandro ("Mano"), for their love, loyalty, and inspiration. I hope that I have been successful in imparting some basic values and in transmitting part of our rich legacy as a family and a people.

Alfredo Mirandé

Introduction

Several years ago I was awarded a Rockefeller Foundation research fellow-ship to carry out a study of Latino men and the role of the father in the fam-ily. I took a leave of absence from my job at the University of California at Riverside and was in residence as a post-doctoral fellow at Stanford Univer-sity. I was a professor of sociology and ethnic studies at the time and had written a number of books and articles on the Chicano experience and the Chicano family and gender. Indeed, one of the factors that led me to under-take this study was the experience of co-authoring a book about Mexican women in the United States with Evangelina Enríquez.

La Chicana proved to be very successful and we each took a great deal of pride and satisfaction in the product; it was like a child that resulted from a dynamic, volatile, and incredibly stimulating relationship.[1] When we undertook the project we were certainly not prepared psychologically for the daily conflict and tension that would ensue. We noted in the preface to the book that while the Aztec codices detail a neat division in the social order and in the roles of men and women, they do not provide a prescrip-tion for harmony between the sexes (Mirandé and Enríquez 1981, ix).

> There was never any question at the outset of this endeavor that we had an inherent respect for our undertaking and for each other; but, alas, we had failed to anticipate the tension and lack of harmony that could arise when two modern-day members of the opposite sex decide to undertake a book together about one sex (1981, iv–v).

To say that there was "a lack of harmony" is undoubtedly understated. The truth is that we fought constantly about the book. Our relationship became a microcosm of the larger societal issues and tensions that we were describ-ing, a story within a story.[2]

While working on La Chicana, I learned many important lessons. But by far the most important lesson I learned was that as a man I was obviously limited in my ability to understand the Chicana experience. When I used the word chingar or chingada, for example, I was only able to do so in a some-what clinical and detached way without fully understanding its symbolism for women. Though Evangelina and I agreed that the verb chingar was an

1

important one for Mexicans, we responded differently to the word. I was fascinated by the word because it contained numerous and diverse meanings, but it was not a term that I found personally offensive or repugnant. *Chingar* is an aggressive form of sexual intercourse with numerous connotations of power. A man might say, for example, *"me chingaron!"*, meaning I was "fucked over," "screwed," or "had"; or he might say with admiration that someone was *chingón* or *chingona*, meaning they were important or had power. In Mexican folklore *La Chingada* was the "Great Whore," our symbolic mother who represented the thousands of Indian women who were raped, violated, and otherwise demeaned by the conquering Spaniards.[3]

I learned that for Evangelina and other women these words were powerful cultural metaphors that elicited very negative images of women as abject, passive, inert creatures—indeed, as passive objects of male sexuality. For women, the imagery was so powerful that in every instance in which a man was controlled or subjugated, he metaphorically assumed the female, passive role. But I also learned that, if one looked more closely, it appeared that many of the prevailing stereotypes about *la mujer* had their counterparts in stereotypes about Latino men. If the woman was not the weak, passive, self-sacrificing, abject figure that we had been led to believe she was, then perhaps the man was not the all-powerful and unquestioned lord and master of the household, as he is often depicted in traditional social science literature and popular conceptions. In a very real sense, in rejecting stereotypes about Chicanas we were beginning to reject stereotypes about men, or at a minimum, to entertain the possibility that Chicano men might also be stereotyped not only by the dominant society but by ourselves. Finally, I learned that because of my academic and personal experiences I might have some special insights into the topic of Chicano/Latino men.

As I began to write about Latino men and masculinity, I realized that my interest in the topic was obviously both academic and personal. I was a man, after all, a father and a *mexicano*, and since childhood I had been taught, largely by women, how to be "a man." I was taught how a man acts or should act in various situations. I was also exposed to a wide range and variety of images of masculinity and manhood (and womanhood), images that were at once complex, subtle, and often contradictory.

My formative years were spent in México City in the *colonia* of Tacuba, near *el árbol de la noche triste* (the tree of the night of sorrows), the tree where Hernán Cortés reputedly wept after his forces were soundly routed by the Aztecs. The "tree" was this large and famous *árbol*, which over centuries had been bent by the force of its own weight and was now almost parallel to the ground. *El árbol* was located about four blocks from my house in a plaza outside of the church that we attended on Sundays. As a child I didn't really understand why such a big deal was made about the old tree, but it was very much a part of my daily existence.

We lived as an extended unit with my mother's family, *los* González-Ochoa, a family that originated in the village of Sayula, a historic community in the state of Jalisco. We lived in three rented houses on the same lot. Inside the large iron gate, a gate that was normally open during the day, the first house on the right was occupied by my mother's oldest brother, Tío Roberto, his wife Adriana, and their two children, Chema (José María) and Macaco (Manuel). The second house was occupied by my mother's oldest sister, Tía Márgara, her husband Ricardo, and my two cousins, Pete (Mercedes) and Chayo (Rosario). I lived in the last of the houses, *"el tres,"* a modest two-bedroom house, with my parents, Xavier and Rosa María, and my older brothers, Alex (Alejandro Rovier[4]) and Gordo (Hector Xavier).

One of the things that I remember most about my *tíos* is that they were sort of *matones* (tough guys), burly, pot-bellied men who smoked, swore, drank tequila, carried weapons, and were not averse to using them, much like the Mexican bad guys in films like *El Mariachi* and *Desperado*. Tío Ricardo was a general in the Mexican army, *El Ejército Nacional*. He was usually in uniform, and usually carried his military pistol. Roberto was in the business of selling tequila and sometimes packed a gun and carried a shoulder holster. Another *tío*, Carlos, lived in Puebla and was married to my mother's sister, María Luisa. Tío Carlos was also a military man. He had been in the Mexican Revolution and had reputedly executed hundreds of men, during and after the revolution, executions that were both formal and informal. It was said that Tío Carlos always slept with one eye open and with a pistol next to the bed. My father was never in the military and never carried a weapon. He was athletic and strong and did not smoke, drink, or swear.

Our extended family and neighborhood was like a small community. One of the most vivid memories that I have of Tacuba occurred when I was around six years old. It was in the afternoon. There was a lot of commotion as the whole neighborhood gathered around Tío Roberto's house. We could hear yelling, screaming, and swearing. Roberto was drunk and beating Tía Adriana. I recall how my father jumped over the back fence and stopped the beating. Because it was unusual for one household to intervene in the private affairs of another and because we could sense the danger, it was a very dramatic moment as we watched my drunken uncle coming after my father. He would hit and jab Roberto and then deftly circle around him, intending more to dissuade him than to hurt him. As my uncle's face bloodied and it became clear that my father was getting the better of the encounter, Roberto ran into the house and emerged from the kitchen with a butcher knife. My father continued to dance and jab with Roberto pursuing, but he looked frightened as Roberto came after him with the menacing knife. What happened at this point was incredible. My mother had somehow entered the

Xavier Mirandé and his three sons. México City. Left to right: Héctor Xavier (Gordo), Alfredo (Bebo), Alejandro (Alex).

yard and stepped between her husband and older brother. She proceeded to belittle Roberto, asking:

> How can you call yourself a man if you go around beating up defenseless women? What kind of a man needs a knife to fight an unarmed man? Put down the knife and let's see what kind of a man you really are.[5]

Shamed by my mother's intervention, Roberto put down the knife and went inside the house. I didn't see Tío Roberto for several days but I believed that he was profoundly humiliated by the incident.

I will not dwell on the implications of this incident except to say that in retrospect it must have had a profound effect on my masculine development and my notions of what was considered good and bad behavior in a man— and in a woman. I learned early, for example, that one of the worst or lowest things that a man could do is to hit a woman. I learned that it is important and honorable to stick up for and defend people who are wronged, abused, or treated unjustly. Finally, I learned from this incident that strength of character and valor are not gendered qualities. I could not have imagined my father hitting my mother, not only because he did not believe in hitting women, but because she wouldn't have tolerated such treatment.

The Study

Though I present findings from a study of Latino men, based on in-depth personal interviews with men, in the end the book probably reveals as much about me and my biography as it does about the men that I studied. On the surface at least, the reason that I undertook this study is that precious little research has been conducted on Latino men and masculinity and even less quality research. Though much has been said and written about machismo or "excessive masculinity" among Latinos in general and Mexicans in particular, until recently such generalizations were based on meager, nonexistent, and misinterpreted evidence.

At a deeper and more personal level, I believe that I undertook this study because I was dissatisfied with the images of Latino men and masculinity that prevailed not only in the social science literature but also in the society at large. I felt that these images were used to perpetuate negative conceptions of Mexicans and to legitimate our economic and political subordination. Until recently much of the literature on machismo and on the Mexican family was based either on anthropological field studies carried out by outsiders who lacked a basic understanding of the nuance and complexity of Mexican and Latino cultures or on small, clinical samples of psychiatric patients. Whether ethnographic or clinical, such studies were carried out by culturally insensitive and linguistically limited outsiders who saw machismo and Latino masculinity as pathological manifestations of societal and familial dysfunction and essentially as indices of sickness or disease. Because much of this early research used dominant societal values as the yardstick for evaluating Chicano/Latino culture and gender, Mexican culture and Mexican people were rendered "defective" and were free to vary only in the degree of pathology they showed.

My overriding goal then was to undertake a study of Latino men that did not begin with the premise that Latino culture and Latino masculinity were inherently negative or pathological. A related goal was to look at Latino men in a way that reflected the richness and complexity of Latino masculinities—a study, in other words, that would incorporate men who were as different and diverse as my father and uncles. A third goal was to articulate an insider's perspective that would reflect the images that Latino men themselves have of machismo, masculinity, and fatherhood. I felt it was very important to learn more about how Latino men see their roles as fathers, as husbands, and as men and the qualities or attributes that they most respect and admire in men in general and in husbands and fathers.

In reporting, analyzing, and interpreting the findings, I have sought to place them within a meaningful historical and theoretical context. Because conventional studies of Mexican and Latino men have been carried out by outsiders who often did not contextualize the phenomenon they were studying, looking at the world through the insider's voice is necessary in order to understand their experience. Is machismo a uniquely Latino and specifically Mexican cultural trait and value system, as was suggested by the traditional literature? Or is it synonymous with male dominance and patriarchy, which are more universal phenomena? Do all Latino men subscribe to the ethic of "hypermasculinity," or are there different types and varieties of masculinities? Is there a difference between being "macho" and being "machista"? Are there social class and regional differences in the expression of manhood and masculinity?

An Overview

Rather than uncritically accepting the existence of the "masculine cult" or assuming that the Latino male is the unquestioned "lord and master" of the household, I hope to examine and reevaluate the male role in *la familia* and *cultura*. The first chapter presents an overview of research on Latino men, some background on the Bem and Mirandé scales, and a theoretical and biographical context for the study. Chapter 2 is a historical overview of Latino men and masculinity. My intent is not to provide a history of Latino men but to place contemporary images and issues within a larger historical context. Three different, though overlapping, explanations of the origin of the so-called cult of masculinity are isolated and discussed. I also examine relevant historical circumstances that might enhance our understanding of contemporary manifestations of masculinity and manhood.

In the middle chapters (3, 4, and 5), I summarize the major findings of the study. Chapter 3 looks at how Latino men themselves perceive the words "macho" and "machismo." Two prevailing conceptions of machismo emerge from the data that roughly correspond with the traditional or compensatory view and a new, emergent revisionist perspective. Chapter 4 provides a systematic analysis and comparison of the Bem (BSRI) and Mirandé (MSRI) sex role inventories. In Chapter 5 an in-depth analysis of regional, occupational, income, and language usage differences in the BSRI and the MSRI is presented. The chapter also includes responses to open-ended questions pertaining to perceptions of masculinity and the father role. In Chapter 6 I offer a critique and synthesis of an emerging field, the new men's studies, and call for the development of a profeminist Chicano/Latino men's studies. The epilogue attempts to summarize and integrate the major findings of the study and to critically assess prevailing conceptions of men and masculinity in Latino culture.

1

Latino Men and Masculinity: An Overview

Perhaps the most fundamental question that cuts across the various chapters of this book is whether prevailing academic and popular conceptions of masculinity and femininity are adequate for understanding the Mexican/Latino experience. In much of the social science literature the world is typically divided into masculine and feminine spheres that correspond with superordinate and subordinate elements in society. According to this view, the masculine sphere is ambitious, assertive, rational, analytical, individualistic, competitive, dominant, and aggressive, whereas the feminine is warm, affectionate, emotional, understanding, cooperative, compassionate, sympathetic, loyal, and affectionate. I critically examine these conceptions of gender and suggest that they are inadequate explanations of Mexican/Latino masculinity.

This chapter presents the parable, or simple story with a message, to illustrate how masculinity and femininity have traditionally been defined in the social sciences and in law. After discussing the parable of "Amy and Jake," two eleven-year-old sixth graders who exhibit very different conceptions of morality and different analytical reasoning skills, the parable of "economic man and literary woman" in law and economics, and the parable of the "reasonable man and the Mexican" in law, I conclude that rather than being universal, these constructs reflect a very limited and culturally specific conception of masculinity.

The Parable of Amy and Jake

In 1982 Carol Gilligan published *In a Different Voice*. The book proved to be extremely influential and provided the theoretical underpinnings for much feminist gender role theory in psychology, sociology, and law. Gilligan began with the basic premise that there is research that supports the position that there are essential differences in the worldviews and moral reasoning capacities of men and women. Men, she argued, are more analytical, concrete, and have a preference for detached, objective, and rational reasoning, whereas women are less analytical, more subjective, more connected to others, and more contextual in their reasoning abilities. Gilligan was not suggesting that one gender is superior, merely that there are essential differences between men and women in analytical reasoning and moral judgment capacities. In addition, Gilligan argued that our educational system and society at large place a greater premium on the analytical and reasoning skills that men are more apt to exhibit. Rather than seeing these gender-specific characteristics as different and complementary views of morality, however, psychology has traditionally defined them as hierarchical stages of development, with men exhibiting a higher level of moral development (Gilligan 1982, 33).

Gilligan used the parable of Amy and Jake to illustrate gender-based differences in moral development. Amy and Jake are both eleven-year-old sixth graders who come from very similar educational and social class backgrounds. They are both intelligent and defy traditional sex role stereotyping, given that Amy is interested in becoming a scientist, while Jake prefers English to math (1982, 25). In the experiment subjects are asked to resolve a hypothetical moral dilemma in which a man ("Heinz") must decide whether to steal a drug that he cannot afford to buy in order to save his wife's life.

From the outset Jake concludes that Heinz should steal the drug. Using logical reasoning, Jake sees the moral dilemma very much like a math problem involving humans and proceeds to derive a logical solution (1982, 26). Stealing is a logically rationalized course of action for Jake because saving a human life is clearly worth more than money and because a human life is irreplaceable, whereas money is not (1982, 26). Jake takes law into account but sees the law as "man-made and therefore subject to error and change" (1982, 26). Jake, moreover, assumes that there is a societal consensus about these moral values that enables one to recognize "right from wrong" (1982, 26). Because of this consensus, the judge would likely see Heinz's actions as morally justified.

According to Gilligan, Jake's "ability to bring deductive logic to bear on the solution of moral dilemmas, to differentiate morality from law, and to see how laws can be considered to have mistakes, points toward the principled conception of justice" that is equated by psychologists with social maturity (1982, 26).

But the same traditional "developmental theory" that exonerates Jake sees Amy as exhibiting a "stunted" or arrested level of development because she demonstrates a failure to use logic and to "think for herself" (1982, 26–27). Amy thinks through the problem and appears uncertain and unsure as to whether Heinz should steal the drug. She pauses to consider other possibilities. Rather than stealing, Heinz could borrow the money or perhaps even talk to the druggist about the problem. For Amy this is ultimately a human problem, not a math or logic problem, and in trying to resolve the moral dilemma, she focuses on relationships and the social context.

Just as Jake is confident the judge would agree that stealing is the right thing for Heinz to do, so too is Amy confident that "if Heinz and the druggist had talked it out long enough, they could reach something besides stealing." Just as he considers the law to "have mistakes," so she sees this drama as a mistake, believing that "the world should just share things more and then people wouldn't have to steal" (1982, 29).

Both Jake and Amy are aware of the need for consensus but each views it as mediated in different ways. For Jake law is mediated impersonally and formally through systems of logic and law; for Amy law is mediated through human communication and personal relationships (1982, 29). Placing the parable of Amy and Jake in a broader societal and historical context, Gilligan concluded that for centuries the voices of women have been muted by the voices of men, which have been presented as a universal voice. The muting of women's voices has occurred not only within developmental psychology but also within society as a whole.

> As we have listened for centuries to the voices of men and the theories of development that their experience informs, so we have come more recently to notice not only the silence of women but the difficulty in hearing what they say when they speak. Yet in the different voice of women lies the truth of an ethic of care, the tie between relationship and responsibility, and the origins of aggression in the failure of connection. The failure to see the different reality of women's lives and to hear the differences in their voices stems in part from the assumption that there is a single mode of social experience and interpretation. (1982, 173–174)

In law the application of different voice theory would lead to greater emphasis on context and on relationships and to less emphasis on individual independence and autonomy. Women would provide an alternative morality that would emphasize broad standards over narrow rules, long-term relationships over short-term contracts, and mediation over dispute resolution.

The Parable of Economic Man and Literary Woman

One of the most direct extensions of Gilligan's *In a Different Voice* is Robin West's discussion of "economic man" and "literary woman." West proposes "literary woman" as a counterpart to the prototypical "economic man" found in the law and economics movement. Economic man is characterized by two basic attributes that clearly differentiate him from literary woman. First, as depicted in modern legal economics, economic man is "an infallible 'rational maximizer' of his own utility" (West 1989, 868). A basic assumption of law and economics, for example, is that "people are rational maximizers of their satisfactions" (1989, 868, note 3).[1] Second, economic man is characterized by what West terms "empathic impotence" (1989, 869). Although economic man is perfectly rational with regard to his own needs and subjective well-being, he lacks empathetic knowledge of the well-being of others. In other words, he is incapable of making what economists term "intersubjective comparisons of utility" (1989, 869). Economic man is thus "both peculiarly capable and peculiarly disabled: he ostensibly knows everything there is to know about his own subjective life, and nothing whatsoever about the subjective lives of others" (1989, 869). individualistic

Literary woman is presented by West as a corrective for economic man. Though literary woman is capable of rational action, she lacks the "Herculean rationalism" of economic man. Unlike economic man, she is capable of empathizing with the pains and pleasures of others and engaging in what economists term "interpersonal comparisons of utility." West rejects the view that economic man is motivationally unidimensional and suggests that people are "dual motivational" and capable of pursuing egoistic and/or altruistic motives.

Rather than being dual dimensional, literary woman is, in fact, multidimensional and multimotivational, according to West. Drawing on the law and literature movement, she proposes that although intersubjective comparisons and empathetic understanding are sometimes difficult to attain, literature can assist us in achieving the moral promise of transcending our own subjective condition. It is difficult to understand or empathize with someone whose life experiences are radically different from our own; for example, it is difficult for the heterosexual to understand what it is like to be gay or for a white person to understand the experiences of a Black person (1989, 873). Although it may be difficult to transcend our own experience and to know and empathize with the experience of others, "narrative literature, when it is good, is the bridge that facilitates empathetic understanding. . . . Metaphor and narrative are the means by which we come to understand what was initially foreign" (1989, 874). Narrative thus enables us to overcome the limitations of economic man, to transcend our own reality and make "intersubjective comparisons of utility" and pain.

The Parable of the Reasonable Man and the Mexican

The idea of the "reasonable man" in law is parallel to the construct of economic man in law and economics. Since this is a book about masculinity and not law, I will not dwell much on the reasonable man. However, as it is perhaps the single most important construct in law and jurisprudence, I will attempt to show how this theory or concept informs our discussion of masculinity. The "reasonable man" is a standard used to evaluate all conduct, ranging from whether specific acts are judged to be negligent in a civil action to whether the police acted reasonably in using force to subdue a suspect or in initiating a search of someone's property or person. Interestingly, "reasonableness" is not an empirical standard. It does not refer to how the average man acts or even to how most of us would have behaved in a particular situation. Rather, it is a moral construct that assesses how a person "should have acted." The reasonable man is not driven by passion or emotion but by logic and reason. He is not impulsive or irrational but analytical, cool, detached, and calculating, and always, always reasonable. In the context of masculinity, what is significant about Gilligan's Jake, West's economic man, and the construct of the reasonable man in law is that each is used to transform a very limited and culturally specific conception of masculinity into either a universal standard or into a higher order of moral development.

When I entered Stanford Law School several years ago, I was immediately troubled by the elusive idea of the "reasonable man." Though I was not certain that I fully understood the concept, two things struck me as problematic about the reasonable man. First, it didn't take long for me to realize that whatever the reasonable man was, he was definitely not Mexican. No one in my family or community acted reasonably, it seemed. My father, in particular, seemed to me to be the paragon of unreasonableness and arbitrariness. Certainly no reasonable person would have felt a duty to jump the fence to confront my drunken uncle. In fact, in Anglo-American law there is no duty to help someone in peril or distress, but once assistance is rendered or attempted, a legal duty is created. Second, in reflecting on the reasonable man and on Jake and Amy and in observing law students at a fancy law school, it seemed to me that many of the white women acted a lot more like Jake than Amy. Can we assume that the parable of Amy and Jake is applicable to Latinos? Are María and Juan the same as Amy and Jake? Intuitively, the Amy and Jake distinction appeared to be an Anglo distinction, one based more on race and class than on gender. If masculinity was defined as being cold, analytical, rational, and dispassionate and femininity as being warm, impulsive, emotional, and passionate, Latino men, it seemed, were essentially more feminine than masculine.

My recollection of my father is that he was much warmer, emotional, and affectionate than my mother. I don't mean to suggest that my mother was not nurturing, but my father was more overtly emotional and demonstrative in his affection. He would always hug us and kiss us. When I was a child, *Pa* and I would play a game together. He would roll on the floor or the bed with me, saying, "*Dame una manzana*" (give me an apple), then, "*Dame una pera*" (give me a pear), then, "*Dame un platano*" (give me a banana). As I turned and screamed with laughter, trying to get away, he would persist and alternately bite one of my cheeks (apple/pear) or my nose (banana). He would bite pretty hard and my cheeks would be all red, but it was one of his ways of showing affection.

The Bem Sex Role Inventory

Using a conceptual framework that is consistent with the dichotomous view of sex roles found in the parable of Amy and Jake, psychologist Sandra Bem (1974) developed the Bem Sex Role Inventory, or BSRI, a scale designed to measure masculine and feminine traits. Each item on the BSRI is scored on a seven-point scale of 1 ("never or almost never true") to 7 ("always or almost always true"). There are sixty items on the scale: twenty masculine, twenty feminine, and twenty so-called neutral or non-gendered items. Bem computed an "androgyny" measure based on the difference between a person's masculine and feminine score. The less the difference between the masculine and the feminine components, irrespective of the score, the more androgynous a person is presumed to be. A highly androgynous person would be one who scores about the same on either the masculine or feminine components, whereas a non-androgynous person would score high on one and low on the other. The masculine and feminine items are listed in Table 1.1 (Bem 1974, 156).

Although the BSRI is widely used, I initially considered not using it because the instrument has not been proven to be applicable to Latinos and because it seemed to lack validity. I felt that masculinity was defined differently and more contextually in Latino culture. By this I mean that I believe masculinity is a more fluid, nuanced, and idealized response to various social situations, whereas Bem sees masculinity and femininity as personal character traits, attributes that are fixed across time and social context. In the end, however, rather than rejecting the Bem scale a priori, I opted to include the BSRI to see how Latino men would respond, to examine internal differences on an established measure of masculinity and femininity, and to compare this instrument to one that I developed, one that I felt was a more culturally sensitive measure.

In this study I introduce a measure of masculinity, the Mirandé Sex Role Inventory (MSRI), one that I believe is not only more consistent with my own experience but also with the nuance and complexity of Mexican/Latino cultures. The MSRI is derived from fifty items that were culled from traditional Mexican and Latino cultural beliefs and values regarding the appropriateness and inappropriateness of various behaviors.[2] What is significant is that rather than having respondents rank themselves on various

TABLE 1.1   BSRI Masculinity and Femininity

Masculinity	Femininity
1. Ambitious	1. Warm
2. Aggressive	2. Tender
3. Has Leadership Abilities	3. Affectionate
4. Dominant	4. Compassionate
5. Individualistic	5. Sympathetic
6. Competitive	6. Loyal
7. Acts as Leader	7. Understanding
8. Willing to Take a Stand	8. Eager to Soothe Hurt Feelings
9. Strong Personality	9. Cheerful
10. Makes Decisions Easily	10. Does Not Use Harsh Language
11. Assertive	11. Feminine
12. Willing to Take Risks	12. Sensitive to Needs of Others
13. Independent	13. Loves Children
14. Self-Sufficient	14. Flatterable
15. Defends Own Beliefs	15. Childlike
16. Self-Reliant	16. Gullible
17. Athletic	17. Gentle
18. Analytical	18. Shy
19. Masculine	19. Soft-Spoken
20. Forceful	20. Yielding

psychological traits—such as being "assertive," "strong," "aggressive," "affectionate," "loving," or "warm"—the MSRI asks respondents to assess the appropriateness of certain behaviors for men and women in various social situations and contexts. For example, one item asks respondents whether they agreed or disagreed with the notion that "the worst thing that a woman can do to a man is to embarrass or contradict him in front of his friends." Some agreed, but others disagreed and noted that this was not "the worst thing" that a woman could do to a man.

The MSRI includes both "traditional" and "nontraditional" items and provides four possible responses: "strongly agree," "agree," "disagree," and "strongly disagree." Traditional items include statements such as "One should always defend the family honor, even if it means death," and "A man should never back down from a fight," whereas examples of nontraditional or antitraditional statements include "A real woman does not need to be dependent on a man" and "It is natural for a woman to 'fool around' after marriage."

Social scientists worry that respondents might begin to answer questions automatically or give a "canned" response. One way to try to avoid such a bias, or "response set," is to vary the questions. This will ensure that the person does not fall into a particular rhythm and begin to give automatic, unreflective responses, essentially entering an "agree" or "disagree" response irrespective of the content of the question. Varying the type of question helps to avoid the response set. On the Bem Scale, for example, masculine and feminine items were interspersed. Traditional and nontraditional statements on the MSRI were also mixed and the wording of some items reversed. For example, with regard to whether it is appropriate for men to show emotion, one item states that "Men should never cry or show their feelings" and another that "A father should not kiss or be too emotional with his sons," but another counters that "It is good for a man to cry or show his emotions." To answer a question consistently with due consideration, then, the respondent would be forced to reverse the response by agreeing with one question and disagreeing with the other.

Research on Machismo and Mexican/Latino Masculinity

Prior to the emergence of revisionist scholarship in the 1970s, Chicano/Latino women and men were depicted in the social science literature as heirs to a cultural heritage that was ostensibly driven by machismo and an obsessive concern with masculinity and hierarchical gender relations. Both historical experience and cross-cultural accounts suggest that machismo and the so-called cult of masculinity may not be unique to Mexican or Latino men.

Some writers suggest that machismo and excessive displays of masculinity and male sexuality are found in all Mediterranean cultures (Brandes 1979, 10). David Gilmore notes that in a large number of societies throughout the world there is an ideology of masculinity and concern with the state of being a "real man" or "true man" (1990, 1).

Sociologist Scott Coltrane cautions against the tendency to universalize masculine displays, arguing that though societies that seek to affirm men's masculinity are more common, they are not universal. There are societies that are relatively unconcerned with gender demarcation and they exist in every major region of the world (Coltrane 1992, 88). Using coded ethnographic data from ninety-three nonindustrialized societies, Coltrane found that outward displays of male dominance are significantly related to patterns of child rearing and property control. Societies in which women control the use and distribution of property and men participate in child rearing are more apt to exhibit behavioral and normative equality between husbands and wives and much less likely to require that women show ritualized deference to men (1992, 163).

There is also evidence that "family stage migration," in which one member of the household, generally the man, migrates to blaze the trail for the rest of the family, may work to reduce patriarchal authority. Men who migrate without their families, after all, are usually forced to live with other men in modified communities in which they must assume many traditional feminine tasks and activities such as cooking and cleaning. In a case study of forty-four adult women and men in twenty-six families in a San Francisco Bay area community, Pierrette Hondagneu-Sotello found that lengthy spouse separation altered patriarchal authority and the traditional division of labor. Men who migrated prior to 1965 more often lived in predominantly male communities and had lived in the United States for a long period of time without their wives (1992, 393). In families that had experienced a lengthy separation, "an unorthodox, more egalitarian gender division of labor emerged when the families were reunited" (1992, 407).

But perhaps the most significant conclusion that can be drawn from recent research and writing is that Latino men do not constitute a homogeneous, monolithic, unvarying mass, as was depicted in the traditional model. This suggests that there is not one masculine mode but a variety of modalities and masculinities that are not only different, but often contradictory.

In a recent ethnographic study Matthew Gutmann (1994) found an enormous diversity of male identities among residents of Santo Domingo, a neighborhood on the outskirts of México City. Gutmann noted that generic terms such as "Mexican men" or "Latino men" mask important regional, class, age, and ethnic differences that exist throughout México, Latin America, and Spain (1994, 21). Gutmann used the behavior of young boys at the local nursery school in Santo Domingo to illustrate recent and dramatic changes in gender role expectations. Today most of the five-year-old boys cheerfully participate in a game called *"el baño de la muñeca"* (the doll bath), whereas a decade earlier most of the boys in Santo Domingo would have protested, "Only *viejas* [women] do that!" (1994, 21).

The most prevalent explanation offered by residents of *Colonia* Santo Domingo for men assuming greater responsibility for various household duties was *"por necesidad,"* or by necessity (1994, 23). After the 1982 economic crisis it was necessary for a large number of women to enter the labor force, requiring men to assume some of the tasks that were traditionally performed by women alone. Generally, it was the women who first changed; they then pressured their husbands to change and to assume more responsibility for household tasks (1994, 23).

In the United States studies of decisionmaking and the division of household tasks among husbands and wives have also begun to challenge traditional and stereotypical conceptions of the Chicano family (see Hawkes and Taylor 1975; Cromwell and Cromwell 1978; Ybarra 1982; Zavella 1987; Baca Zinn 1989). Though the ideology of patriarchy persists and women continue to assume primary responsibility for most household tasks, decisionmaking is generally egalitarian and men are beginning to assume a number of traditionally female household tasks such as ironing, cooking, dishwashing, and housecleaning.

Scott Coltrane and Elsa Valdez conclude that recent research on Chicano families supports the view that gender relations are more egalitarian than was assumed by the traditional model (1993, 153). Their study of dual earner couples found considerable sharing in a number of areas. Though couples described their relationships as being fairly egalitarian, the relative earning power of each spouse was significantly related to the allocation of household tasks. In those families in which the wife earned less than a third of the family income, the husband assumed few of the household or child-rearing tasks (1993, 169–170), but among couples "sharing significant amounts of housework and child care, a preponderance had relatively balanced incomes" (1993, 170).

"Insiders" and "Outsiders": Issues in Studying Latino Men

Though my postdoctoral fellowship provided a modest stipend and a limited budget for research costs incurred during the study, there was no funding for interviewers. I personally conducted about two-thirds of the interviews. The other interviews were completed by two interviewers who worked closely with me. One of the interviewers was my adult nephew, Armando Mirandé (Alex's son); the other was my good friend and *compadre* (my son's godfather), Enrique López.

In retrospect, I believe that these budgetary restrictions had both positive and negative effects. Because the interviews were long and time-consuming, the sample is not as large as I would have wished. The positive side of this limitation was that it required that I become intensely involved with all aspects of the research process. I participated in all phases of the study, from designing the interview schedule to analyzing the data. This could sound like a justification for having limited funds, or "sour grapes," but I firmly believe that although my restricted budget may have made for a less efficient research operation, it gave me the opportunity to gain invaluable insights—an opportunity that I would not have had as a principal investigator directing a larger and more bureaucratic research team in which many of these activities would have been delegated to research assistants or clerical staff. I felt, in other words, that I learned a great deal and gained incredible insights from my personal involvement in the study.

Several months were devoted to preparation of the interview schedule. The first phase required an extensive review of relevant literature on Latino men and, specifically, on the participation of fathers in the family. Pertinent literature on men and various measures of masculinity were also appraised, and colleagues were consulted during each phase of preparation. The end result was a lengthy twenty-page interview schedule that included many questions concerning masculinity, family decisionmaking, participation and involvement in child rearing and child care, and parental aspirations and expectations.

Traditionally, most of the generalizations concerning Latino culture and Latino men were derived from research typically carried out by white men who lacked genuine knowledge and understanding of the cultural patterns they observed. In this study the principal investigator and staff were bilingual and, I think, sensitive to and knowledgeable about Latino cultural and linguistic patterns. Spanish and English versions of the interview schedule were prepared, and respondents were given the option of being interviewed in either language. Though a substantial number of respondents were limited in their English-speaking ability and a few were limited in Spanish, most were bilingual, and Spanish and English were often intermingled. Approximately one-third of the interviews were conducted in Spanish and two-thirds in English. Some persons who clearly spoke Spanish still opted to do the interview in English because they felt that their formal Spanish was not "good" or "proper" Spanish. They spoke "Chicano Spanish," or *caló*, in other words, with a lot of code switching and intermingling of the two languages. Of the 105 completed interviews, one-third were carried out in each of three locales—northern California (San José, Redwood City, East Menlo Park, and San Francisco), southern California (Riverside, Upland, Ontario), and San Antonio, Texas. All of the persons interviewed were *Latino Americanos* and the vast majority were of Mexican origin.

Although interviews conducted by "insiders" helps to create a more culturally sensitive interview setting, it does not grant one automatic access to or legitimation in the Latino community. Maxine Baca Zinn (1979a) observed that minority researchers do have a number of advantages in carrying out research in minority communities, but they also encounter a number of obstacles. The most immediate problem we faced was gaining legitimacy from potential respondents.

How does one approach or elicit confidence from strangers in a research setting? Because we did not live in the communities where the interviews were conducted, in most cases we were considered "insider-outsiders" rather than "insider-insiders" (Merton 1972, 29). This was compounded by the fact that many of the questions in the interview schedule dealt with personal or private matters that Latino men might not readily discuss with strangers. We anticipated that the topic of "machismo" would prove to be sensitive and controversial and were surprised to find that it was not.

Several years ago I conducted a study in the Casa Blanca barrio in Riverside, California. We selected a random sample of households in the community, using available U.S. census tracks. Because our funds were limited and because we knew women tended to be overrepresented as respondents in social science studies, we decided at first to interview men and women in alternate households. When a man answered the door and the house was one in which we were scheduled to interview the wife, I recall how difficult it was having to explain to the man that we were interested in talking to his wife, not to him. In México, if a man approaches a couple in public and does not know either party well, it would be considered rude and inappropriate for him to approach the woman directly without first addressing the man or, at least, acknowledging his presence. Because our initial plan went against the grain of cultural expectations, then, we quickly abandoned it and decided to use male and female teams of interviewers who would interview both partners.

Two additional factors set limits on the study. First, as noted, we had severe budgetary limitations. We did not have adequate resources to employ interviewers or to draw a very large sample. Second, the nature of our study population—married Latino fathers living in an intact household—made it impossible to identify the total universe from which a sample could be drawn. Because of these limitations, I decided to use a "snowball sample" that would be both diverse and purposely selected.[3] The sample would include both working-class and middle-class respondents, foreign and native-born persons, and residents of three different geographic regions—northern California, southern California, and San Antonio. Thus, while the sample is not representative, it is diverse and includes a broad cross section of the Latino population.

An advantage of the snowball sample is that it enabled us to utilize key resource persons to identify and contact potential respondents. Resource persons were first approached and briefed on the nature of the study. I presented myself to them as a professor conducting a study of Latino fathers and the role of the man in the family and indicated that I was interested in identifying participants for the study. The basic criteria for inclusion in the sample was that the person be a Latino father with at least one child between the ages of four and eighteen living at home and that he be willing to be interviewed.

Sometimes the resource person contacted potential interviewees and stimulated some initial interest in the project prior to their interview, but more often I approached the potential respondent directly by telephone. The objectives of the study were explained and the person was asked to participate in the project. At the conclusion of the interview, interviewees in turn became resource persons and were asked if they could identify other *padres de familia* who might be willing to participate. The study gained additional legitimacy when would-be respondents were informed that the person who recommended them for the study had already been interviewed.

The resource person was someone who knew or trusted me or someone who knew someone I knew and trusted. Resource persons, therefore, served an essential function—a bridge, in a sense, between us and potential study respondents. They were "insider-insiders" who acted as liaisons between the study respondents and the interviewer. The interviewee, in turn, became a resource person and was asked to recommend friends, relatives, *compadres*, neighbors, co-workers, or acquaintances.

Obtaining *confianza* (trust) or legitimacy is critical in carrying out research in the Latino community. When I told a potential participant that I was a personal friend of Señor Mendoza, for example, and that *el señor* had given me his name and recommended him for the study, the individual would be more likely to respond favorably. The response to the study, in fact, was overwhelmingly positive. A common reply to my request to set a time and place for an interview was, *"Si como no, sería un honor para nosotros"* (Yes, of course, we would be honored), or, *"¡Seguro que sí!"* (Yes, of course!). This was especially true of respondents who preferred to speak Spanish and who were relatively unassimilated into American society.

The positive response to the study was very gratifying. Our experience differed markedly from that of past researchers, who have left the field feeling that the research relationship was inherently asymmetrical or unequal. In social science research it is often assumed that the respondent is doing the researcher "a favor" by cooperating with the study. Maxine Baca Zinn (1979a), for example, has noted that the issue of reciprocity in social science research has not been adequately addressed and that researchers, even insiders, invariably receive far more than they give to respondents. She adds that "gestures of reciprocity do not by themselves, alter the nature of research relationships. Nor is having research conducted by insiders sufficient to alter the inequality that has characterized past research" (1979a, 218).

In this study, at least, I did not find the research relationships to be inherently unequal. Our relationships with respondents were not totally one-sided and appeared to entail a genuine mutual exchange and reciprocity. As researchers, we were obviously obtaining valuable knowledge and information and establishing rewarding relationships with our study respondents, but the respondents also appeared to have benefited from the association. First, they often seemed to be pleased, if not honored, to have been selected as participants. Second, those whom I interviewed seemed flattered that a *profesór* would come to their home to ask their opinions about their role as *padres de familia* (parents). Finally, and perhaps most significantly, the interview process often appeared to have had a cathartic or therapeutic effect.

Respondents volunteered that their position as men in the family was not only an important area of study but also an important part of their lives and that they welcomed the opportunity to reflect on their duties and responsibilities as fathers. The interview seemed to provide them with an outlet to think about issues and express feelings and concerns that they had not had an opportunity to express elsewhere. In a sense, the interview gave them an opportunity to vent. The interview covered many significant aspects of their lives, such as childhood experiences, marriage, child-rearing practices, conceptions of masculinity, and their duties and responsibilities as fathers, about which they had strong feelings and beliefs. Even men who felt that they could be better fathers welcomed the opportunity to reassess their relationships with their children and their positions as fathers and men in the family.

Respondents told us they did not often have an opportunity to express their feelings. Some seemed very much aware of and dissatisfied with prevailing conceptions of Latino males in the media and the public at large. One said, "There is a big lie out there about us that people have bought." In short, the interview situation provided a forum for expressing views on issues that are a central part of their lives. Respondents were so willing to participate that the interviews were completed with few refusals. One person in San Francisco failed to show up for the interview at a café on three separate occasions, but when he was subsequently contacted by telephone, he apologized profusely and indicated that because he worked as a courier, it was difficult for him to know exactly when he would return home from work. Two men who had recommended him for the study felt that this courier was a very good father. Two or three others were not able to meet with us as we had scheduled the interviews on a busy holiday. Virtually none of those we approached, however, rejected our requests outright.

Fieldwork: Bias, Neutrality, and Detachment

Within conventional social science, the prototypical researcher was expected to be objective, indifferent, and completely detached from the "objects" of study.[4] One of the unfortunate implications of this view was that as "insiders," people of color would somehow have difficulty conducting unbiased research in their respective communities. Because of their emotional involvement and lack of objectivity and detachment, Chicanos would have difficulty carrying out research on Chicanos and Black people would have difficulty carrying out research on Blacks. Chicanos and other "insiders," in other words, were viewed as inherently limited in their ability to carry out objective, neutral, and scientifically valid social science research. In retrospect, the popularity of the conventional view is not surprising, given that research in minority communities was typically carried out either by "outsiders" or by "insider-outsiders" who had somehow been trained by their mentors to be objective, detached, and indifferent to the communities they studied.[5]

Two things strike me as flawed about this view. First, had the norm been applied universally, and it was not, it would have led to the conclusion that members of the dominant group were also incapable of studying themselves—in other words, that only non-white researchers could study or understand white people.

In a classic article Howard Becker (1967) made the insightful observation that the issue of "bias" is generally raised only when one takes the side of the poor or the oppressed or the side of members of subordinated communities. Ironically, then, research from the perspective of the dominant groups—those in positions of power, authority, or responsibility—is apt to be viewed as objective, balanced, and devoid of values. According to Becker, there is a hierarchy of credibility such that "in any system of ranked groups, participants take it as a given that members of the highest group have the right to define the way things really are" (1967, 241). It is generally assumed, for example, that the statements of police are somehow more credible than those of criminals; those of hospital personnel more credible than those of psychiatric patients; those of city officials more credible than those of the homeless; and those of the dominant group more credible than those of people of color.[6] What is critical, according to Becker, is that the issue of bias is generally raised when the subordinate perspective is assumed, which occurs when both the hierarchy of credibility and conventional wisdom are being called into question.

Second, the norms of objectivity, value neutrality, and moral detachment strike me as incredibly consistent with the Anglo-American masculine ethic found in Gilligan's Jake, the reasonable man in law, and in the way masculinity has been conceptualized in the social sciences. I submit that "scientific man," like his counterparts economic man and the reasonable man, is ultimately a veiled manifestation of Anglo-American masculinity, an attempt to institutionalize and legitimate a specific, culturally bound masculinity as a universal, scientific norm.

Over the past two decades or so, the traditional model has been called into question by a growing number of social scientists who argue that it is neither possible nor desirable to conduct research that is objective, detached, or free of personal or political values (Mirandé 1978, 1985). If to have values is to be human, the value-free ethic has posed a false dichotomy between objectivity and subjectivity. The issue, then, is not whether to take sides, since we inevitably will, but deciding which side we will take (Becker 1967, 239). Those who plead neutrality, knowingly or unwittingly, take the side of the dominant group.

When I undertook this study I did not seek to be objective or detached, nor do I think it would have been possible for me to be so. And I certainly was not indifferent. As a Latino, as a man, and as a father, not only do I think the issues addressed in this book are important, but I believe also that my academic preparation and my experience provide me with a unique perspective on Latino men and masculinity, a perspective not reflected either in Chicano/Latino scholarship or in the new men's studies. I undertook this project precisely because I was dissatisfied with the way that Latino men had been depicted by social scientists and because prevailing limited and stereotypic images of men and masculinity did not mesh with my own experience. I don't believe that it is possible or desirable for me to be objective, detached, or indifferent about these issues. Ironically, all too often the rhetoric of objectivity and scientific detachment has been used to veil pejorative and culturally myopic portrayals of Latino culture and Latino men.

Being a Latino man and a father offered a number of advantages in conducting the research, but it also created certain problems. The fact that I am a Latino man, especially a mature Latino man and a father, facilitated approaching other men and developing a rapport with them. When I approached prospective respondents about the study, I explained that one of my objectives was to present an "insider" view of Latino masculinity and fatherhood. I also explained that though there is much that has been written and said about Latino men and their position in the family, much of what has been written is negative, stereotypical, and unsupported by research. My goal in undertaking the study was to provide an inside look at Latino men that captured the reality and complexity of the Chicano/Latino masculine experience.

I introduced myself as a *profesor* and a social scientist, but mostly I presented myself as a man, a fellow Latino. I did not want the men to see me as a detached, indifferent, or neutral academic. I was a concerned person, a man who wanted very much to learn about their opinions *as men* on a number of issues and questions. I wanted to know what they thought about "machos" and "machismo," whether they had positive or negative impressions of these terms. I wanted to know which qualities or traits they respected and admired in men, how decisions were made in their families, and to what degree they participated in household tasks and in child care. I told them that their opinions mattered and that by sharing them with me, they would be contributing to the development of a more accurate, less stereotypical, and more complete understanding of Latino men.

In addition to objectivity and value neutrality, conventional social science—or "scientism," as it has been called—subscribed to the norm of universalism, the idea that to be valid, scientific generalizations had to apply to many individuals across time and space. Science was assumed to be universal, not particularistic. One of the oldest and most extreme adherents of this norm was Robert Merton. According to Merton, the norm of universalism held that "the acceptance or rejection of claims entering science is not to depend on the personal or social attributes of their protagonist; his race, nationality, religion, class and personal qualities are as such irrelevant" (Merton 1963, 553).

I propose that universalism is not only a dominant group norm but a dominant white male norm. It is a norm that is clearly at odds with Mexican and Latino cultural values, which are characterized by particularism and personalism. My respondents generally could not relate to the idea that they were anonymous, faceless, and nameless "subjects" of a scientific study. When I first contacted potential respondents, I told them either that their name had been given to me by a mutual acquaintance (resource person) or that they had been personally "recommended" as possible participants in the study. In many cases simply mentioning the name of the resource person was sufficient to elicit a positive response and an expression of willingness to participate in the study. I remember in particular Rudy Torres, a young man in his mid-twenties from San Antonio, sort of a "born again" Catholic who confided that he had been fairly wild and irresponsible in the early stages of his marriage.[7] Rudy had been referred to us by a woman in his parish, Mary Sánchez, a woman whom he very much valued and respected. His response was that he would look favorably on *any* person or project that Mrs. Sánchez had recommended because she had helped him out when he and his family were down on their luck.

The importance of personal contacts and referrals can be illustrated by relating two negative experiences. In the first instance, Mr. Art Gonzalez was contacted and told that he had been recommended by Mr. Ray Ortiz. Mr. Gonzalez responded that he did not know anyone by that name and admonished the caller (me) "to get his facts straight before he went around contacting people." I learned subsequently that Mr. Gonzalez apparently did know Mr. Ortiz but did not remember him when I called. In other words, they were simply casual acquaintances, not close or intimate friends.

The second case involved a woman who had given me the names of several Mexican nationals, laborers who worked for her ex-husband at a furniture factory. Since she only knew them by their first names and did not have their home telephone numbers, she suggested that I call and ask to speak to them at her ex-husband's shop. Unfortunately, her "ex" answered the telephone. When I asked to speak to the men, he responded very aggressively and wanted to know my reasons for contacting them. I proceeded to explain the project and identified his "ex" as the person who had suggested that I contact the workers. He became very irate, perhaps jealous about any relationship that I might have had with his "ex." He refused to let me speak to the employees, even though I assured him that I had just met his wife, that she was not involved in the project in any way, and that she had simply given me a list of potential interviewees that had included his workers. The ex-husband said that a part of him wanted to help me out. He could see that the project was important, that it had nothing to do with him personally, and that, as a fellow Chicano, it would have been in his interest to help me out. On the other hand, the project *did* have something to do with him (and presumably her). In retrospect, it is clear that simply mentioning her name was "the kiss of death" and that he would have been much more receptive if someone other than his ex-wife had been the contact person. These incidents are exceptions that prove the rule that in a culture that emphasizes personal relations, a negative or weak referral is worse than no referral at all. In both instances I would have been better off approaching the party without a referral.

As I was a postdoctoral fellow at Stanford when the project was initiated, like other researchers affiliated with the university, I was required to submit the interview schedule to the campus Human Subjects Committee. It was necessary for me to prepare a standard caveat about eliciting cooperation from respondents. The caveat explicitly indicated that they would be guaranteed anonymity and that they would not be identified in the results of the study. This is standard procedure in social science research, but it is a procedure that I think goes against the grain of prevailing Mexican and Latino values. Although few of these respondents would have wanted very intimate or personal aspects of their lives to be revealed in print, neither did they wish to be anonymous. Most were proud fathers and believed strongly in the views they shared in the interviews.

In Latino culture a strong value is placed on being *una persona que cumple con su palabra* (a person of his word). A person is, therefore, expected to "back up" or "stand behind" what he says or believes. The response to my "pledge of anonymity" was often indifference or reassurance that they did not seek, expect, or want anonymity as a condition of participation. One man, for example, said, "Hey man, use my name, it's okay!" The point simply is that, except when discussing intimate personal or family problems, the Latino ethic is to be proud of and to stand behind one's beliefs. It should be noted that many of the questions dealt with general attitudes and beliefs that most respondents would be not only willing, but eager to reveal and discuss publicly. Another way of viewing this is that from a Latino perspective, it is incomprehensible why one would take the time to complete a two-hour interview expressing one's attitudes and beliefs and then opt to remain anonymous.

An essential ingredient of Latino culture is personal and collective pride, not so much in oneself and one's individual accomplishments but in the accomplishments of family and friends. Many individuals were clearly proud to have been "selected" to participate in the project, proud that a fellow Latino was writing a book about them, and proud to have the opportunity to express their views on masculinity and fatherhood. Respondents actually showed a keen interest in or curiosity about the book, and many of the men wanted to know how they could get a copy. Some said they wanted a copy even if their name was not going to be mentioned in it! One man told me at the beginning of the interview, "Listen, Mirandé, one thing I wanted to tell you is that a condition of doing this is that I get a copy of the book when it comes out, and I'm willing to pay for it. Is that understood?" Another said, "Even though you are not going to use any names, I'm very interested in seeing how you are going to interpret all of this information that you're getting."

Although some interviews were conducted in public places such as restaurants and bars, most were held in the respondents' homes. The wife was often present when I arrived, but she would usually excuse herself and go about her business while I sat in the living room or dining room and interviewed the husband. Some women, however, were very curious about the study and wondered why I was not interviewing them, almost as though they had been slighted. As I felt bad about this, I apologized and explained that although it would be ideal to interview both husband and wife, my resources were very limited and as a result I was unable to interview women at this time.

One case stands out as an example in which the women were very vocal in expressing their displeasure at not being included in the study. I was interviewing a man at the home of his *compadre*. The *compadre*, who had already been interviewed and was now serving as a resource person, was barbecuing fajitas on the patio and serving members of the two families outdoors. As we sat in the living room doing the interview, the *compadre* came in and out of the house as he prepared the meal, each time locking the sliding door behind him and restricting access into the house. After the interview I visited with the two couples and their children outside. The women started kidding the *compadre* and chastising him for not letting anyone into the house. The women also wanted to know more about what I was doing, what I had found out so far, and how their husbands "ranked." They wondered whether it was possible to get the full picture without also interviewing women. In a sense they were complaining because they were not interviewed.[8] It seemed "unfair" that "he" got to "listen in" and they did not. The *compadre* said, and I believed him, that he was not listening and that he was just being respectful by trying to keep the noise down while the interview was in progress. Curiously, the *compadre* prepared and served the entire meal, even while the women were complaining about his chauvinism.

Another incident illustrates how the norm of "universalism" in social science is often used to perpetuate dominant societal values. The following protocol, used as an introduction to the interview, was submitted to the Human Subjects Committee of the university for approval:

> We are carrying out a study of men and their attitudes toward different issues. You can help us a great deal by simply answering some questions. There are no right or wrong answers. We are interested in what you think about these things. Please give us your honest opinion on each question. We will not ask your name or attempt to identify you in any way. *Your answers are strictly confidential and will not be given out to anyone. You are free to not answer any question that you do not want to.*

The response of the committee members was revealing. They felt that both the protocol and the interview schedule were acceptable, but they were concerned that I did not indicate anywhere that I was doing a study of Latino men. They felt that the protocol should say that I was studying Latino men only. I wrote back to the chair to ask whether the Human Subjects Committee would have required someone who was studying Anglo men to also indicate this on a protocol. I never heard from the Human Subjects Committee again.

The Bem Sex Role Inventory (BSRI) was normalized and validated on a predominantly Anglo population of college students, ironically also conducted at Stanford and at a nearby community college. Yet the issue of race is not typically raised when evaluating the validity of Bem's instrument or other instruments designed by white researchers and validated on white subjects. This experience illustrated not only the norm of universalism but the hierarchy of credibility. Chicano/Latino men *are* men, no more or less so than Anglo men. There appears to be a prevailing, though unstated, assumption in social science that findings and generalizations obtained with white samples and reflecting dominant theories, perspectives, and ideologies are generalizable to the population as a whole, whereas studies of Latinos, African-Americans, Asians, or American Indians are studies of subpopulations or specialized groups. Why is a study of Latino, African-American, Asian, or American Indian men somehow viewed as being less universal than a study of Anglo men? Is it that Anglo men are ethnically or racially neutral? Is it that they are simply generic men? Would the Human Subjects Committee have requested that Bem call her instrument the Bem Anglo Sex Role Inventory or that Michael Kimmel's recent book, *Manhood in America*, be titled *Anglo Manhood in America*? Somehow, I don't think so.

2

Genesis of
Mexican Masculinity

While growing up in México City, I didn't know a lot about my pre-Columbian heritage, though I lived in Tenochtitlán—the capital of the Aztec empire—and was literally immersed in that heritage. I recall that one of my childhood hobbies was to collect pictures of Aztec warriors and other Mexican heroes like the Aztec king Cuauhtémoc, who was captured and tortured by the Spaniards. I should add that none of these heroes were Spanish. My brothers and I would go to a little store in our neighborhood near *el árbol de la noche triste* on *avenida México-Tacuba* and buy candy. Each package of candy contained a picture card of a Mexican historical figure that we would paste into an *album,* or scrapbook. Since the pictures would repeat themselves in the candy packages, we would trade them with other kids in order to collect a variety. It was kind of like a baseball card collection because some of the cards were rare and more valuable than others. The goal, of course, was to complete *El Album,* a pictorial history of México. I collected these books without fully understanding that I was living in the Aztec capital and honoring my pre-Columbian heritage.

My *vecindad,* Tacuba, formerly Tlacopan, is located at the west edge of the city. After my parents separated, I moved south with my father to my grandmother Anita's house in Tacubaya, near Chapultepec. My brothers and I would go almost daily to play in Chapultepec, where there was a huge park with a lake and numerous attractions, including the internationally renowned Museum of Anthropology and the majestic Castle of Chapultepec. But we didn't go to Chapultepec because of the museums and tourist attractions. We went because it was green and because there were places to play, a lake, hills to climb, and places to hide. We went because Chapultepec was our back yard—our private playground, as it were.

El Castillo[1] was the Castle where the Hapsburg emperor Maximilian and his wife Carlota resided during the French intervention in the 1860s and, more importantly, where *Los Niños Héroes* leaped to their death. After the

U.S. invasion in 1847, with the Mexican forces severely depleted, a group of military school boys valiantly defended the Castle. These boys emerged not only as heroes and patriots but also as symbols of Mexican manhood. On September 13, 1847, rather than surrendering, the six military cadets died defending their country. Juan Escutia is perhaps best known because he leaped to his death wrapped in the Mexican flag. Like every other Mexican schoolboy, I learned about and deeply identified with these young Mexican patriots. I admired them in my pictorial collection without realizing at the time that both of my neighborhoods, Tacuba and Chapultepec, were an integral part of the ancient capital.

The Aztecs, or *Mexicas,* were the last of the nomadic tribes to enter the valley of México from the north in the middle of the thirteenth century. After a number of defeats and humiliations they were able to establish themselves in 1325 on an island in a lake, according to the ancient codices (León-Portilla 1962, xiv). Founded on a low-lying island that other tribes had not bothered to occupy (León-Portilla 1962, xv), Tenochtitlán had emerged by the time of the arrival of Cortés as a bustling metropolis, dazzling the Spaniards with its size and beauty. Bernal Díaz del Castillo, famous chronicler of the Conquest, was so taken that he concluded that "the wonders must be a dream." The Spaniards were welcomed to the city as guests by the Aztec king himself. Motecuhzoma II climbed to the top of the pyramid in the main temple and pointed out the magnificent sights for all to see. Bernal Díaz remarked:

> So we stood looking around us, for that huge and cursed temple stood so high that from it one could see everything very well, and we saw the three causeways which led into México, that is the causeway of Iztapalapa by which we had entered four days before, and that of Tacuba, along which later on we fled on the night of our great defeat . . . and we saw the fresh water that comes from Chapultepec which supplies the city, and we saw the bridges on the three causeways which were built at certain distances apart through which the water of the lake flowed . . . and we beheld on that lake a great multitude of canoes, some coming with supplies of food and others returning loaded with cargoes of merchandise. . . . Some of the soldiers among us who had been in many parts of the world, in Constantinople, and all over Italy, and in Rome, said that so large a market place and so full of people, and so well regulated and arranged, they had never beheld before. (Díaz del Castillo 1908, 2:74–75)

When the Spaniards entered the Aztec capital on November 8, 1519, arriving from the direction of Tlalpan in the south and having crossed the causeway of Iztapalapa, they were welcomed not only as honored guests but heralded also as returning deities by the Aztec king, who mistook them for the returning deposed white god Quetzalcóatl and other gods (León-Portilla 1962, vii). This would be the first encounter "between one of the

Boy soldier, México, 1915 (*Jefes, Héroes y Caudillos*, Sistema Nacional de Fototecas Del Instituto Nacional de Antropología E Historia, Fondo Casasola. México: Fondo de Cultural Económica, 1996).

FIGURE 2.1 The valley of México. From *The Broken Spears* by Miguel León-Portilla. © 1962, 1990 by Beacon Press. Expanded and updated edition © 1992 by Miguel León-Portilla. Reproduced by permission of Beacon Press, Boston.

most extraordinary pre-Columbian cultures and the strangers that would eventually destroy it." The Aztec capital would fall within two years, on August 13, 1521, but only after a fierce struggle and with the aid of Indian allies such as the Tlaxcalans, who joined forces against the Aztecs.[2]

The Cempoal, for example, dreaded the Aztecs and proposed intermarriage with the Spaniards in order to insure their own protection and survival. Bernal Díaz noted that when a fat Cempoal *cacique*, or noble, offered eight of the finest young women of the elite families to Cortés and his men, Cortés told the Indians that before he could accept their friendship or the women, they must renounce their idolatrous practices, cease their sacrificial offerings, and free themselves from sodomy (1908, 1:186). It was also necessary that the women undergo the ceremony of baptism.

Much of what has been said and written about the Conquest has been from the perspective of the conquerors, who saw the Indians as heathens who believed in false idols and were badly in need of conversion. The codices, or Indian chronicles, however, present the Indian view of the Conquest. When Cortés left the capital, he left one of his lieutenants, Pedro de Alvarado, in command. In a surprise and unprovoked move Alvarado proceeded to attack and mutilate thousands of defenseless people as they celebrated a feast to Huizilopochtli, a very important feast that Fray Bernardino de Sahagún likened to Easter for Christians (León-Portilla 1962, 70). The Indian chronicles describe how the Spaniards entered the sacred patio and proceeded to massacre the celebrants.

> They ran in among the dancers, forcing their way to the place where the drums were played. They attacked the man who was drumming and cut off his arms. Then they cut off his head, and it rolled across the floor.
>
> They attacked all the celebrants, stabbing them, spearing them, striking them with their swords. They attacked some of them from behind, and these fell instantly to the ground with their entrails hanging out. Others they beheaded; they cut off their heads or split their heads to pieces.
>
> They struck others in the shoulders, and their arms were torn from their bodies. They wounded some in the thigh and some in the calf. They slashed others in the abdomen, and their entrails all spilled to the ground. Some attempted to run away, but their intestines dragged as they ran; they seemed to tangle their feet in their own entrails. (León-Portilla 1962, viii–ix)

The Aztecs revolted against this brutal massacre. After a fierce battle that raged for four days, Cortés was forced to abandon Tenochtitlán. He attempted to withdraw at night down the Tlacopan (now the Tacuba) but was discovered, and the Aztecs avenged the massacre of Tlatelolco. According to Sahagún's informants, the rout was so disastrous that it came to be know as *la noche triste*, the night of sorrows (León-Portilla 1962, 83).

FIGURE 2.2   The massacre in the main temple (Codex Duran).

Alternative Explanations
of Hypermasculinity

My intent here is not to provide a history of pre-Columbian México and the Conquest, for that would be beyond the scope of this chapter. My intent is to reexamine the ensuing conflict not only as one between two very different cultures and races, but also ultimately as a conflict between men, one that would expose contrasting images of masculinity and manhood. I present three explanations for the emergence of hypermasculinity, or outward masculine displays, among Mexicans.

By far the most prevalent and the most negative explanation for the Mexican preoccupation with masculinity is that it is the direct result of the Spanish Conquest, an event so devastating that it produced a form of "masculine protest," an almost obsessive concern with images and symbols of manhood, among Indian and mestizo men. The view is negative, or pathological, because it assumes that the so-called Mexican protest is a response to intense and persistent feelings of powerlessness and weakness. A second, related view, is that the cultural emphasis on masculinity was a characteristic of Spanish society prior to the Conquest that was imposed on the native population. The emphasis on masculinity and patriarchy were, therefore, imposed on the Indian in the same way that Catholicism, horses, pork, and deadly diseases such as the "great plague" were imposed. A third and final explanation is that masculine displays may have had pre-Columbian origins that predated the arrival of the Spaniards. The Aztec universe, after all, was sharply divided into masculine and feminine spheres. From birth Aztec men were told that their vocation was to wage war on and to subdue their enemies. According to this view, excessive masculine displays were, therefore, a part of Aztec society long before the arrival of the Spaniards.

Before examining each of these explanations, several caveats are in order. First, though the views are treated separately, they are not in fact separate or mutually exclusive. What I present under each explanation is a very extreme description or prototype. The truth is that though there is much overlap among the three, I believe that the theories or explanations are distinct enough to deserve separate treatment and discussion. Second, I want to reiterate that I am *not* suggesting that masculine displays or hypermasculinity are either unique to Mexicans or pathological manifestations of the Mexican psyche, unlike conventional theories or what has been termed the "deficit model." As noted in the previous chapter, a large number of societies are concerned with manhood and masculinity and with assessing who is a "real man" or a "true man." According to Gilmore, "Many societies build up an elusive or exclusionary image of manhood through cultural sanctions, ritual, or trials of skill and endurance" (1990, 1). Finally, though I critically examine each explanation, it is not possible to say which is the "true" or "correct" explanation for Mexican displays of masculinity.

A Response to the Conquest: *Hijos de la Chingada*

In *The Labyrinth of Solitude* the renowned Mexican philosopher, poet, and Nobel laureate Octavio Paz attributed the Mexican's deep-seated feelings of "inferiority" to the spiritual rape and conquest of México—a defeat that was so devastating that it proved to be not only a military conquest but a spiritual and moral downfall as well. Our anxiety, tension, and rage is captured by a solitary phrase that is uttered as follows: "When anger, joy or enthusiasm cause us to exalt our condition as Mexicans: '¡Viva México, hijos de la chingada!'" (Long live México, children of the great whore!) (1961, 74). Significantly, this phrase becomes a battle cry on Mexican Independence Day, September 16, as all Mexicans are symbolically acknowledged as offspring of a single mythical mother, *La Chingada*.

It is important to note, parenthetically, that not everyone agrees with the view that the Conquest was totally effected. León-Portilla (1990, 56), for example, noted that shortly after the Conquest, the Spanish friars stressed the widespread acceptance of Christianity among the natives, but by the second half of the sixteenth century many began to have serious doubts about the efficacy of the conversion. In addition, there are numerous native testimonies and indigenous expressions that indicate a hostility toward and profound criticism of the procedures used to impose the Christian faith (León-Portilla 1990, 56).

According to Paz, in Mexican folklore *La Chingada* is not our real mother but our mythical, violated, metaphorical "mother," who is symbolized by the thousands of native women raped by the conquistadores. The counterpart to *La Chingada* is the great macho, or *Gran Chingón*, who is powerful and aggressive and goes about committing *chingaderas* and ripping up the world. Extending the sexual analogy further, whereas *La Chingada* is passive and inert, *El Chingón* is wounding and penetrating. Thus the Mexican male is said always to be distrustful of others *para que no se lo chinguen* (so that he is not "fucked over").

La Chingada is symbolized in Mexican folklore by *La Malinche,* or Doña Marina, an Indian woman who was given as a slave to Hernán Cortés at the age of fourteen and who went on to serve as his translator and concubine (see Mirandé and Enríquez 1981, 24–31). Although she was apparently an articulate young woman who was respected by both the Spaniards and Indians, Mexican folklore has erroneously labeled her a traitress, whore, and mother of a bastard mestizo race. She is despised for somehow "opening herself up" to the conqueror and humiliating and thereby emasculating the male, despite the fact that she was actually sold into slavery and literally "given" as a gift to Cortés shortly after his arrival.

According to this view, the so-called cult of machismo developed as Mexican men found themselves unable to protect their women from the Conquest's ensuing plunder, pillage, and rape. Native men developed an overly masculine and aggressive response in order to compensate for deeply felt feelings of powerlessness and weakness. Machismo, then, is nothing more than a futile attempt to mask a profound sense of impotence, powerlessness, and ineptitude, an expression of weakness and a sense of inferiority.

The renowned Mexican psychologist Samuel Ramos also used the concept of "inferiority" to explain Mexican character. By systematically using and applying Alfred Adler's psychological theories, Ramos concluded that the Mexican's hypermasculinity is a form of masculine protest designed to mask feelings of inferiority[3] (Ramos 1962, 56).

> One must presuppose the existence of an inferiority complex in all those people who show an excessive concern with affirming their personality, who take vital interest in all things and situations that signify power, and who demonstrate an immoderate eagerness to excel, to be first in everything.

FIGURE 2.3   Tenochtitlán: Malinche and Cortés. Courtesy of the Bancroft Library, University of California.

It is important to note Ramos was not saying that the Mexican *is* inferior "but rather that he *feels* inferior" (1962, 57).

For Ramos the prototype of Mexican national character is the *pelado*, a term that defies translation but literally means "plucked," "naked," or "stripped" and connotes a "lowly person" or "nobody." Like the *chingón* he has an intense phallic obsession and attributes not only sexual potency but also every type of power to the reproductive organ (Ramos 1962, 60). Thus the success of any man is always attributed to his "balls." The *pelado* may lack economic power and social status but he consoles himself by strutting around holding his genitals and exclaiming, "*¡Tengo muchos huevos!*" (I have a lot of balls). The phrase "*Yo soy tu padre*" (I am your father) is likewise used to assert power and dominance over others in a patriarchal society in which the father is the ultimate symbol of power and control (1962, 60). The *pelado*, however, is a study in contradiction. He is not, in fact, strong and brave but is weak and cowardly, and his aggressiveness, assertiveness, and bravado are designed to conceal insecurity, distrust, and inferiority.

The appearance he shows us is false. It is a camouflage by which he misleads himself and all those who come into contact with him. One can infer that the more show he makes of courage and force, the greater is the weakness that he is trying to hide. (Ramos 1962, 61)

Ramos, like Paz, believed that the most striking aspect of Mexican national character, at first sight at least, is distrust (1962, 64). The Mexican does not distrust anyone in particular, he distrusts everyone (1962, 64). This so-called a priori form of oversensitivity is so pervasive that the distrust is not limited to the human race but "embraces all that exists and happens" (1962, 62).

There are several problems with Ramos's characterization of the *pelado*. First, the characterization is clearly classist because the *pelado* is a low-life, poor, or proletarian Mexican. One wonders what form false or ingenuine courage and bravado takes among middle- or upper-class Mexican men. Ramos acknowledged that feelings of inferiority are also found among middle-class, educated Mexicans, and that when a middle-class Mexican loses control, he is chastised by peers for "acting like a *pelado*" (1962, 68). In fact, "the main psychic disparity between upper-class Mexicans and those of the lower classes is due to a complete dissimulation by the former of their sense of inferiority. . . . On the other hand, the *pelado* flaunts with impudent frankness his psychological idiosyncrasies, and the connection in his soul between the conscious and unconscious is quite simple" (1962, 68–69). The middle-class Mexican masks feelings of inferiority through imitation, especially imitation of European, and specifically French, institutions and culture (1962, 18).

When a Mexican compares his own nullity to the character of a civilized foreigner, he consoles himself in the following way: "A European has science, art, technical knowledge, and so forth; we have none of that here, but . . . we are very manly." (1962, 61)

In other words, though we may not have art and high culture, ultimately we have the only thing that really counts—"balls!" But we are men only in a very limited zoological sense, in the sense of the male exhibiting "complete animal potency" (1962, 61).

A second problem with Ramos's characterization is that because the *pelado* is seen as a negative response of Mexican manhood that is rooted in feelings of inferiority, the limited and unidimensional character that emerges is a caricature, one that serves to mask possible positive manifestations of this masculine response to subordination. In his films the beloved Mexican comic Cantinflas, for example, captured what one might term—for lack of a better word—a good or benign *pelado*, or at a minimum, a humorous, comic *pelado*. Cantinflas's characters were invariably poor Mexicans who encountered oppression, classism, and internal racism against Indians. But Cantinflas always managed to outsmart and certainly outwit his more pretentious, well-educated, and rich adversaries. He was the master of double-talk, or *albur*, a form of verbal art common among Mexicans, and he symbolized a positive quality of the uncultured, witty, but infinitely resourceful Mexican *pelado*.[4]

The popular Mexican singer and actor, Pedro Infante, also symbolized a positive version of the *pelado*. In classic films such as *Nosotros los Pobres* (We the Poor), *Ustedes los Ricos* (The Wealthy Talk), and *Pepe el Toro* (Pepe the Bull), Pedro Infante represented a positive image of the poor Mexican male who is depicted as strong, honest, moral, loyal, and compassionate. Though proud and *muy hombre* (very manly), the poor Mexican is neither loud, boisterous, nor insensitive. He is sensitive, loving, and loyal, and demonstrates his manliness through action, not by abusing people or holding his genitals and proclaiming his manhood.

The Spiritual Conquest and Machismo.   From Paz and Ramos it is clear that the literature linking the origin of machismo to the spiritual conquest of México often assumes a psychoanalytic model in which the outward expression of courage and bravado is based on subconscious feelings of impotence and inadequacy. Psychoanalyst Aniceto Aramoni (1965), for example, defined machismo as "the expression of exaggerated masculine characteristics, ranging from male genital prowess to towering pride and fearlessness. It also is a specific counter phobic attitude toward women" (Aramoni 1972, 70). Ultimately, the *machista* (male chauvinist) is propelled to dominate and subdue others in order to deny his own weakness, dependency, and regressiveness. Aramoni believed that the cultural emphasis on hyper-manliness, or machismo, "is a uniquely Mexican answer—albeit a disturbed one—to the universal quest for individuation, dignity and relatedness" (1972, 73). Aramoni noted that though machismo is not a universal Mexican trait, it is a fairly common feature of Mexican culture and certainly not rare among Mexican males.

Similarly, for American psychoanalyst Marvin Goldwert (1980, 1983, 1985), the cult of male virility and machismo, characteristic not only of México but all of Spanish America, is a mechanism of denial, reaction formation, and sublimation used to repress persistent feelings of femininity. Extending the sexual metaphor further, Goldwert (1985, 161) argued that mestizo society was a product of some form of "metaphysical bisexuality" whereby the Spanish conquistadores assumed the active, aggressive male role in metaphorically raping or sodomizing the passive or feminine Indian. In other words, one might say *que el español chingó al indio* (that the Spaniard metaphorically violated or "fucked" the Indian). The contemporary macho who incessantly strives to prove his masculinity to himself and

Center, movie star and singer Jorge Negrete; *right,* Xavier Mirandé.

others is, according to Goldwert, a tragic figure—the product and victim of this "metaphysical bisexuality."

> The conquest was, then, a time of "kairos," a time of trauma shaping all ensu-
> ing human relationships. Stemming from the conquest there now exists in
> every Mexican male a culturally stereotyped polarity in which "masculinity" is
> synonymous with the active/dominant personality and "femininity" is pas-
> sive/submissive. (1985, 162)

The mestizo macho, haunted by the bisexual quality of the Conquest, seeks not only to be dominant and aggressive in his household but also to con-quer all women outside his household. In contrast, the chastity and purity of his "own" women (i.e., wives, mothers, daughters) must be protected at all costs, even if the cost is death. It is interesting to note that a man who is a *mujeriego,* or "womanizer," is also referred to as a conquistador, for he is seen not only as seducing but also as symbolically "conquering" women.

Although machismo was associated with the sexual sphere during the colonial period, once independence from Spain was attained, it was transferred to the political arena as symbolized by the caudillo, or political strongman (Goldwert 1985, 163). Porfirio Díaz, who ruled México with an iron hand from 1876 to 1910, personified the supreme macho, authoritarian father figure. The Mexican Revolution in 1910, in turn, produced its own brand of machismo, unleashing "an orgy of machismo, sexual rampages, and destructiveness" (1985, 163). Revolutionary leader Pancho Villa, for example, was considered to be the epitome of Mexican manliness. According to Aniceto Aramoni, Villa embodied the attributes of machismo:

> *hipertrofia compensadora de la personalidad, narcisismo, petulancia, agresividad, destructividad intensa, odio importante hacia el superior . . . , desprecio profundo y temor por la mujer* (An extreme, compensatory exaggeration of the personality, narcissism, petulance, aggressiveness, intense destructiveness, considerable hatred of superiors . . . , a deep contempt for and fear of women). (Aramoni 1965, 151)

Two Zapatistas in Sanborns. México, D.F., December 1914 (*Jefes, Héroes y Caudillos*, Sistema Nacional de Fototecas Del Instituto Nacional de Antropología E Historia, Fondo Casasola. México: Fondo de Cultural Económica, 1996).

Firing-squad executions of Arcadio Jiménez, Hilario Silva, and Marcelino
Martínez (Chalco). Edo. de México, April 28, 1909 (*Jefes, Héroes y Caudillos,*
Sistema Nacional de Fototecas Del Instituto Nacional de Antropología E Historia,
Fondo Casasola. México: Fondo de Cultural Económica, 1996).

Villa appealed to the masses because, like the *pelado* and Cantinflas, he
symbolized the peon or lower-class person taking a stand against the dominant classes. Mexicans seem to identify vicariously with the person who
"bears with it," who is brave, *que no se deja* (who doesn't take anything
from anyone), and *que no se raja* (who doesn't back down), especially if the
person is depicted as an underdog and of poor or humble origins (1965,
163). Villa's invasion of the United States, for example, was celebrated
because it demonstrated his audacity in taking on the most powerful nation
in the world. In the end, what mattered was not that the battle was won or
lost or that numerous casualties were incurred but that Villa *tenía huevos*
(he had "balls") and was man enough to take on the hated yanquis. Francisco I. Madero assumed the presidency after Porfirio Díaz was toppled.
Madero's personality and physique contrasted sharply with those of Villa
and Díaz, as he was small in stature, idealistic, and gentle. When Madero
appeared hesitant and indecisive, Villa told him in a letter to assert himself
and show them *que tenía pantalones* (that he wore the pants) (Villa 1913).

General Francisco ("Pancho") Villa and wife (Austreberta Rentería) (*Jefes, Héroes y Caudillos*, Sistema Nacional de Fototecas Del Instituto Nacional de Antropología E Historia, Fondo Casasola. México: Fondo de Cultural Económica, 1996).

Fray Bernardino de Sahagún: Father of Modern Ethnography. Before discussing the next two explanations of the Mexican "masculine cult," it is important to discuss the source of much of the Indian perspective on the Conquest. Fray Bernardino de Sahagún belonged to the "second wave" of preacher ethnographers, arriving in 1529, only eight years after the downfall of Tenochtitlán (Klor de Alva 1988, 34). Sahagún used native informants and proceeded to systematically gather information on the ancient practices, rituals, and political, religious, and moral beliefs of the people. His *Historia General de las cosas de la Nueva España* (in English, the *Florentine Codex*) and other texts yielded important insights into Aztec culture and pre-Columbian society. Klor de Alva described Sahagún as the father of modern ethnography, noting that "the Sahaguntine corpus undoubtedly constitutes the most thorough, objective, and complete study of another culture that has ever been attempted" (Klor de Alva 1988, 34). Moreover, because Sahagún used a dialogical method in creating the corpus of his ethnography, "authorship and authority must be primarily attributed to the informants and trilingual native scholars, the *colegiales,* who worked with him" (1988, 34). In order to convert the Nahua (Aztec) natives to Christianity, he quickly learned Náhuatl and immersed himself in Nahua culture and, like a modern ethnographer, he used natives as "informants" and trained them in ethnographic methods. It soon became clear that his interest in Nahua culture extended well beyond ordinary pastoral concerns (1988, 34). The *Historia General* and other texts provide a rich description of pre- and post-Conquest Nahua culture as seen from the perspective of the Nahua themselves (1988, 35).

Others are less generous in their interpretation of Sahagún's work. Louise Burkhart, for example, identifies many "doctrinal" aspects to Sahagún's *Coloquios,* noting that "Sahagún the pioneer ethnographer cannot be fully separated from Sahagún the zealous missionary" (Burkhart 1988, 65). Not only did Sahagún compile a "doctrinal encyclopedia" to go along with the ethnographic encyclopedia, but he also openly acknowledged that the purpose of the *Historia General* "was the education of fellow religious in order that they recognize idolatries" (1988, 65). The intent of Sahagún's ethnographic work was to present Nahua culture to a European audience, whereas his catechistic writing presented Christianity to his indigenous converts (1988, 65). Nonetheless, Indian influences are found throughout his doctrinal writing. According to Burkhart,

> Aside from Sahagún's reliance on native assistants, the very process of presenting Christian material in Nahuatl forced a recasting of Christian concepts according to Nahua categories. With their medieval world view and rigid moral absolutism, the friars especially in the beginning, were insensitive to the nuance of language and classification. They sought synonyms, one-to-one cor-

respondence between Nahua and Christian terms, and used whatever Nahuatl words they could find.[5] (1988, 65)

One drawback of the codices is that they have both a class and a racial bias, reflecting the worldview not only of the Spanish clerics but also of the Aztec elite, or *pipiltin*. Despite these limitations, the *Florentine Codex* is a powerful pictographic document that provides extensive information about a wide variety of roles in Aztec society. It characterizes, for example, the good noblewoman and the bad noblewoman as well as the "good" and "bad" weaver of designs. Yet what is most notable in this document is the rigidity of the social structure, apparent in the detailed descriptions of behaviors and attitudes one should assume in various roles. The Aztec universe was based on dualities, and the division of the universe into masculine and feminine components was a central duality.

The Conquistadores as the First Machos: *Caballeros con Huevos de Oro*

Rejecting the explanation that machismo was a response to emasculation wrought by the Conquest, some have argued that machismo and the cult of masculinity were introduced to the New World by the Spanish conquistadores, who were themselves extremely macho. According to this view, Mexican masculinity was not a form of masculine protest that emanated from feelings of inferiority but was, like Indian conversion, an assimilation of the value system and worldview of the conquistador. Marvin Goldwert (1980, 59; 1983, 1) argued that the Spanish were not only the "first machos" but also the prototype and model for the contemporary Mexican macho. Octavio Paz observed that

> It is impossible not to notice the resemblance between the figure of the macho and that of the Spanish conquistador. It is the model—more mythical than real—that determines the images the Mexican people form of their men in power. . . . They are all *machos, chingones*. (Paz 1961, 82)

Chicano playwright Luis Valdez (1972, xvi) similarly depicted *los conquistadores* as being larger than life itself—"Fifty foot caballeros with golden huevos" (balls). The Spaniards were the last *caballeros* (knights or gentlemen; literally, "horsemen"), and Cortés and his men were representative of the best *caballería* (knighthood or cavalry) that Spain or any other nation had ever assembled (Aramoni 1965, 128). They were depicted as a handful of daring, robust, and valiant men of action who, after their ships had been destroyed, overcame numerous adversities to conquer a vast continent and millions of Indians, in the process committing numerous *chingaderas*.

Fray Bernardino de Sahagún wrote one of the most complete and author-itative accounts of the Indian life, culture, and customs, but he was un-doubtedly biased and seeking to justify the Conquest. He described Cortés as "God's valiant soldier" who was selected by God to fulfill the difficult and important mission of converting the Indians to Catholicism.

> *A este negocio muy grande y muy importante, tuvo nuestro Señor Dios por bien de que hiciese camino y derrocase el muro conque esta infidelidad estaba cercada y murada, el valentísimo capitán D. Hernando Cortés, en cuya pres-encia y por cuyos medios, hizo Dios nuestro Señor muchos milagros en la con-quista.* (In this very great and very important enterprise, our Lord God willed that a path be blazed and that the wall with which this godlessness was sur-rounded and enclosed be pulled down; through the figure and deeds of the valiant captain D. Hernando Cortes, our Lord performed many miracles in this conquest.) (Sahagún 1946, 3:10)

Because Cortés was an emissary of the king and was seen as an instru-ment of God, the subjugation and conversion of the Indian was seen not only as morally defensible and justified but also as divinely willed and ordained. Before war was waged, efforts were made to convert the Indians to Catholicism and to persuade them to abandon the worship of "pagan deities." In his dispatches to the king, Carlos V, Cortés indicated that he had

> overturned the idols in which these people believe the most and rolled them down the stairs. Then I had those chapels cleansed, for they were full of blood from the sacrifices; and I set up images of Our Lady and other Saints in them. . . . I made them understand by the interpreters how deceived they were in putting their hope in idols made of unclean things by their own hands. I told them that they should know there was but one God, the Universal Lord of all, Who had created the heavens and earth and all things, and them, and us. (Blacker and Rosen 1962, 57)

This missionary zeal was reinforced by foreboding elements in Aztec reli-gion and mythology that had foretold the destruction of the Aztec empire. Incredibly, the Spaniards' arrival coincided with the prophesied return of the deposed god Quetzalcóatl. Eight signs, or omens, in Aztec mythology predicted the Aztec demise some ten years prior to Cortés's arrival. The Aztec emperor Motecuhzoma initially mistook Cortés to be Quetzalcóatl, who had promised to return from the East. Miraculously, the date of the prophesied return coincided with Cortés's arrival (Caso 1958, 25). There was even a physical resemblance between Cortés and Quetzalcóatl, as both were said to be fair-haired, light-skinned, and bearded.

Representatives of the Aztec emperor were sent to greet the returning god and to present him with the treasure of Quetzalcóatl. They were to treat him with the respect and reverence that would be accorded a deity (León-Portilla 1962, 21–26). Cortés accepted the lavish gifts from the five messengers and asked, with incredible arrogance, "And is this all?" Then he had the messengers chained by their feet and necks and, in a demonstration of cruelty, brute power, and force, Cortés ordered the great cannon fired. The frightened messengers returned to the capital, giving the following graphic account of the incident to the emperor:

> A thing like a ball of stone comes out of its entrails; it comes out with shooting sparks and raining fire. The smoke that comes out with it has a pestilent odor. . . . This odor penetrates even to the brain and causes the greatest discomfort. . . . If it is aimed against a tree, it shatters the tree into splinters. This is a most unnatural sight, as if the tree had exploded from within. (León-Portilla 1962, 30)

Motecuhzoma was astonished not only by reports of the Spaniards' firearms but by the description that they rode animals that looked like deer and that they had large dogs.

As the Spaniards moved inland toward Tenochtitlán, the Aztec capital, they acquired many allies by force and persuasion. Tribes such as the Totonacs and Tlaxcalans were bitter enemies of the Aztecs and lived under their rule and domination. They, therefore, readily allied themselves with Cortés. Other Indians were awed by the weapons and the numerous daring feats of the Spaniards and thought them to be *Teules,* or gods (Díaz del Castillo 1963, 116–117). Because these tribes lived in constant fear of the Aztecs, they could not believe the deference and respect that the Aztecs accorded the Spaniards. The natives were astonished that, rather than sending his armies to destroy the intruders, Motecuhzoma sent them presents and declared the Aztecs to be the Spaniards' servants (1963, 116–117).

It should be noted that Motecuhzoma and the great lords of Tenochtitlán debated whether to welcome the Spaniards. Motecuhzoma called together his nephew Cacama, his brother Cuitláhuac, and the other great lords. Cuitlahuac cautioned against welcoming the Christians in any way, but Cacama disagreed. Motecuhzoma's nephew felt that

> it would show a want of courage to deny them entrance once they were at the gates. He added that it was not proper for a great lord like his uncle to turn away the ambassadors of another great prince. If the visitors made any demands which displeased Motecuhzoma, he could punish their insolence by sending his hosts of brave warriors against them. (León-Portilla 1962, 61)

Motecuhzoma agreed with his nephew, disregarding his brother's admonition that the strangers would overthrow his rule (León-Portilla 1962, 61).

One confrontation occurred when five Aztec tax collectors entered the Totonac city of Cempoala, and Cortés ordered the Totonac natives to arrest them. The Totonacs were overwhelmed by this daring suggestion, but they reluctantly complied, arresting the tax collectors and beating one who resisted being tied. According to Bernal Díaz del Castillo, "The Act they had witnessed was so astonishing and of such importance to them that they said no human being dared to do such a thing, and it must be the work of *Teules*" (1963, 112).

When Cortés arrived in Tenochtitlán on November 8, 1519, Motecuhzoma willingly accepted his right and authority to subjugate the Aztecs, noting that his people believed that someday

> those who descended from him [Quetzalcóatl] would come to subjugate this country and us . . . and according to the direction from which you say you come, which is where the sun rises, and from what you tell us of your great lord, or king, who has sent you here, we believe and hold for certain, that he is our rightful sovereign. . . . Hence you may be sure that we shall always obey you, and hold you as the representative of this great lord . . . you will be obeyed and recognized and all we possess is at your disposal. (Blacker and Rosen 1962, 43)

As noted earlier, had Pedro de Alvarado not massacred several thousand Indians in an unprovoked attack as they celebrated a religious festival, the Conquest may have been effected with very little additional bloodshed (León-Portilla 1962, 74–76). The massacre in the main temple resulted in an all-out war and the routing of the Spaniards after a furious attack. The downfall of Tenochtitlán came on August 13, 1521, but only after a fierce struggle and with the help of the Tlaxcalans, who nursed Cortés and his men back to health after the Night of Sorrows and joined forces with them in the final siege of the Aztec capital.

In retrospect, then, it is clear that despite the Spaniards' arrogance and cruelty, or perhaps because of it, the extraordinary feats of the conquistadores established them not only as warriors and fearless soldiers but also as symbols of masculinity. Like Pancho Villa and his *Dorados* (Golden Ones), Cortés and his followers from Estremadura embodied personal qualities that have come to be associated with negative machismo. In a word, they were *chingones*. According to Aniceto Aramoni, they were truly the last genuine knights, but they differed from other knights in that they were not mythical or legendary figures, but real men of blood and bones.

Cortés y los conquistadores son estrictamente 'personajes en busca de un autor'; viven la caballería y la escriben con su sangre, sus heridas y sus obras

(Cortés and the conquistadores are strictly 'characters in search of an author'; they live knighthood and write it with their blood, their wounds and their actions). (Aramoni 1965, 129)

Pre-Columbian Roots of Machismo

A third perspective is that *machista* tendencies were clearly evident in Aztec society long before the arrival of the Europeans and that the Spanish emphasis on *caballería* and *hombría* had their counterparts in Indian culture. There are, in fact, striking parallels between the two groups. According to Aramoni (1965, 280), both social systems were patriarchal. They were warring, conquering, predatory, military nations in which men were dominant and women subordinate. The Aztec man was first and foremost a warrior.

> *El hombre iba a la guerra como a la fiesta, a lucir su fuerza, obtener honores y vestir con lujo; se le recompensaba por la labor realizada, calificada por el número de prisioneros que hiciera y el valor desplegado* (The man went to war as if to a party, to demonstrate his strength, receive honor and to dress elegantly; his efforts were rewarded and measured by the number of prisoners he took and the valor he displayed). (Aramoni 1965, 283)

Aztec women assumed a largely domestic role and their status in society was determined by how well they performed their feminine duties. According to the *Florentine Codex,*

> *Habéis de estar dentro de casa, como el corazón dentro del cuerpo, no habéis de andar fuera de casa, no habéis de tener costumbre de ir a ninguna parte; habéis de ser la ceniza con que se cubre el fuego del hogar; habéis de ser las trebedes, donde se pone la olla, en este lugar os entierra nuestro señor; aquí habéis de trabajar, y vuestro oficio ha de ser traer agua, y moler el maíz en el metate; allí habéis de sudar junto a la ceniza y el hogar* (You should be inside the home, as the heart is inside the body; you should not tread outside the home, nor should you make it a habit to go anywhere; you should be like the ashes that cover the hearth of the home; you should be the trivet [tripod] on which the pot is placed; our Lord inters us in this place; you should work here, and your job should be to carry water and to grind the corn on the *metate;* you should sweat there, next to the ashes and the hearth). (Sahagún 1946, 1:603–604)

The exhortation to the male Aztec child proved to be even more revealing. He was told that this house where he was born was not his home; he was a soldier, a warrior, and a bird destined to leave the roost.

> *Eres pájaro que llaman zaquan y también eres ave y soldado del que está en todas partes; pero esta casa donde has nacido no es sino un nido, es una posada*

donde has llegado, es tu salida para este mundo; aquí brotas y floreces, aquí te apartas de tu madre . . . tu propia tierra otra es; para otra parte estás prometido, que es el campo donde se hacen las guerras, donde se traban las batallas, para allí eres enviado, tu oficio y facultad es la guerra, tu obligación es dar a beber al sol sangre de los enemigos, y dar de comer a la tierra . . . con los cuerpos de tus contrarios (Thou art like the zaquan bird and thou art also a bird and a soldier that is everywhere; this house where you were born is but a nest, a resting place where you have arrived, it is your entry into this world; here you blossom and flower, here you separate from your mother . . . your true land is not here; you are promised elsewhere, on the field where wars are waged, where battles are fought, you are to be sent there, your calling and duty is war, you are obliged to quench the sun's thirst with the blood of thine enemies, and to feed the earth . . . with the bodies of thine adversaries). (Sahagún 1946, 1:601–602)

The man was exhorted to be a warrior and to struggle on the field of battle, whereas the woman was to struggle within the home. During the female baptismal ceremony a spindle and a shuttle—symbols of the feminine trades of spinning and weaving—were placed in the center of the patio along with a tiny skirt and smock. The symbols of the boy's vocation, by contrast, were a tiny bow and arrow.

Because the woman's procreative function was central, women who died in childbirth enjoyed a special kind of immortality and were called *mocihuaquetzque*, or "valiant women." They were seen as having fought a fierce battle equivalent to that fought by the male warriors, and they shared residence with brave warriors in a heavenly realm. Whereas procreation fell within the feminine sphere, death corresponded to the male domain. As the culture of the Aztecs was, according to Aramoni (1965, 71), male-oriented and patriarchal, theirs was a masculine world in which men ruled and determined death.

The Aztec codices provide insights not only into various social roles and vocations but also into the rhetoric and moral philosophy of the people. Chapter 20 of Book 6 of the *Florentine Codex,* for example, contains the exhortations of the father, ruler, or nobleman to his son. The son is admonished to follow the humble life and to behave in a manner that is pleasing to his ancestors, to the gods, and to man. He is told to heed the examples and teachings of "our forefathers," the old men and women who are white-headed. The forefathers came to be honored and revered. Although they enjoyed prosperity and all manner of drink and food and were honored by many who came to see them and bring them marvelous gifts, they did not become brazen or presumptuous, but humble and contrite. "The more they were honored, the more they wept, suffered affliction, sighed; they became most humble, most meek, most contrite" (Sahagún 1969, 6:107). Interestingly, those who became the rulers were not the loudest, strongest, or most boastful. Those who oversaw the vassals, who directed the eagle warriors and the ocelot warriors "were the weepers, the sighers, those who humbled themselves . . . the peaceful, the calm, the gentle" (Sahagún 1969, 6:110). Whatever a son's station in life, he was admonished to take it to heart and to behave with humility and meekness.

> Do not praise thyself, . . . be not vain, be not proud, be not presumptuous. Vanity, presumption, pride truly [provoke] the annoyance, the anger of the lord of the near, of the night. . . . Perhaps thou will be something, perhaps thou will be nothing. Just conduct thyself; especially be thy head bowed, thy arms folded, thy head lowered. (1969, 6:111)

In Chapter 21 of Book 6, a father advises his son to observe a life of chastity. The father likened the "pure life" to a jewel, a well-smoked, precious green stone without a blotch or blemish. Thus the son was also admonished to be good of heart, worthy of confidence, and to "not lust for vice, for filth; thou are not to take pleasure in that which defileth one, which corrupteth one, that which, it is said, driveth one to excess, which harmeth, destroyeth one" (1969, 6:116). Because the Lord of the Near, or the Lord of the Night, had ordained one woman for each man, the son was cautioned to avoid sexual excesses and to avoid "ruining" himself impetuously. He was admonished that "thou art not to devour, to gulp down the carnal life as if thou wert a dog" (1969, 6:117). Contrary to the double standard that today is associated with the cult of masculinity and machismo, temperance was called for in the carnal life of the Aztecs.

> And if thou ruinest thyself impetuously, if too soon thou seducest, thou discoverest [women] on earth, verily the old men went saying, thou wilt interrupt thy development, thou wilt be stunted, thy tongue will be stunted, thy tongue will be white, thy mouth will become swollen, puffed; . . . thy nasal mucus will go dripping, thou wilt go coughing, thou wilt be enfeebled, weakened, emaciated . . . very soon to be old, old and wrinkled. (1969, 6:117)

Sex, then, was somehow viewed as existing in a limited quantity, and those who gave themselves excessively to the carnal act endangered themselves. They were said to be like a maguey that has been sucked excessively, or a cape that has been wetted, washed, tightly wrung, and quickly dried. The *Florentine Codex* recounts an incident about two old white-headed women who had committed adultery with two young priests. When the ruler asked why they had betrayed their husbands, the old women replied:

> Ye men, ye are sluggish, ye are depleted, ye have ruined yourselves impetuously. It is all gone. There is no more. There is nothing to be desired. But of this, we who are women, we are not the sluggish ones. In us is a cave, a gorge,

whose only function is to await that which is given, whose only function is to receive. . . . and of this, if thou has become impotent, if thou no longer arouses anything, what other purpose will thou serve? (1969, 6:118–119)

Fidelity in marriage was expected for both husbands and wives. Transgressions brought shame to one's family, and ancestors and were punished by death. The penalty, moreover, was applied uniformly to both the common people, *macehualtin,* and to the nobility, *pipiltin* (Zorita 1963, 130). A jealous husband who beat his wife because he suspected her of adultery was in violation of Aztec law, which specified that she was to be judged and punished by the state. A wife who was beaten unjustly could complain to authorities, and divorce was permissible under such circumstances (Bonilla García 1959, 265). A woman could also obtain a divorce if she proved that her husband did not provide for her nourishment or sustenance. The man, on the other hand, had legitimate grounds for divorce if his wife was sterile, did not carry out her domestic duties, or abandoned the family (1959, 265).

Although fidelity was expected in marriage and monogamy was the prevailing pattern, polygyny was permitted under certain circumstances. In reality it appears to have been practiced only among the *pipiltin,* who were able to absorb the added financial burden (1959, 264). The practice had a practical dimension, as it provided the man with more hands to carry out needed work and afforded him more leisure time. Much of this leisure time was spent playing and gambling, as Aztec men were fond of playing and betting on a particular ball game. They also enjoyed a dice game called *patoliztli.*

Although it was not unusual for the *pipiltin* to have one or more secondary wives and concubines, a distinction was made between the principal wife, who took part in an elaborate marriage ceremony, and secondary wives. Only the children of the principal union were legitimate, but sometimes noble families offered children of secondary unions a place in the affairs of the state (1959, 265).

Prudence and moderation were called for in all aspects of life. One was to sleep in moderation, to be prudent in one's travels, not to hang one's head or incline it too much, to speak very slowly and deliberately, not to dwell upon that which is done, not to gossip, to come the first time one is summoned, not to dress vainly, and, above all else, to be prudent in drink and food. One should not eat hastily or impetuously or break up one's tortillas, but eat them calmly, slowly, and quietly.

In Chapter 14 of Book 6 of the *Florentine Codex* the ruler admonished all residents of the city not to become drunk, to steal, or to commit adultery. The people were warned to leave the jimsonweed alone and to avoid *octli,* or liquor.

It is like a whirlwind, like a severe wind, for it cometh rolling together the bad, the evil. Behold: one [desireth] another's woman; one committeth adultery; one coveteth, one stealeth, one pilfereth. . . . [Because of] the pulque he braggeth falsely of his noble lineage; he thinketh himself superior; he vaunteth himself; he esteemeth himself; he is grandiose; he regardeth on one with much consideration; he valueth no one, praiseth no one; he is disrespectful. (Sahagún 1969, 6:68–69)

Drunkards had no purpose and for this reason the rulers who gave forth the word of the lord would stone or hang people who used pulque to excess (1969, 6:69).

Book 10 of the *Florentine Codex* outlined additional virtues and vices of the people and spoke also of the role of the father. The first chapter speaks of the inherent qualities of those related through lineage or blood. Whereas the good father is depicted as the "sincere one," sympathetic, compassionate, and diligent, the bad father is lazy, uncompassionate, untrustworthy, unfeeling, and neglectful of duty. The good father is also a careful administrator of the household.

He rears, he teaches people. . . . He advises, he admonishes one. He is exemplary; he leads a model life. He stores up for himself; he stores up for others. . . . He is thrifty—he saves for the future, teaches thrift, looks to the future. He regulates, distributes with care, establishes order. (1969, 10:1)

The *Florentine Codex* also outlined the virtues and vices of noble persons and rulers. The good ruler was seen as a protector, one who carries his subjects in his arms and unites them. He carries his subjects in his cape and assumes responsibilities and burdens for their welfare (1969, 10:15). The good noble person similarly was seen as loving, merciful, and compassionate. "He loves others, benefits others, merits respect" (1969, 10:15).

Despite the hierarchical quality of Aztec society and the division of the universe and the society into masculine and feminine realms, there is evidence that calls into question the view that male dominance and patriarchy were endemic to Aztec society and culture. June Nash (1978) rejected the view that male dominance is somehow universal and unvarying, suggesting that the relative dominance of men or women is linked historically to economic and structural conditions. She argued that Aztec society evolved from a society organized around kinship with little status differentiation to a highly specialized empire based on a highly differentiated class structure. According to Nash, there was an "interrelationship between male specialization in warfare, predatory conquest, a state bureaucracy based on patrilineal nobility supported by an ideology of male dominance, and the differential access to its benefits between men and women" (Nash 1978, 350). Throughout its nomadic period and in the early years of residence in the central plateau, Aztec society was governed by the *calpul,* or territorially based kinship group. The *calpul* elected a chief to be in charge of war and another to be in charge of civil and religious acts. In Toltec and early Aztec society women occupied important positions within the economy, had equal rights before the law, and served as priestesses. The society, moreover, was organized around matrilineal descent. According to Jacques Soustelle, "In former times women had held the supreme power, as at Tula" (1968, 183).

Although war occupied a central role in the society and men were destined from an early age to be warriors, war also had a symbolic and ritual meaning. In an interesting article Inga Clendinnen (1985) provided considerable insights into the role of ritual, war, and courage in Aztec society. The first gathering of the agricultural harvest and the fine frosts signaled the beginning of the Aztec season of war and was celebrated with the Feast of the Flaying of Men. According to Clendinnen,

> Eighty days after that harvest, the first crop of warrior captives was killed, and eighty days after that, as the first sign of spring indicated the beginning of the planting season, came the Feast Day of the Flaying of Men. (1985, 68)

The feast featured the great warriors and honored Xipe Totec, the Flayer or the Flayed One. The less important war captives were killed on the first day of the festival. After the body was dismembered it was given to the captor, who gathered his kin at his house. "There, amid weeping and lamentations, the kinsmen of the captor each ate a small piece of flesh served with a dish of 'dried' (unsoftened?) maize kernels" (1985, 69). The captor, however, would not participate in the feast. He would refuse to eat the maize stew and the flesh of his captive, saying "Shall I perchance eat my very self?" (1985, 69). The captor would not eat the flesh of his victim because he ideally hoped to someday die in battle. Since death in battle was rare, ritualized executions took place and victims were sacrificed on the stone.

Violence was ritualized and socially sanctioned. The person who was "furious in war" and went into battle blindly was valued and rewarded but was not accorded a position of authority or unqualified social support. The person who did not know fear was not socially informed. "Admiration was reserved for the warrior who is morally informed; who understands his obligation" (1985, 88).

Thus there was a contradiction between the official rhetoric of self-control and moderation and the reality of public, ritualized displays of violence. This contradiction can only be resolved if we begin to understand the role that violence played in Aztec culture and religion. To describe as "violence" the deliberate sequence

> of bloody acts which we see brought into the frame and focus of ritual action is to assume that their point lay in their destructiveness. But the crucial under-

FIGURE 2.4   Nezahualcoyotl, king of Tetzcoco, dressed in war attire: a feather tunic and kilt (*ehuatl*) usually worn over padded cotton armor (*ichcahuipilli*), greaves (*cozehuatl*), armbands (*matemecatl*), wristlets (*matzopetztli*), sandals (*cactli*), a helmet, and a gold lip plug. He is armed with a feather-fringed shield (*yaochimalli*) and a sword (*macuahuitl*) and carries a small upright drum (*huehuetl*) on his back to signal the attack. Codex Ixtlilxochitl 106r. Courtesy of the Bibliothèque Nationale, Paris.

standings which grounded those killings and slow dismembering were that human flesh and maize—"maize" as metonym for all vegetable sustenance—were the same matter in different transformations; that the transformations were cyclic, and the cycles constantly in jeopardy; and that men's actions played a part . . . in maintaining the sequence. (1985, 89)

Indian and Spanish Images of Men: A Comparison and Critique

Although it is not possible from this brief historical overview to determine which explanation of the development of the cult of masculinity or machismo in Latino culture is ultimately the best or "correct" explanation, it is possible to compare and contrast Indian and Spanish images of men. Aztec society was militaristic, hierarchical, and at the time of the Conquest, undoubtedly patriarchal. At the same time, prevailing conceptions of masculinity in Aztec society appear to have been dramatically at odds both with the contemporary masculine cult and with the Spanish conception of *hombría* and *caballería*. Unlike the conquistadores, who were *chingones*, and like the negative *pelado*, brazen in their displays of masculinity, Indian men were exhorted to be humble and contrite rather than boastful and vain. Vanity, presumptuousness, and pride provoked the anger of the Lord of the Night. Prudence and moderation were expected in all realms of existence, including eating, drinking, and the carnal life. Although adultery occurred, it was not sanctioned and was severely punished by society.

The *Florentine Codex* reveals that the good father was sincere, diligent, and compassionate. Although the Aztec universe was based on the concept of dualities, and although the male sphere was the battlefield and the female sphere centered on domestic duties, women, especially in the early period, were certainly not confined to the home. Women of all social classes participated at all levels of Aztec society (see Mirandé and Enríquez 1981, 14–52). Noblewomen were recognized for their good deeds on behalf of the less fortunate, whereas lower-class women contributed to the more basic and mundane needs of society as weavers, spinners, and cooks. "Perhaps the highest status in the domestic realm was accorded the *partera*, or midwife" (1981, 16), who was recognized not only for her medicinal and obstetrical skills but also for her spiritual and religious role. Women also accompanied men to battle and served as cooks and carriers of supplies. Although male priests occupied the most privileged positions, women participated actively in the religious sphere and served as priestesses, or *ciuatlamacazqui* (Soustelle 1968, 54–55). The genesis of the Aztec universe was feminine, as embodied by the "Lady of the Serpent Skirt" (Coatlicue). This goddess was awesome, the creator and destroyer of all life and matter. In addition, almost half of the eighteen months in the Aztec calendar contained feast days in honor of feminine deities or cults (Clendinnen 1991, 295–300). The ceremonies on such days were conducted by priestesses and celebrated mostly by women (Mirandé and Enríquez 1981, 18).

The view propagated by Paz, Ramos, and Goldwert—which sees excessive masculine displays as attempts to compensate for subconscious feelings of impotence and inferiority—is based on a psychoanalytic model that assumes that the Spanish Conquest had a very profound and disturbing impact on contemporary Mexican culture. Although this view may be interesting and provocative, there are a number of problems that make it difficult to accept as an adequate explanation of contemporary expressions of machismo in Latino culture. One is that it is based on a metaphysical theory that assumes events and incidents that transpire in one historical period can have a direct and unchanging effect on the psyche of subsequent generations. The view holds, as Goldwert noted, that the Conquest was a time of "kairos," or trauma, that shaped all ensuing human relationships. An additional difficulty with this explanation is that it is inherently and primarily pathological, essentially treating all of Mexican history and culture as a manifestation of dysfunction, sickness, and disease. For example, the title of Goldwert's (1980) book on paternalism and machismo in Latin America is *History as Neurosis*. Finally, the view is problematic in that it derives from a form of genetic transnational determinism that assumes events that occurred in México in the course of the Conquest have a direct impact not only on all of Latin America but also on persons of Mexican descent residing in the United States (i.e., Chicanos).

Although it cannot be denied that our pre-Columbian heritage and the Conquest have had a substantial impact on Mexican culture and on expressions of masculinity, the explanation that appears most plausible is that machismo and the cult of masculinity, in their most extreme and negative form, were introduced to the New World by the Spanish conquistadores. They provided the model of the figure of the negative macho—daring, arrogant, dominant, insensitive, warring, irreverent, lewd, unpredictable, and lustful men of action who committed numerous *chingaderas* in the course of the Conquest and in the name of their Christian god. The Aztecs were warriors, but their military activities had a religious thrust and justification—to satisfy the gods and feed the sun.

This discussion is not meant to suggest that negative machismo was directly transplanted to the New World and immediately adopted by the indigenous population, but rather that the conquistadores embodied many of the traits traditionally associated with the masculine cult. They had power and were *chingones*. By contrast, Indian society represented a very different and less pathological ideal of masculinity, one that stressed attributes such as modesty, virtue, responsibility, caring for children, wisdom, and judiciousness. A good man in Indian society was not loud, boastful, pretentious, irresponsible, or vain. And he certainly did not go about committing *chingaderas*. In Chapter 6 of Book 10 of the *Florentine Codex*, the "bad brave man" is depicted as

> One who leads others to destruction by his deception, who secretly puts one in difficulty; who visits others' houses; who yells; who slays others viciously, who treacherously forsakes one, who swoons with terror. He becomes frightened, he swoons with terror, he secretly puts one in difficulty (*In tlaueliloc oquichtli tenaoalpoloani, tetlanaoaltequiliani, tecacalaquini tlaoio, teauilmictiani texiccaoani, mauhcaçonequini, momauhtia, mauhcaçonequi tetlanaoaltequilia*). (1969, 10:23)

Nepantla and the Concept of Ecosis

The notion that the Conquest was not only a military defeat but also a total moral and spiritual downfall is consistent with the missionary zeal that led the conquering friars to overestimate the success of the mass conversion of the Indians. The very use of terms like "conquest," "pacification," or "conversion" to describe what transpired may serve to underestimate the extent to which pre-Columbian society either resisted conversion to European civilization and Christian precepts or incorporated them into existing indigenous institutions and worldviews.

León-Portilla noted that the accounts of the spiritual conquest left by the friars were designed to support the assertion that they had succeeded in bringing about widespread acceptance of Christianity among the natives (León-Portilla 1990, 56). In the first decade following the fall of Tenochtitlán the missionaries were said to be "euphoric" about the success of conversion campaigns (1990, 57). Father Motolinía, for example, maintained that between 1521 and 1536, more than four million souls were baptized (1990, 57–58). Motolinía claimed that the forty or so active Franciscan fathers at the time had each baptized more than one hundred thousand individuals and that some had baptized as many as three hundred thousand (1990, 58).

Though native accounts are rare, there is growing evidence that there was massive resistance to the Conquest and the imposition of Christianity. The Indians reputedly accepted the *Virgen de Guadalupe* as the patron saint of the Mexican people because her apparition occurred on the hill of Tepeyac near a shrine to the Indian goddess *Tonantzín*. The Spanish clergy expressed concern, however, that the Indians continued to worship Indian idols rather than *Nuestra Señora* (Our Lady, or the Virgin Mary).

In the introduction to *Procesos de Indios Idolatras y Hechiceros* Luis González Obregon notes that one of the problems with the mass conversions of the Indians was that they were accomplished through interpreters who, though intelligent, were not equipped to explain the subtlety and depth of the Catholic religion (*Procesos de Indios Idolatras y Hechiceros* 1912, vi). As a result, many Indians were brought before inquisitorial tribunals for continuing to adhere to false idols and failing to follow the Christian faith. On June 28, 1836, Bishop Zumárraga initiated the inquisitorial process against "Indian Heretics and Sorcerers."

Following the death of his wife, an Indian named Tacatecle, for example, was accused of incest after allegedly marrying his daughter (1912, 10–11). He was also accused of hiding eight bloodied idols in a cave and secretly conducting sacrifices to them. Tacatecle acknowledged knowing the idols and said they represented his gods. During the tribunal various witnesses testified against Tacatecle, including his daughter María. The daughter said that she had been baptized five years earlier by a father in Tula, but that she had not attended church or been exposed to church doctrine. María confessed that she was married and had two children with her father and that she knew this was a grave sin (1912, 14).

In a trial that drew a great deal of attention and notoriety, Don Carlos Ometochitzin, a local leader and lord of Tetzcoco, was charged in 1539 by the *Proceso Inquisitorial* with continuing his idolatry even after having been baptized (León-Portilla 1990, 75–76). Named *Yoyontzin* in his native language and Mendoza in Spanish and having assumed the title of *Chichiemecatecutli* as one of the lords of Tetzcoco, Don Carlos Ometochitzin was the nephew of the great and wise poet Nezahualcóyotl and son of the chronicler Netzahualpilli (*Proceso Inquisitorial del Cacique de Tetzcoco* 1910, x). Although acknowledging that he too had been raised in the faith, Don Carlos called into question the authority of the Spanish fathers, their teachings, and their god, asking:

> *¿Esos padres son nuestros parientes ó nacieron entre nosotros? Si yo viese que lo que mis padres y antepasados tuvieron conformaba con esta ley de Dios, por ventura la goardaría y la respetaría. Pues, hermanos, goardemos y tengamos lo que nuestros antepasados tuvieron é goardaron. . . . y esto que los predicadores nos enseñan oyámoslo y echémoslo atrás, y no curemos de ello, y ninguno ponga su corazón en esta ley de Dios ni ame a Dios. ¿Qué certidumbre véis é halláis en esta ley? Yo no lo entiendo; mira, hermano, que pecas en hacer creer á los viejos y viejas esta ley, pues sábete que nuestros antepasados dixieron muy de cierto, que la ley que ellos goardaron que en el cielo tuvo principio, y que los dioses que ellos tenían, solo aquellos eran los verdaderos, y su ley era la buena y verdadera.* (Are these fathers our relatives or were they born amongst us? If I saw that what our parents and ancestors taught us was consistent with this law of God, I would guard and respect it. Well, my brothers, let us guard and nurture the teachings that our ancestors had and guarded. . . . and let us hear what these preaching fathers tell us and put it aside, and let us not believe in it, and let no one put his heart in this law of God nor love God. What truth is there in this law? I do not understand it; recognize my brother that you sin in making our elders believe in this law, for you know that our ancestors said with certainty that the law which they guarded and which originated in heaven, and the gods that our ancestors had, they were the true ones, and their law was good and true). (Proceso Inquisitorial del Cacique de Tetzcoco 1910, 49)

Another example of Indian resistance is found in the *Coloquios*, or dialogues, between the twelve Franciscan friars and some of the native wise men. These Náhuatl texts, which were gathered by Sahagún, reveal the Indian concern with the destruction of their worldview and religion.

> Our Lord, very esteemed lords:
>   You have endured hardship to arrive in this land. Here before you, we ignorant people contemplate you. . . . And now, what shall we say? What shall we raise to your ears? We are merely common people. . . .
>   Through an interpreter we respond, we return the breath and word of the Lord of the Near and of the Surrounding (Tloque Nahuaque).. . .
>   Because of him we put ourselves at risk, for Him we put ourselves into danger. . . . Perhaps we are to be taken to our ruin, perhaps to our destruction.

[But] where are we to go now? We are common people, we are destructible, we are mortal. Le us die now, let us perish, since our gods have already died. (León-Portilla 1990, 68–69)

Mexican anthropologist León-Portilla introduces two innovative concepts that may help to explain the Indian resistance to conversion: *nepantla* and ecosis. *Nepantla* is a Náhuatl word that means "in the middle," or "neutral." In the mid-sixteenth century a Dominican friar named Diego Durán had reprimanded an Indian for his behavior, noting that it was at odds both with Christian precepts and with indigenous customs and morals (León-Portilla 1990, 10). The wise old native answered: "Father, don't be afraid, for we are still *'nepantla.'*" The trauma of "nepantlism" was also captured by the response of indigenous wise men after hearing the words condemning their ancient beliefs.

We cannot be tranquil, and certainly we still do not believe, we do not accept as true that which you say, even though this might offend you. . . . It is enough already that we have lost, that it has been taken from us, that our ancient way of life has been impeded. If we remain in this place, we will not only be made prisoners. . . .
    Allow us to die, allow us to perish, since our gods have already died. (León-Portilla 1990, 10)

Borrowing from the historian Thucydides, León-Portilla also introduced the term "ecosis" to his study of human communities. Initially, ecosis meant the process of making or organizing a house, but León-Portilla expanded the concept to include "the whole set of transformations that a human community makes for its own well-being, by acting upon the geographic area where it has settled in order to develop there" (León-Portilla 1990, 11). According to this view, Mexican society existed as an ecosis prior to the Conquest. Rather than being destroyed by the Conquest, it has continued to adapt and change for its well-being by acting on the geographic area in order to develop in this locale or environment. More precisely, through the term ecosis,

one seeks to underline the antecedents and consequences, as well as the forms of development, of the processes of contact between a human group and a particular natural context. Elements that appear common to all ecoses involve the purposeful actions of a group, such as seeking the advantageous exploitation of environmental resources and the establishment of a foundation that transforms the area into a home or place or residence. (León-Portilla 1990, 11)

The concepts of *nepantla* and ecosis stand in sharp contrast to such dominant societal conceptions as assimilation and acculturation. The problem with concepts like assimilation and acculturation is that, like "conquest" or "conversion," they reflect the view of the dominant group—the views of the conqueror rather than those of the subordinate group or the vanquished. The point is that though the European invasion and the military defeat were undoubtedly painful and traumatic experiences for the Indian, the natives actively resisted and only reluctantly accepted the imposition of Spanish culture and Christianization and the destruction of their way of life and gods. Contemporary México is *México-Tenochtitlán*, an indigenous people, culture, and civilization that has incorporated elements of Christianity and Western civilization. It would remain *México-Tenochtitlán* after the arrival of Cortés, during my childhood, through the current *crisis*, and beyond.

3

"Macho": Contemporary Conceptions

Mi Noche Triste

My own *noche triste* occurred when my father returned from location on the film *Capitán de Castilla* (Captain from Castille). I remember that he had been gone for a long time, that he came back from Morelia with a lot of presents, and that at first, I was very happy to see him. Then there was a big fight; my parents argued all night, and they separated shortly thereafter.[1] One night when my mother was very sad and depressed, she went to *el árbol de la noche triste*. As she cried by the tree she thought about how she and Hernán Cortés both had been in the same situation: depressed, weeping, and alone.

After my parents separated, my brothers and I went with my father and moved to Tacubaya to live with his mother, Anita, and her mother (my great-grandmother), Carmela (Mamá Mela). Grandmother Anita, or *Abillá*, as we called her, was a petite, energetic little woman, but Mamá Mela was tall, dark, and stately. In Tacubaya we were also surrounded by family, but now it was my father's family, Mirandé-Salazar. His family was smaller because he was an only child and because his father's two siblings, Concha (Consuelo) and Lupe (Guadalupe), never married or had children. My grandfather, Alfredo, died when I was about two years old, but I remember him.

In Tacubaya we first lived in a big, long house with a large green entrance, *El Nueve* (nine), on a street called Vicente Eguía, before moving to an apartment house, *El Trece* (thirteen), down the street. At *El Trece* we lived in the first apartment, and my great-aunts, Concha and Lupe, lived in *El Seis* (six). Concha had been an elementary school teacher and Lupe was an artist. They were retired but very active; both did a lot of embroidering and Lupe was always painting. I was very fond of *las tías*. To me *las tías* always seemed old and very religious, but I was very close to my aunts and

63

loved them deeply. They wore black shawls and went to church early each morning. When I wasn't playing in the courtyard, I was often visiting with my aunts. They taught me catechism, and Tía Lupe was my *madrina*, or godmother, for my first communion.

I would spend hours with *las tías*, fascinated by their conversation. It seemed that every minute was filled with stories about the Mexican Revolution and about my grandfather, Alfredo. I especially liked it when they spoke about him, as I had been named Alfredo and identified with him. They said he was a great man and that they would be very proud and happy if I grew up to be like him someday. No, it was actually that I had no choice—I was destined to be like him. Because I had the good fortune of being named after Alfredo, I had to carry on his name, and, like him, I too would be a great man someday. I should add that my aunts stressed *man* when they talked about him. In other words, I had a distinct impression that my grandfather and I were linked not only because we were both named Mirandé and Alfredo, but also because we were both men. I did not realize it at the time, but my teachers (who were mostly women)—*las tías*, my *Abillá*, Mamá Mela, and my mother—were socializing me into my "sex role." But I don't remember anyone describing Grandfather Alfredo as "macho." Perhaps my *tías* took his being "macho" for granted, since he was obviously male.

I do not know very much about Alfredo's family, except that his father, Juan, or *Jean*, came to México from France and married a *mexicana*, María. I also learned from my mother that Alfredo was of humble origins and was, in a very real sense, a self-made man who studied and pursued a career as a civil engineer. He was committed to bringing about social justice and distributing the land held by the *hacendados* (landowners) among the Mexican *peones*. As a civilian he served under Emiliano Zapata, making cannons and munitions. According to historian John Womack (1968, 291), Alfredo Mirandé was one of Zapata's key assistants and worked as a spy in Puebla for some time under the code name "DELTA." While he was in hiding, my *Abillá* would take in other people's clothes to mend and to launder to earn money so that the family could survive. My grandfather grew to be disillusioned, however, as the Revolution did not fulfill its promise of bringing about necessary economic and social reforms.

My *tías* had a photograph of Alfredo standing proudly in front of a new, experimental cannon that he had built. They related that a foolish and headstrong general, anxious to try out the new cannon, pressured Alfredo to fire it before it was ready. My grandfather reluctantly complied and received severe burns all over his body, almost dying as a result of the explosion. It took him months to recover from the accident.

As I think back, most of the stories they told me had a moral and were designed, indirectly at least, to impart certain values. What I learned from my *tías* and, indirectly, from my grandfather was that although one should

Alfredo Ignacio Mirandé and Ana María Salazar de Mirandé.

stand up for principles, one should attempt to avoid war and personal conflicts, if at all possible. One should also strive to be on a higher moral plane than one's adversaries. Alfredo was intelligent, strong, and principled. But what impressed me most is that he was said to be incredibly just and judicious. Everyone who knew him said he treated people of varying educational and economic levels fairly, equally, and with dignity and respect.

I realize that Alfredo lived in a society and a historical period in which women were relegated to an inferior status. Yet I also know that he and my grandmother shared a special intimacy and mutual respect such as I have never personally encountered. By all accounts they loved and respected each other and shared an incredible life together. I have read letters that my grandfather wrote to my grandmother when they were apart, and they indicate that he held her in very high regard and treated her as an equal partner.

"Macho": An Overview

Mexican folklorist Vicente T. Mendoza suggested that the word "macho" was not widely used in Mexican songs, *corridos* (folk ballads), or popular culture until the 1940s (Mendoza 1962, 75–86). Use of the word was said to have gained in popularity after Avila Camacho became president. The word lent itself to use in *corridos* because "macho" rhymed with "Camacho."

While "macho" has traditionally been associated with Mexican or Latino culture, the word has recently been incorporated into American popular culture, so much so that it is now widely used to describe everything from rock stars and male sex symbols in television and film to burritos. When applied to entertainers, athletes, or other "superstars," the implied meaning is clearly a positive one that connotes strength, virility, masculinity, and sex appeal. But when applied to Mexicans or Latinos, "macho" remains imbued with such negative attributes as male dominance, patriarchy, authoritarianism, and spousal abuse. Although both meanings connote strength and power, the Anglo macho is clearly a much more positive and appealing symbol of manhood and masculinity. In short, under current usage the Mexican macho oppresses and coerces women, whereas his Anglo counterpart appears to attract and seduce them.

This chapter focuses on variations in perceptions and conceptions of the word "macho" held by Mexican and Latino men. Despite all that has been written and said about the cult of masculinity and the fact that male dominance has been assumed to be a key feature of Mexican and Latino culture, very little research exists to support this assumption. Until recently such generalizations were based on stereotypes, impressionistic evidence, or the observations of ethnographers such as Oscar Lewis (1960, 1961), Arthur Rubel (1966), and William Madsen (1973). These Anglo ethnographers were criticized by noted Chicano folklorist Américo Paredes (1977) for the persistent ignorance and insensitivity to Chicano language and culture that is reflected in their work. Paredes contended, for example, that although most anthropologists present themselves as politically liberal and fluent in Spanish, many are only minimally fluent and fail to grasp the nuance and complexity of Chicano language. There is, it seems, good reason to be leery of their findings and generalizations regarding not only gender roles but also all aspects of the Mexican/Latino experience.

Utilizing data obtained through qualitative open-ended questions, I look in this chapter at how Latino men themselves perceive the word "macho" and how they describe men who are considered *"muy machos."* Although all of the respondents were living in the United States at the time of the interviews, many were foreign-born and retained close ties with Mexican/Latino culture. Since they had been subjected to both Latino and American influences, I wondered whether they would continue to adhere to traditional Mexican definitions of "macho" or whether they had been influenced by contemporary American conceptions of the word.

Specifically, an attempt was made in the interviews to examine two polar views. The prevailing view in the social science literature of the Mexican macho is a negative one. This view holds that the origins of excessive masculine displays and the cult of masculinity in México and other Latino countries can be traced to the Spanish Conquest, as the powerless colonized man attempted to compensate for deep-seated feelings of inadequacy and inferiority by assuming a hypermasculine, aggressive, and domineering stance. There is a second and lesser-known view that is found in Mexican popular culture, particularly in film and music, one that reflects a more positive, perhaps idyllic, conception of Mexican culture and national character. Rather than focusing on violence and male dominance, this second view associates macho qualities with the evolution of a distinct code of ethics.

Un hombre que es macho is not hypermasculine or aggressive, and he does not disrespect or denigrate women. Machos, according to the positive view, adhere to a code of ethics that stresses humility, honor, respect of oneself and others, and courage. What may be most significant in this second view is that being "macho" is not manifested by such outward qualities as physical strength and virility but by such inner qualities as personal integrity, commitment, loyalty, and, most importantly, strength of character. Stated simply, a man who acted like my Tío Roberto would be macho in the first sense of the word but certainly not in the second. It is not clear how this code of ethics developed, but it may be linked to nationalist sentiments and Mexican resistance to colonization and foreign invasion. Historical figures such as Cuauhtémoc, El Pipíla, Los Niños Héroes, Villa, and Zapata would be macho according to this view. In music and film positive macho figures such as Pedro Infante, Jorge Negrete, and even Cantinflas are patriots, but mostly they are muy hombres, men who stand up against class and racial oppression and the exploitation of the poor by the rich.

Despite the apparent differences between the two views, both see the macho cult as integral to Mexican and Latino cultures. Although I did not formulate explicit hypotheses, I entered the field expecting that respondents would generally identify with the word "macho" and define it as a positive trait or quality in themselves and other persons. An additional informal hypothesis proposed was that men who had greater ties to Latino culture and the Spanish language would be more likely to identify and to have positive associations with the word. I expected, in other words, that respondents would be more likely to adhere to the positive view of macho.

Findings: Conceptions of Macho

Respondents were first asked the following question: "What does the word 'macho' mean to you?" The interviewers were instructed to ask this and all other questions in a neutral tone, as we wanted the respondents to feel that we really were interested in what they thought. We stressed in the interviews that there were no "right" or "wrong" answers to any of the questions. This first question was then followed by a series of follow-up questions that included: "Can you give me an example (or examples) of someone you think is really macho?"; "What kinds of things do people who are really macho do?"; and "Can a woman be macha?"

Each person was assigned an identification number, and the responses to the above questions were typed on a large index card. Three bilingual judges, two men and one woman, were asked to look at the answers on the cards and to classify each respondent according to whether they believed the respondent was generally "positive," "negative," or "neutral" toward the word "macho." Those respondents classified as "positive" saw the term as a desirable cultural or personal trait or value, identified with it, and believed that it is generally good to be, or at least to aspire to be, macho. But those respondents classified as "negative" by the judges saw it as an undesirable or devalued cultural or personal trait, did not identify with being macho, and believed that it is generally bad or undesirable to be macho. In the third category, respondents were classified as "neutral" if they were deemed to be indifferent or ambivalent or to recognize both positive and negative components of the word "macho." For these respondents, macho was "just a word," or it denoted a particular male feature without imputing anything positive or negative about the feature itself.

Overall there was substantial agreement among the judges. In 86 percent of 105 cases the judges were in complete agreement in their classifications, and in another 12 percent two out of three agreed. In other words, in only two instances was there complete disagreement among the judges in which one judge ranked the respondents positive, another negative, and still another neutral.

One of the most striking findings is the extent to which the respondents were polarized in their views of macho. Most had very strong feelings; very few were neutral or indifferent toward the word. In fact, only 11 percent of the 105 respondents were classified as neutral by our judges. No less surprising is the fact that, contrary to my expectations, very few respondents viewed the word in a positive light. Only 31 percent of the men were positive in their views of macho, compared to 57 percent who were classified as negative. This means, in effect, that more than two-thirds of the respondents believed that the word "macho" had either negative or neutral connotations.

My expectation that those individuals with greater ties to Latino culture would be more likely to identify and to have positive associations with "macho" was also not supported by the data. Of the thirty-nine respondents who opted to be interviewed in Spanish, only 15 percent were seen as having a positive association with macho, whereas 74 percent were negative and 10 percent were neutral toward the term. In contrast, of the sixty-six interviewed in English, 41 percent were classified as positive, 47 percent as negative, and 12 percent as neutral toward the term.

Although negative views of the word "macho" were more prevalent than I had expected, the responses closely parallel the polar views of the word "macho" discussed earlier. Responses classified as "negative" by our judges are consistent with the "compensatory" or "deficit" model, which sees the emphasis on excessive masculinity among Mexicans and Latinos as an attempt to conceal pervasive feelings of inferiority among native men that resulted from the Conquest and the ensuing cultural, moral, and spiritual rape of the indigenous population. Those classified as "positive," similarly, are roughly consistent with an "ethical" model, which sees macho behavior as a positive, nationalist response to colonization, foreign intervention, and class exploitation.

Negative Conceptions of "Macho"

A number of consistent themes are found among the men who were classified as viewing the word "macho" in a negative light. Though I divide them into separate themes to facilitate the presentation of the findings, there is obviously considerable overlap between them.

Negative Theme 1: Synthetic/Exaggerated Masculinity. A theme that was very prevalent in the responses is that machos are men who are insecure in themselves and need to prove their manhood. It was termed a "synthetic self-image," "exaggerated masculinity," "one who acts tough and is insecure in himself," and an "exaggerated form of manliness or super manliness." One respondent described a macho as

> one who acts "bad." One who acts tough and who is insecure of himself. I would say *batos* [dudes] who come out of the *pinta* [prison] seem to have a tendency to be insecure with themselves, and tend to put up a front. [They] talk loud, intimidate others, and disrespect the meaning of a man.

Another person described it as

> being a synthetic self-image that's devoid of content. . . . It's a sort of facade that people use to hide the lack of strong, positive personality traits. To me, it often implies a negative set of behaviors. . . . I have a number of cousins who fit that. I have an uncle who fits it. He refuses to have himself fixed even though he was constantly producing children out of wedlock.

Negative Theme 2: Male Dominance/Authoritarianism. A second, related theme is that of male dominance, chauvinism, and the double standard for men and women. Within the family, the macho figure is viewed as authoritarian, especially relative to the wife. According to one respondent, "They insist on being the dominant one in the household. What they say is the rule. They treat women as inferior. They have a dual set of rules for women and men." Another respondent added:

> It's someone that completely dominates. There are no two ways about it; it's either his way or no way. My dad used to be a macho. He used to come into the house drunk, getting my mother out of bed, making her make food, making her cry.

A Spanish-speaker characterized the macho as follows:

> *Una persona negativa completamente. Es una persona que es irresponsable en una palabra. Que anda en las cantinas. Ese no es hombre. Si, conozco muchos de mi tierra; una docena. Toman, pelean. Llegan a la casa gritando y golpeando a la señora, gritando, cantando. Eso lo vi yo cuando era chavalillo y se me grabó. Yo nunca vi a mi papá que golpeara a mi mamá* (A completely negative person. In a word, it's a person who is irresponsible. Who is out in the taverns. That's not a man. Yes, I know many from my homeland; a dozen. They drink, fight. They come home yelling and hitting the wife, yelling, singing. I saw this as a child and it made a lasting impression on me. I never saw my father hit my mother).

Negative Theme 3: Violence/Aggressiveness. A third, related theme is macho behavior manifested in expressions of violence, aggressiveness, and irresponsibility, both inside and outside the family. It is "someone that does not back down, especially if they fear they would lose face over the most trivial matters." Another person saw macho as the exaggeration of perceived masculine traits and gave the example of a fictional figure like Rambo and a real figure like former president Ronald Reagan. This person added that it was "anyone who has ever been in a war," and "it's usually associated with dogmatism, with violence, with not showing feelings." A Spanish-speaking man summarized it succinctly as *"el hombre que sale de su trabajo los viernes, va a la cantina, gasta el cheque, y llega a su casa gritando, pegándole a su esposa diciendo que él es el macho"* (the man who gets out of work on Friday, goes to a bar, spends his check, and comes home yelling and hitting his wife and telling her that he is the macho [i.e., man]). Still another felt that men who were macho did such things as "drinking to excess," and that associated with the word "macho" was "the notion of physical prowess or intimidation of others. A willingness to put themselves and others at risk, particularly physically. For those that are married, the notion of having women on the side."

One of our Spanish-speaking respondents mentioned an acquaintance who lost his family because he would not stop drinking. *"Él decía, 'La mujer se hizo para andar en la casa y yo pa' andar en las cantinas'"* (He used to say, "Woman was made to stay at home and I was made to stay in taverns"). This respondent also noted that men who are real machos tend not to support their families or tend to beat them, to get "dandied up," and to go out drinking. Another said that they "drink tequila" and "have women on their side kissing them."

Negative Theme 4: Self-Centeredness/Egoísmo. Closely related is the final theme, which views someone who is macho as being self-centered, selfish, and stubborn, a theme that is especially prevalent among respondents with close ties to México. Several men saw machismo as *un tipo de egoísmo* (a type of selfishness) and felt that it referred to a person who always wanted things done his way—*a la mía.* It is someone who wants to impose his will on others or wants to be right, whether he is right or not. It is viewed, for example, as

un tipo de egoísmo que nomás "lo mío" es bueno y nomás mis ideas son bue-
nas. Como se dice, "Nomás mis chicharrones truenan." . . . Se apegan a lo que
ellos creen. Todo lo que ellos dicen está correcto. Tratan que toda la gente entre
a su manera de pensar y actuar, incluyendo hijos y familia (a type of selfishness
where only "mine" is good and only my ideas are worthwhile. As the saying
goes, "Whatever I say goes." . . . They cling to their own beliefs. Everything
they say is right. They try to get everyone, including children and family, to
think and act the way they do).

Some respondents who elaborated on the "self-centeredness" or *egoísta* theme noted that some men will hit their wives "just to prove that they are machos," while others try to show that they "wear the pants" by not letting their wives go out. One person noted that some men believe that wives and daughters should not be permitted to cut their hair because long hair is considered "a sign of femininity," and another made reference to a young man who actually cut off a finger in order to prove his love to his sweetheart.

Because the word "macho" literally means a "he-mule" or a "he-goat," respondents often likened macho men to a dumb animal such as a mule, goat, or bull: "Somebody who's like a bull, or bullish"; "The man who is strong as though he were an animal"; "It's an ignorant person, like an animal, a donkey or mule"; and "It's a word that is outside of that which is human." One person described a macho as

the husband of the mule that pulls the plow. A macho is a person who is dumb
and uneducated. *Hay tienes a* [There you have] Macho Camacho [the boxer].
He's a wealthy man, but that doesn't make a smart man. I think he's dumb! . . .
They're aggressive, and they're harmful, and insensitive.

Another respondent said, "Ignorant, is what it means to me, a fool. They're fools, man. They act bully type." Another similarly linked it to being "ignorant, dumb, stupid," noting that they "try to take advantage of their physical superiority over women and try to use that as a way of showing that they are right."

Given that these respondents viewed "macho" in a negative light, it is not surprising to find that most did not consider themselves macho. Only eight of the sixty men in this category reluctantly acknowledged that they were "somewhat" macho. One said, "Yes, sometimes when I drink, I get loud and stupid," and another, "Yes, to an extent because I have to be headstrong and bullish as a teacher."

Positive Conceptions of Macho:
Courage, Honor, and Integrity

As previously noted, only about thirty percent of the respondents were classified as seeing macho as a desirable cultural or personal trait or value, and those who did so were much more apt to conduct the interview in English. Some 82 percent of the men who had positive conceptions were interviewed in English.

As was true of men who were classified as negative toward the word "macho," several themes were discernible among those classified as positive. And as with the negative themes, they are separate but overlapping. A few respondents indicated that it meant "masculine" or "manly" (*varonil*), a type of masculinity (*una forma de masculinidad*), or male. The overriding theme, however, linked machismo to internal qualities like courage, valor, honor, sincerity, respect, pride, humility, and responsibility. Some went so far as to identify a distinct code of ethics or a set of principles that they saw as being characteristic of machismo.

Positive Theme 1: Assertiveness/Standing Up for Rights. A more specific subtheme is the association of machismo with being assertive, courageous, standing up for one's rights, or going "against the grain" relative to other persons. The following response is representative of this view:

> To me it means someone that's assertive, someone who stands up for his or her rights when challenged. . . . Ted Kennedy because of all the hell he's had to go through. I think I like [Senator] Feinstein. She takes the issues by the horns. . . . They paved their own destiny. They protect themselves and those that are close to them and attempt to control their environment versus the contrast.

It is interesting to note that this view of being macho can be androgynous. Several respondents mentioned women who exemplified "macho qualities" or indicated that these qualities may be found among either gender. Another man gave John Kennedy and Eleanor Roosevelt as examples and noted that people who are macho

> know how to make decisions because they are confident of themselves. They know their place in the world. They accept themselves for what they are and they are confident in that. They don't worry about what others think. . . . They know what to do, the things that are essential to them and others around them.

A Spanish-speaking respondent added:

> *En respecto a nuestra cultura es un hombre que defiende sus valores, en total lo físico, lo emocional, lo psicológico. En cada mexicano hay cierto punto de macho. No es arrogante, no es egoísta excepto cuando tiene que defender sus valores. No es presumido* (Relative to our culture, it's a man that stands up for what he believes, physically, emotionally, and psychologically. Within every Mexican there is a certain sense of being macho. He is not arrogant, not egoistic, except when he has to defend his values. He is not conceited).

Positive Theme 2: Responsibility/Selflessness. A second positive macho theme is responsibility, selflessness, and meeting obligations. In direct opposition to the negative macho who is irresponsible and selfish, the positive macho is seen as having a strong sense of responsibility and as being very concerned with the welfare and well-being of other persons. This second positive macho theme was described in a number of ways: "to meet your obligations"; "someone who shoulders responsibility"; "being responsible for your family"; "a person who fulfills the responsibility of his role . . . irrespective of the consequences"; "they make firm decisions . . . that take into consideration the well-being of others." According to one respondent,

> A macho personality for me would be a person that is understanding, that is caring, that is trustworthy. He is all of those things and practices them as well as teaches them, not only with family but overall. It encompasses his whole life.
> It would be a leader with compassion. The image we have of Pancho Villa. For the Americans it would be someone like Kennedy, as a strong person, but not because he was a womanizer.

Positive Theme 3: General Code of Ethics. The third theme we identified embodies many of the same traits mentioned in the first and second themes, but it differs in that respondents appear to link machismo not just to such individual qualities as selflessness but to a general code of ethics or a set of principles. One respondent who was married to an Israeli woman offered a former defense minister of Israel as exemplifying macho qualities. He noted that

> It's a man responsible for actions, a man of his word. . . . I think a macho does
> not have to be a statesman, just a man that's known to stand by his friends and
> follow through. A man of action relative to goals that benefit others, not
> himself.

Another said that it means living up to one's principles to the point of
almost being willing to die for them. One of the most extensive explications
of this code of ethics was offered by the following respondent:

> To me it really refers to a code of ethics that I use to relate values in my life
> and to evaluate myself in terms of my family, my job, my community. My belief
> is that if I live up to my code of ethics, I will gain respect from my family, my
> job, and my community. Macho has nothing to do with how much salsa you
> can eat, how much beer you can drink, or how many women you fuck!
>   They have self-pride, they hold themselves as meaningful people. You can be
> macho as a farmworker or judge. It's a real mixture of pride and humility.
> Individualism is a part of it—self-awareness, self-consciousness, responsibility.

Positive Theme 4: Sincerity/Respect.   The final positive theme overlaps
somewhat with the others and is often subsumed under the code of ethics
or principles. A number of respondents associated the word "macho" with
such qualities as respect for oneself and others, acting with sincerity and
respect, and being a man of your word. One of our interviewees said,

> *Macho significa una persona que cumple con su palabra y que es un hombre
> total. . . . Actúan con sinceridad y con respeto* (Macho means a person who
> backs up what he says and who is a complete man. . . . They act with sincerity
> and respect).

Another mentioned self-control and having a sense of oneself and the situation.

> Usually they are reserved. They have kind of an inner confidence, kind of like
> you know you're the fastest gun in town so you don't have to prove yourself.
> There's nothing to prove. A sense of self.

Still another emphasized that physical prowess by itself would not be sufficient to identify one as macho. Instead, "It would be activities that meet the
challenge, require honor, and meet obligations." Finally, a respondent
observed:

> Macho to me means that you understand your place in the world. That's not
> to say that you are the "he-man" as the popular conception says. It means you
> have respect for yourself, that you respect others.

Not surprisingly, all of the respondents who viewed machismo in a positive light either already considered themselves to have macho qualities or saw it as an ideal they hoped to attain.

Neutral Conceptions of Macho

Twelve respondents could not be clearly classified as positive or negative in their views of "macho." This so-called neutral category is somewhat of a residual one, however, because it includes not only men who were, in fact, neutral but also those who gave mixed signals and about whom the judges could not agree. One said that "macho" was just a word that didn't mean anything; another said that it applied to someone strong like a boxer or a wrestler, but he did not know anyone who was macho, and it was not clear whether he considered it to be a positive or negative trait. Others were either ambivalent or pointed to both positive and negative components of being macho. A street-wise young man in his mid-twenties, for example, indicated that

> The word macho to me means someone who won't take nothing from no one. Respects others, and expects a lot of respect from others. The person is willing to take any risk. . . . They always think they can do anything and everything. They don't take no shit from no one. They have a one-track mind. Never want to accept the fact that women can perform as well as men.

Significantly, the judges were divided in classifying this respondent; one classified him as negative, another as positive, and the third as neutral. The fact is that rather than being neutral, this young man identifies both positive ("respects others and self") and negative ("never want to accept the fact that women can perform as well as men") qualities with being macho.

Another person observed that there were at least two meanings of the word—one, a brave person who is willing to defend his ideals and himself, and the other, a man who exaggerates his masculinity—but noted that "macho" was not a term that he used. Another respondent provided a complex answer that distinguished the denotative (i.e., macho) and connotative (i.e., machismo) meanings of the term. He used the word in both ways, differentiating between being macho or male, which is denotative, and machismo, which connotes male chauvinism. He considered himself to be macho but certainly not *machista*.

> *Ser macho es ser valiente o no tener miedo. La connotación que tiene mal sentido es poner los intereses del hombre adelante de los de la mujer o del resto de la familia. Representa egoísmo. . . . Macho significa varón, hombre, pero el machismo es una manera de pensar, y es negativo* (To be macho is to be brave or to not be afraid. The connotation that is negative is to put the interests of

the man ahead of those of the woman or the rest of the family. It represents selfishness. . . . Macho means male, man, but machismo is a way of thinking, and it is negative).

Another person similarly distinguished between being macho and being *machista*.

Pues, en el sentido personal, significa el sexo masculino y lo difiere del sexo femenino. La palabra machismo existe solamente de bajo nivel cultural y significa un hombre valiente, borracho y pendenciero (Well, in a personal sense, it means the masculine gender and it distinguishes it from the feminine. The word machismo exists only at a low cultural level and it means a brave man, a drunkard, and a hell-raiser).

Six of the twelve respondents who were classified as neutral considered themselves to be at least somewhat macho.

Regional and Socioeconomic Differences in Conceptions of Macho

Conceptions of the word "macho" do not vary significantly by region, but there are significant differences according to socioeconomic status. Men with more education, with a higher income, and in professional occupations were more likely to have a positive conception of the word. This is not to suggest that they are necessarily more *machista,* or chauvinistic, but that they simply see the word in a more positive light. Almost half (42 percent) of the respondents who were professionals associated the word "macho" with being principled or standing up for one's rights, whereas only 23 percent of nonprofessionals had a positive conception of the word.[2]

Place of birth and language were also significantly associated with attitudes toward machismo, but, ironically, those respondents who were born in the United States and those who were interviewed in English were generally more positive toward the word "macho." Forty-two percent of those born in the United States gave positive responses, compared with only 10 percent of those who were foreign-born.

An English-speaking respondent said that "macho equals to me chivalry associated with the Knights of the Round Table, where a man gives his word, defends his beliefs, etc." Another noted that machos were people who "stand up for what they believe, try things other people are afraid to do, and defend the rights of others." But one Mexican man saw it as the opposite—"*Mexicanos que aceptan que la mujer 'lleve los pantalones,' irresponsables, les dan mas atención a sus aspectos sociales que a sus responsabilidades*" (Mexicans who accept that the woman 'wear the pants,' they are irresponsible, these men pay more attention to their social lives than to their responsibilities).

Regional and Socioeconomic Differences in "How Machos Act"

After defining the word "macho," respondents were asked to give an example of how people who are macho act or behave. The answers ranged from drinking to excess, acting "bad" or "tough," being insecure in themselves, to having a "synthetic self-image," a code of ethics, and being sincere and responsible. Because responses typically were either negative or positive rather than neutral or indifferent, they were grouped into two broad categories.

Regional differences were not statistically significant, although southern Californians were more likely than Texans or northern Californians to see macho behavior as aggressive or negative and to associate it with acting tough, drinking, or being selfish.

The general pattern that was observed with regard to occupation, education, and income was that professionals, those with more education, and those with higher incomes were less likely to associate the word "macho" with negative behaviors such as drinking and trying to prove one's masculinity.[3]

Place of birth and the language in which the interview was conducted were also related to the type of behavior that was associated with the word "macho." Men born in the United States and those who opted to conduct the interview in English were significantly more likely to associate such positive behaviors as being responsible, honorable, or respectful of others with people they considered to be macho.

Conclusion

These data provide empirical support for two very different and conflicting models of masculinity. The compensatory model sees the cult of virility and the Mexican male's obsession with power and domination as futile attempts to mask feelings of inferiority, powerlessness, and failure, whereas the second perspective associates being macho with a code of ethics that organizes and gives meaning to behavior. The first model stresses external attributes such as strength, sexual prowess, and power; the second stresses internal qualities like honor, responsibility, respect, and courage.

Although the findings are not conclusive, they have important implications. First, and most importantly, the so-called Mexican/Latino masculine cult appears to be a more complex and diverse phenomenon than is commonly assumed. But the assumption that being macho is an important

Mexican cultural value is seriously called into question by the findings. Most respondents did not define macho as a positive cultural or personal trait or see themselves as being macho. Only about one-third of the men in the sample viewed the word "macho" positively. If there is a cultural value placed on being macho, one would expect that those respondents with closer ties to Latino culture and the Spanish language would be more apt to identify and to have positive associations with macho, but the opposite tendency was found to be true. Respondents who preferred to be interviewed in English were much more likely to see macho positively and to identify with it, whereas the vast majority of those who elected to be interviewed in Spanish viewed it negatively.

A major flaw of previous conceptualizations has been their tendency to treat machismo as a unitary phenomenon. The findings presented here suggest that although Latino men tend to hold polar conceptions of macho, these conceptions may not be unrelated. In describing the term, one respondent observed that there was almost a continuum between a person who is responsible and one who is chauvinistic. If one looks more closely at the two models, moreover, it is clear that virtually every trait associated with a negative macho trait has its counterpart in a positive one. Some of the principal characteristics of the negative macho and the positive counterparts are highlighted in Table 3.1.

The close parallel between negative and positive macho traits is reminiscent of Vicente T. Mendoza's distinction between genuine and false macho. According to Mendoza, the behavior of a genuine machismo is character-

TABLE 3.1   Negative and Positive Macho Traits

Negative	Positive
Bravado	Brave
Cowardly	Courageous
Violent	Self-Defensive
Irresponsible	Responsible
Disrespectful	Respectful
Selfish	Altruistic
Pretentious	Humble
Loud	Soft-Spoken
Boastful	Self-Effacing
Abusive	Protective
Headstrong/Bullish	Intransigent
Conformist	Individualistic
Chauvinistic	Androgynous
Dishonorable	Honorable
External Qualities	Internal Qualities

ized by true bravery or valor, courage, generosity, stoicism, heroism, and ferocity; the negative macho simply uses the appearance or semblance of these traits to mask cowardliness and fear (Mendoza 1962, 75–86).

From this perspective much of what social scientists have termed "macho" behavior is not macho at all, but its antithesis. Rather than attempting to isolate a modal Mexican personality type or determining whether macho is a positive or a negative cultural trait, social scientists would be well served to see Mexican and Latino culture as revolving around certain focal concerns or key issues such as honor, pride, dignity, courage, responsibility, integrity, and strength of character. Individuals, in turn, are evaluated positively or negatively according to how well they are perceived to respond to these focal concerns. But because being macho is ultimately an internal quality, those who seek to demonstrate outwardly that they are macho are caught in a double bind. A person who goes around holding his genitals, boasting about his manliness, or trying to prove how macho he is would not be considered macho by this definition. In the final analysis it is up to others to determine the extent to which a person lives up to these expectations and ideals.

It is also important to note that to a great extent, the positive internal qualities associated with the positive macho are not the exclusive domain of men but extend to either gender. One can use the same criteria in evaluating the behavior of women and employ parallel terminology such as *la hembra* (the female) and *hembrismo* (femaleness). *Una mujer que es una hembra* (a woman who is a real "female") is neither passive and submissive nor physically strong and assertive, for these are external qualities. Rather, *una hembra* is a person of strong character who has principles and is willing to defend them in the face of adversity. Thus, whereas the popular conception of the word "macho" refers to external male characteristics such as exaggerated masculinity or the cult of virility, the positive conception isolated here sees being macho as an internal, androgynous quality.

4

Masculinity: Traditional and Emergent Views

A Declaration of War

One of the things that I remember most about my father is that he always made us confront our fears. He used to say *"Al mal paso, darle prisa,"* a saying that literally translates as "The bad step shall be taken quickly." It is different than "Don't put off until tomorrow what you can do today" because it emphasizes that one should not put off negative or unpleasant situations. My father taught us to swim by throwing us into the swimming pool to see if we would sink or swim. Of the three brothers, I was the only one, I think, who literally sank.

Our house on *la calle Colegio Militar* in Tacuba was near the house of two brothers, Samuel and *El Chapulín* (the grasshopper) Sánchez, who were roughly the same age as my older brothers (Alex and Héctor, or *Gordo*). Though we eventually became friends, at first *Chapulín* and Samuel were our bitter enemies. We used to be afraid of going by the Sánchez house because the brothers and their friends would yell out things, trying to scare and intimidate us. There was definitely a class difference between us and the Sánchez family. The Sánchezes were very poor, and I recall that my mother would take them in periodically, bathe them, and rid their hair of lice.

I also remember that *Chapulín* was crazy. The boys lived right near the railroad tracks and *Chapulín* would put coins on the track so that they would be mangled by the train. But his craziest stunt was to stand on the track waiting for an oncoming train, daring the engineer to hit him. At the last minute, he would throw himself down on the tracks and wait for the train to pass over him. He was fearless. We always thought he would get killed, but *Chapulín* would get up after the train passed, grinning from ear to ear, dust himself off, and go about his business as though nothing had happened.

One afternoon we were sitting in Tía Márgara's living room, relaxing and singing. It seems strange to write about it now. But the extended family often sat around my *tía's* house listening to her, my mother, and neighbors and friends singing *rancheras* or *corridos*. All of my mother's sisters could sing, but Tía Márgara was the best. She had an incredible voice and knew a lot of songs. One day our seclusion was suddenly interrupted by an avocado pit that came flying through the open bay window. It was a very dramatic moment; my father picked up the strange object from the floor and read a note out loud that had been tied around the projectile with a string. The Sánchez boys had finally declared war, offering a challenge to the Mirandés to come out and fight, if they dared.

My father acted immediately. I don't recall why he picked Héctor, or *El Gordo*. Perhaps it was because he was the same age as *Chapulín* (around ten), or perhaps it was because my father sensed that my brother was scared. He took *Gordo* by the arm and proceeded to go outside to meet the challenge. We met Samuel and *Chapulín* at *La Pila*, a waterless fountain in the center of the street that formed a *glorieta*, or traffic circle, on the dead-end street where we lived. We always played around *La Pila*.

The confrontation near *La Pila* reminded me of a classic gunfight in a western movie, as the entire family and neighborhood accompanied my father and *Gordo* to *La Pila*. It was a dramatic moment as my father, after asking *Chapulín* if he wanted to take on my brother, ordered *Gordo* to fight. I remember that *Gordo* was chunky and bigger than his opponent but that he was not very street-wise. I doubt that he had ever been in a real fight. Though *Chapulín* clearly had an advantage in the beginning, his biggest obstacle, I think, proved not to be my brother, but my family, especially *las tías*. Every time that Héctor landed a punch or even came close to landing a punch, *las tías* would go wild, screaming their approval, shouting: "¡*Orale!*", "Now you've got him!", "He's in trouble now!", or "Look, he's bleeding!" (he wasn't, initially). Rather than concentrating on the fight at hand, *Chapulín* became distracted and looked down to see if there was actually blood and looked at *las tías* as they screamed.

So what Héctor lacked in boxing skills, he made up for in crowd support, perseverance, and enthusiasm. Rushing after his opponent like a small bull, he was unquestionably the crowd favorite. *Gordo* "had heart" and would eventually prevail. He would prevail after *Chapulín* got a bloody nose and ran home crying. My father was pleased but would have been pleased regardless of the outcome. What mattered to him most, I think, was not so much that *Gordo* had won, but that his son, a Mirandé, had accepted the challenge and had conquered his fear of the Sánchez boys.

The Bem Sex Role Inventory and Latino Masculinity

As I reflected on this incident and sought to relate it to my present interest in masculinity, I realized that none of the Bem masculine items really seemed to capture the kinds of qualities that my father sought to foster in us. I don't think my father was trying to make us "aggressive" or "assertive," and though I suppose that being "willing to take a stand" or "defending one's beliefs" come closest to the qualities he valued, they are not quite the same either. In retrospect, I think this incident taught me that my father wanted his sons to be willing to defend the family honor, but mostly he wanted us to overcome our fear of the neighbor boys. He wanted us to face our fear directly and to conquer it. This wasn't just about physical fear, it was about any kind of fear of or hesitation to face a difficult or unpleasant situation.

In deciding whether to include the Bem Scale (BSRI) in the study, I was placed in a catch-22 situation, a dilemma faced by all researchers who are seeking to develop measures that are more sensitive to the nuance and complexity of non-majority cultures. The dilemma essentially is how to reject a measure that appears to lack validity without first utilizing it. Since established measures have typically been validated on the dominant group, people of color have reason to be leery of these measures. They must either ignore established measures or use them and run the risk that they will not be relevant or valid. Though I had some reservations about the validity of the scale for Latinos, I finally decided to include the BSRI to see how the respondents ranked the Bem items.

On a seven point scale, scores on the twenty BSRI masculine items ranged from a high of 6.25 (self-sufficient) to a low of 4.33 (dominant).[1] From the rank ordering of these items it is clear that the men in the sample generally saw themselves as possessing many traditional masculine traits, as only three masculine items received a mean rank of less than 5.00. But more stereotypical macho traits such as being "dominant" (ranked #20), "aggressive" (#18), "individualistic" (#17), and "athletic" (#19) were not as highly endorsed as other traits such as being "self-sufficient" (#1), "self-reliant" (#3), "defending one's beliefs" (#2), and "willing to take a stand" (#4).

The rank order distribution of the BSRI feminine items was even more surprising and not at all consistent with stereotypical depictions of macho men and Latino culture. "Loves children" (#1), for example, was more highly endorsed than any other feminine or masculine item on the scale. Other feminine items receiving a high mean ranking were "loyal" (#2), "understanding" (#3), "sympathetic" (#4), and "compassionate" (#5).

Overall, then, the Latino men in this study tended to view themselves as self-reliant, self-sufficient, and willing to take a stand to defend their beliefs. At the same time, they thought of themselves as loving children, being loyal, compassionate, sympathetic, and sensitive to the needs of others, but not as shy, yielding, childlike, gullible, or feminine.

In order to assess whether the BSRI measures two separate and distinct dimensions, or factors, as Bem suggests, I decided to use a statistical technique called "factor analysis." Factor analysis is used to identify certain items (variables) that tend to cluster together or to be associated with one another in a consistent and predictable way. To the extent that distinct clusters can be identified and the groupings make sense theoretically, they are labeled as "factors." A basic assumption of factor analysis is that relatively complex phenomena can be explained by their underlying dimensions, or factors (Norušis 1990, 322). The goal of factor analysis, then, is to explain the observed correlations with as few factors as possible. Obviously, if many factors are needed to explain, little is gained from the analysis because simplification or summarization has not occurred.

Although factors are not directly observable, factor analysis allows us to identify them or infer their existence from observable variables. Let us say, for example, that we are interested in measuring elusive ideas such as "creativity," "altruism," or "love." One obviously cannot measure a concept like love directly, but such measurement might be inferred from "strongly agree" responses such as she (or he) sends me flowers, listens to my jokes, cares about my feelings, or makes me feel good or special. The phenomenon of love or "being in love" cannot be directly observed, but it is a construct that we believe exists and that may be inferred from other directly observable variables (Norušis 1990, 321).

"Factor loadings" tell us the relative strength of a factor by showing how much of the variation in an item or variable is explained by a particular factor. By squaring the factor loading, we can determine the percentage of the total variation in the variable "explained," or accounted for, by the factor. If the factor loadings for each of the items on a scale are high, say between .50 and .80, we can be confident that a person's total score actually reflects true differences on the dimension that has been identified. It is therefore a common practice to retain items that have at least moderate factor loadings.

Because "masculinity" and "femininity" are separate and independent, according to Bem, the score on one dimension does not necessarily affect the score on the other. Theoretically, at least, one can score high on both masculinity and femininity or low on both dimensions. What makes a person "androgynous," then, is not the absolute value of the score but the fact that there is not much disparity between the total masculinity and femininity components. The initial results of the factor analysis tended to support Bem's contention that there are two distinct masculine and feminine factors underlying the BSRI, although about half of the items on the scale were not related or did not "cluster" (i.e., were not correlated) around either factor.[2]

Because the factor loadings on a number of variables were very low, items with factor loadings under .40 were discarded and the data reanalyzed. Fourteen items emerged from this reanalysis with high factor loadings (.40 or more) on either Factor 1 (masculinity) or on Factor 2 (femininity). However, two masculine and four feminine items were reversed. The last two items with high loadings on masculinity—"flatterable" and "sensitive to the needs of others"—are supposedly "feminine" attributes on Bem's original scale. And four BSRI "masculine" items—"self-reliant," "self-sufficient," "defends own beliefs," and "willing to take a stand"—loaded on femininity with our study respondents (see Table 4.1).[3]

One of the most important inferences that can be drawn from these findings is that certain conceptions of sex-appropriate behavior that have been assumed to be universal by Bem and other researchers appear to be culture specific. The findings suggest that Latino men may score high on traditional masculinity traits such as being independent, assertive, and having leadership abilities, while at the same time remaining sensitive to the needs of others. Conversely, Latino men may endorse traditional "feminine" traits such as being warm, tender, loyal, and affectionate, and still remain self-reliant, self-sufficient, defend their beliefs, and be willing to take a stand. I am not suggesting that these findings can be generalized to all Latinos, but I am suggesting that many traits that are defined as "feminine" in the dominant culture, such as being affectionate, warm, sympathetic, tender, emotional, and sensitive, are much more acceptable behaviors in Latino men than they are in Anglo men. Despite the popular macho stereotype of Latino men as cold, hard, aggressive, and insensitive, it is more culturally acceptable for Latino men to cry, to be emotional, and to demonstrate their feelings.

The concept of loyalty, an item that was highly endorsed by the study respondents, can be used to illustrate cultural differences in conceptions of masculinity and femininity. Anglo culture appears to have a more limited conception of loyalty, one largely associated with monogamy and sexual

TABLE 4.1   BSRI Masculinity and Femininity Factor Loading

Masculinity (Factor 1)			Femininity (Factor 2)		
Mean Rank	*Item*	*Factor Loading*	*Mean Rank*	*Item*	*Factor Loading*
1.	Ambitious	.74	1.	Warm	.73
2.	Aggressive	.73	2.	Tender	.71
3.	Has Leadership Abilities	.68	3.5	Affectionate	.67
4.	Dominant	.65	3.5	Compassionate	.67
5.	Individualistic	.62	5.	Sympathetic	.64
6.	Competitive	.62	6.	Self-Sufficient	*.53
7.	Acts as Leader	.62	7.5	Loyal	.52
8.	Strong Personality	.61	7.5	Understanding	.52
9.	Makes Decisions Easily	.58	9.	Willing to Take a Stand	*.50
10.	Assertive	.57	10.	Soothes Hurt Feelings	.49
11.	Willing to Take Risks	.48	11.5	Cheerful	.47
12.	Independent	.47	11.5	Defends Own Beliefs	*.47
13.	Flatterable	*.45	13.	Loves Kids	.41
14.	Sensitive to Needs of Others	*.37	14.	Self-Reliant	*.40

*Indicates item is reversed.

fidelity. I propose that for Latinos loyalty is a more expansive concept that is grounded in notions of interpersonal commitment and support and that is not necessarily a sex-linked quality. A person who is loyal is one who can be counted on to support one's friends and who will not "bend with the winds," so to speak. Loyalty is a highly valued quality among Latinos.

The fact that some of the items on the BSRI were reversed made me consider the possibility of the presence of a third factor. A factor analysis using three factors revealed that the masculinity factor is essentially unaffected by the introduction of a third factor,[4] but femininity (Factor 2) contains two distinct subfactors. The revised Factor 2 includes the following eight feminine items, all with relatively high loadings (.55 or greater):

Revised BSRI Factor 2 (Femininity)

1. Compassionate (.75)
2. Sympathetic (.72)
3. Tender (.72)
4. Warm (.70)
5. Understanding (.63)
6. Affectionate (.62)
7. Gentle (.57)
8. Soothes hurt feelings (.56)

In addition, a new Bem hypermasculine, or super-macho, Factor 3 emerged, an interesting mixture of traditionally feminine and masculine items. Four of the seven items in Factor 3 were classified as "masculine" on the original Bem scale. Three of these masculine items ("self-reliant," "defends own beliefs," and "self-sufficient") loaded on the femininity factor in our initial two-factor analysis; another (forceful) previously did not load on either factor. The rank ordering and factor loadings on the seven-item Bem hypermasculine component of the three factor loadings were as follows (* indicates loaded on "femininity" on two-factor analysis; <– indicates item is reversed):

Factor 3 (Hypermasculinity)

1. Self-reliant (*.64)
2. Soft-spoken (< –.58)
3. Defends own beliefs (*.55)
4. Self-sufficient (*.54)
5. Shy (< –.49)
6. Forceful (*.41)
7. Gullible (< –.40)[5]

The fact that the three "feminine" items loaded negatively on Factor 3 suggests that this new factor taps what is essentially a hypermasculine, or perhaps more accurately, a distinctly "nonfeminine" dimension. The third factor parallels the negative conception of machismo discussed in the previous chapter and appears to isolate a truly aggressive form of masculinity. In short, "hypermasculine" men see themselves as being self-reliant, self-sufficient, and forceful, as defending their beliefs, and, because the items are reversed, definitely not as being shy, soft-spoken, or gullible.[6]

An Alternative Measure: The Mirandé Sex Role Inventory

Overview of the Items

The Bem Sex Role Inventory defines masculinity and femininity as a series of individual psychological traits or attributes such as "tender," "masculine," or "assertive." But Latino conceptions of masculinity and femininity, I believe, are more situational and are best understood within a collective sociocultural context rather than as individual traits. The Latino sense of masculinity and femininity is often determined by the response of the collective. How a person behaves in public and the images that are projected to others are, therefore, very important, as a value is placed on being *una persona decente* (a decent or respectable person) or *bien educada* (well-bred).

Although the issues of honor and integrity are focal concerns in Latino culture, often it is the behavior of women rather than that of men that is more closely scrutinized and used in assessing honor, decency, and integrity. Men, in turn, are generally expected to respond to violations of honor and integrity. It is in this sense that gender is externalized and encompasses not only prescriptions for male behavior but, more importantly, restrictions on the conduct of women.

Many of the statements in the Mirandé Sex Role Inventory (MSRI) were taken from *dichos* (cultural "truths" or sayings), *consejos* (words of advice or wisdom that elders pass on to youth), *cuentos* (stories), and *corridos* (folk ballads). The statements, therefore, reflect traditional Latino values surrounding the role of men and women in society. The following are examples of such statements: *"El hombre debe tener 'los calzones' en la familia,"* (The man should wear the pants in the family), *"La palabra de un hombre vale más que nada"* (A man's word is his most important possession), *"Es preferible morir parado que vivir de rodillas"* (It is better to die on your feet than to live on your knees), *"El verdadero hombre tiene respeto y autoridad completa en la familia"* (A real man has complete respect and authority in the family).

Other items expressed traditional values regarding female marital fidelity and the role of the male in the family. This dimension included questions such as "A woman should always be faithful to her husband," "Even if a man cannot provide for his family, he should still be the boss," and "A married woman should not dance with another man unless her husband gives his permission."

Although the items on the MSRI are concerned with assessing traditional conceptions of appropriate behavior for women and men, they can be grouped into four distinct subcomponents or categories: (1) a double sexual standard for men and women, (2) the idea that the male is or should be the dominant figure in the home, (3) the importance of maintaining honor and integrity in the family, and (4) toughness and the notion that men should be tough and not cry or be too emotional.

The first component revolves around the double sexual standard that dictates women are to be sexually pure and protected, whereas men are not. Women are expected to be pure before marriage and loyal after marriage, whereas men are seen as inherently promiscuous before and after marriage. This component included items such as:

1. "A woman should always be faithful to her husband."
2. "It is not important for a woman to be a virgin when she marries." (reversed)
3. "A married woman should not dance with another man unless her husband gives his permission."
4. "It is natural for a man to fool around before marriage."
5. "It is natural for a man to fool around after marriage."

Another component of traditional gender roles is related, but it revolves less around sex and more around the power and authority of the man in the family. This second component included items such as:

1. "A woman should honor and obey her husband."
2. "A real man has complete respect and authority in the family."
3. "Even if a man cannot provide for his family, he should still be the boss."
4. "A man's home is his castle."
5. "The father is the more influential parent."
6. "The man should wear the pants in the family."

The third component focuses not on the double sexual standard or on male authority but on the idea of maintaining and, if necessary, protecting personal and collective honor and integrity, at almost any price. It included such items as:

1. "A man should be willing to take a stand or take risks for something that he believes in, even at the risk of losing his life."

2. "Once a man 'gives his word' or agrees to something, he should not change his mind."
3. "A man's word is his most important possession."
4. "One of the worst things that a man can do is to disgrace or dishonor his family."
5. "It is much better to die on your feet than to live on your knees."

The final component revolves around the assumption that men should not cry and that they should not be too emotional or affectionate, especially with male children. Men should be tough, stoical, and unfeeling. Some of the items included were:

1. "A sign of a real man is the ability to withstand pain, hardship, or failure."
2. "Little boys should be taught that men do not cry."
3. "Men should never cry or show their feelings."
4. "A father should not kiss or be too emotional with his sons."

Before analyzing each of the four components, I will present an overview of the responses to the fifty original MSRI items. The mean responses to the original fifty items on the MSRI, ranked in order from the most to the least often endorsed, are found in Appendix B. On the surface, at least, these responses do not appear to be consistent with traditional conceptions of Latino masculinity, especially the belief that men are distant and uninvolved with the family. Almost all of the respondents (98 percent), for example, believed that "a man should be willing to help his wife with the care of children and household chores" (52 percent "strongly agreed" and 46 percent "agreed" with the statement). Fourteen other items were endorsed by 80 percent or more of the respondents. Not surprisingly, most men (95 percent) believed that a woman should always be faithful to her husband, but 90 percent said that a man should also always be faithful to his wife. More than 90 percent agreed that it is not right for a man to get high, stoned, or "wasted."

Several items center around the father's role in the family as the provider and source of emotional support. Eighty-six percent believed both that a good man spends a lot of time with his wife and children and that the worst thing that a man can do is not to take care of them. Another 87 percent agreed that a man should put his wife and children above everything else. Contrary to what was expected, though 91 percent felt that the worst thing that a man could do is to disgrace or dishonor his family, only 76 percent felt that this was the worst thing a woman could do.

Some traditional beliefs as expressed in such items as "A man should be willing to take a stand or take risks for something that he believes in, even at the risk of losing his life" (78 percent) and "It is much better to die on your feet than to live on your knees" (83 percent) were heavily endorsed, but the idea that men must prove their masculinity by showing that they are tougher, stronger, less emotional, and otherwise superior to women was not supported by the data. Only 8 percent, for example, believed that a man should never back down from a fight, 9 percent that the best way to get respect is to be stronger and tougher, 10 percent that a father should not kiss or be too emotional with his sons, and 11 percent that men should never cry or show their feelings. More than nine out of ten respondents said that it is *not* right for a man to get high, stoned, or "wasted" and to look for trouble, another 84 percent that it *is* good for a man to cry or show his emotions, and only 63 percent believed that women are somehow more sensitive and emotional than men.

These preliminary responses also suggest that egalitarian beliefs regarding the marital relationship may be much more prevalent among Latinos than is commonly assumed. Almost nine out of ten respondents indicated that marriage is a fifty-fifty proposition, with the man and the woman having an equal say (87 percent), and that women are equal to men (88 percent). Eighty-three percent, moreover, felt that a man who hits a woman is not really a man. The value of virginity before marriage was not widely endorsed, as 73 percent said it is *not* important for a woman to be a virgin when she marries, and 89 percent said that a woman who is not a virgin at the time of marriage is generally just as good a wife and mother as one who is.

Isolating Factors on the MSRI: "Traditionalism," "Toughness," and "Sensitivity"

Like the BSRI, items on the MSRI were subjected to factor analysis to determine if one or more factors, or components, would emerge. Initially, two fairly distinct factors were identified.[7] The seventeen items with very high factor loadings (.50 or more) on "traditionalism," or Factor 1, appear in Table 4.2. The variables with the highest factor loadings (.78) were "A son should always obey his father" and "A woman should always honor and respect her man." Those with the lowest loadings (.53) were "Women are more sensitive and emotional than men" and "The worst thing a man can do is to not take care of his wife and children."

Perhaps what is most striking about these findings is that the component dealing with the double sexual standard and the cultural emphasis on virginity does not appear to be a significant part of the traditionalism factor. The notion that men should be tough and not cry or be too emotional is also not reflected in the factor, since there is only one item that relates at all to this component (A real man withstands pain, hardship, and failure).

TABLE 4.2   MSRI Factor 1: Traditionalism

Mean Rank	Item	Factor Loading
1.5	Woman should always honor and respect man	.78
1.5	Son should always obey father	.78
3.	Better if married woman does not work	.71
4.5	Woman should always honor/obey husband	.70
4.5	Worse thing woman can do is disgrace family	.70
6.	Man's home is his castle	.68
7.	Woman should always be faithful to husband	.66
8.	Worst thing man can do is disgrace family	.65
9.	Worst thing someone can do is insult mother	.63
10.5	Woman should not dance without permission	.62
10.5	Most important thing father gives is family name	.62
12.	Real man can withstand pain, hardship, and failure	.61
13.	Good man spends time with wife and children	.59
14.	Man should be able to handle all financial responsibilities of marriage	.57
15.	Real man has complete authority in the family	.55
16.5	Women more sensitive and emotional than men	.53
16.5	Worst thing is not to take care of wife and children	.53

It is also worth noting that seven of the seventeen items directly invoke restrictions on the behavior of women. A woman should thus honor and respect her man (mean rank of #1.5), honor and obey her husband (mean of #4.5), not dance with another man without her husband's permission (mean of #10.5), always be faithful to her husband (mean of #7), not disgrace or dishonor the family (mean of #4.5), and, preferably, not work outside the household (mean of #3).

Three items deal with men, but they imply that women have a subordinate status.[8] A man is thus expected to have "complete respect and authority in the family" (mean of #15), "to handle all of the financial and economic responsibilities of marriage" (mean of #14), and to believe that "his home is his castle" (mean of #6). The ideas that the most important thing a father gives his children is the family name (mean of #10.5), that one of the worst things one can do is to insult one's mother (mean of #9), and that a son should always obey his father (mean of #1.5) are based on a patriarchal value system that extols male privilege.

In short, the MSRI appears to tap a traditional conception of gender that holds that the woman should honor, respect, and be faithful to the man, and, ideally, stay home and permit him to handle the economic and financial responsibilities of marriage. Men thus occupy a special and privileged status in the home. Significantly, items that are contrary to this notion, such as "A man should always be faithful to his wife" and "A real woman is strong and independent," did not emerge as significant components of the sex role inventory. On the other hand, very traditional beliefs such as "The father is the more influential parent," "It is natural for a man to 'fool around' after marriage," "The man should 'wear the pants' in the family," and "A man should never back down from a fight" also did not prove to be significant.

Whereas the principal factor in the MSRI measures traditional conceptions of gender that maintain the privileged position of men while restricting the behavior of women, the second factor isolates a machismo or "toughness" component, including the idea that men should not cry, that they should not kiss or be too emotional with male children, that a man should never back down from a fight, and that it is somehow "natural" for men to be more sexually promiscuous before marriage. Factor 2 includes seven items with a factor loading of .50 or greater (see Table 4.3).

Most of these items focus on toughness and a lack of emotion, but one item does not fit conceptually with the rest. Item 6 indicates that a man *should* help with chores and child care.

In order to refine the analysis further, I decided to run another factor analysis using three principle factors instead of two, including all variables with an initial factor loading of .50 or greater. This analysis revealed three distinct factors, although Factor 1 is clearly larger and more reliable than the other two.[9] Factor 1 remains essentially the same as in the two-factor analysis, except for slight variations in factor loadings and the addition of Variable 15 (Item 36—"One should defend the family honor even if it means death") (see Appendix B).

With regard to Factor 2, four of the seven items on the two-factor analysis remain and constitute a shorter, revised, and more refined "toughness" component. It includes the following variables: (1) It is natural for a man to

TABLE 4.3   MSRI Factor 2: Toughness

Mean Rank	Item	Factor Loading
1.	Natural for a man to fool around before marriage	.74
2.	Good for man to cry or show his emotions	.68
3.	Men should never cry or show feelings	.66
4.5	Man should never back down from a fight	.64
4.5	Father should not kiss or be too emotional with children	.64
6.	Man should help wife with chores and child care	.63
7.	Boys should be taught that men do not cry	.50

fool around before marriage (.81), (2) A man should never back down from a fight (.78), (3) A father should not kiss or be too emotional with his children (.70), and (4) Men should never cry or show their feelings (.52).

Interestingly, a third factor emerges that stands at the polar end of "toughness" and that I have termed "sensitivity." This new factor includes two items that previously appeared in Factor 2 A man should help his wife with chores and child care, and It is good for man to cry or show his emotions), and three items that had not previously loaded. The factor loadings on the MSRI sensitivity component were as follows:

1. "Marriage is a fifty–fifty proposition" (.73)
2. "Women are equal to men" (.73)
3. "A man should help his wife with chores and child care" (.63)
4. "It is good for man to cry or show his emotions" (.53)
5. "The worst thing a man can do is to disgrace his family" (< .44)

This new dimension appears to tap male sensitivity or egalitarian gender roles, which hold not only that marriage is a fifty-fifty proposition, that women are equal to men, that the man should help with household chores and child care, and that it is good for a man to cry or show his emotions, but also that disgracing the family is *not* the worst thing that a man can do. This sensitivity component is unique and cannot be readily classified as masculine or feminine.

Regional and Socioeconomic Differences

This section presents an overview of regional, educational, occupational, income, and language usage differences in the BSRI and the MSRI. Based on previous research and social scientific theory, I came into the study expecting that middle- and upper-middle-class men would generally be less traditional and more "androgynous" than working-class men. With regard to regional variations, Californians were expected to be somewhat more "modern" and less traditional in their gender role orientations than Texans, but this was more of a hunch than a formal hypothesis.

Regional and Socioeconomic Differences in the BSRI

There were substantial differences in the BSRI among our respondents, though these differences were surprising and not generally consistent with what had been predicted (see Appendix A, Table 1).[10] The Bem masculinity component (Factor 1), for example, was positively associated with income, education, and occupational status. But contrary to what was expected, men in professional occupations, those with higher incomes, and those with more education were more likely to endorse traditional masculine items than those respondents who had a lower socioeconomic standing. These differences, moreover, tended to be statistically significant.[11] Regional differences in the BSRI also defied our predicted "hunch." Texans scored higher on masculinity than northern or southern Californians, but the differences were slight and not statistically significant. In addition, the BSRI femininity component (Factor 2) did not differentiate clearly. Income, educational, occupational, and regional differences in femininity were generally negligible and statistically insignificant.

With regard to the second, or "super-masculine," component isolated in Factor 3, northern Californians, high school graduates, and men with higher incomes tended to score higher on the factor. They were more apt, in other words, to be self-reliant, self-sufficient, forceful, to defend their beliefs, and to not see themselves as shy, gullible, or soft-spoken. The differences, however, were also not significant.

Regional and Socioeconomic Differences in the MSRI

The findings relative to regional, occupational, and socioeconomic differences on the Mirandé Sex Role Inventory were more consistent with the hypothesized relationships than was the case for the Bem Inventory, suggesting that the MSRI may be a more valid measure (see Appendix A, Table 2).

As expected, our findings indicated that men who are professionals or managers and those with more education or higher incomes are less "traditional." These differences were statistically significant. What was unexpected, however, was the finding that southern Californians are somewhat more "traditional" than northern Californians or Texans.

Factor 2 on the MSRI is a dimension that extends beyond traditional gender roles to measure "toughness," supporting the notions that men are naturally more sexually permissive than women, that men should not cry or show their feelings, and that a man should never back down from a fight.

Factor 2, however, did not generally differentiate among the respondents in either the two- or the three-factor analysis. Differences in Factor 2 by region, education, or occupation were minimal. In fact, the only variable that was statistically significant in Factor 2 was income, as men who earned higher incomes generally did not score as high on the toughness dimension as did those with moderate or low incomes.

Unlike toughness, sensitivity (Factor 3 in the MSRI) includes items that tap a nontraditional orientation toward gender. Men who scored high on "sensitivity" rejected the double standard and believed that women are equal to men, that men should help with chores and child care, and that it is good for a man to cry or show his feelings.

Not only were educational, occupational, and income differences in Factor 3 negligible, but they were also the opposite of what had been predicted. Men who were nonprofessionals, those with a high school education, and those with moderate incomes were somewhat more likely to score high on sensitivity. Regional differences were also significant and contrary to what we expected, as Texans were most sensitive or nontraditional, whereas northern Californians were the least sensitive and most traditional.

Nativity, Language, and Socioeconomic Status Differences

Nativity, Language, and Socioeconomic Status Differences and the BSRI

Because the preliminary analysis suggested that language usage and language preference did not appear to be significantly related to the various factors in the BSRI, I reanalyzed the data without these variables. The revised analysis included the following variables: place of birth, language in which the interview was conducted, education, occupation, and income (see Appendix A, Table 3). The results revealed that these variables were generally significantly related to the original Bem Factor 1 (masculinity) and Factor 2 (femininity) but not to the new Factor 3 (hypermasculinity). Specifically, education and income were significantly related to Factor 1, as men with more education and higher incomes were more apt to endorse traditional masculine traits. Education and income were significantly related to femininity (Factor 2), but, as previously noted, the relationship was inverse so that men with more education and higher incomes generally scored lower on femininity.

Scores on androgyny, the difference in the mean score on the masculine and feminine items, were highly significant. Education again was significantly related to androgyny, whereas occupation and the language in which the interview was conducted approached significance. Contrary to what had been predicted, those with more education, those with higher incomes, and those interviewed in English were less likely to be androgynous than those with less education, those with lower incomes, and those who preferred to be interviewed in Spanish.

Nativity, Language, and Socioeconomic Status Differences and the MSRI

Finally, an analysis was conducted to assess whether factors such as place of birth, language preference, language usage, and the language in which the interview was conducted were related to responses on the Mirandé Sex Role Inventory (see Appendix A, Table 4). Although the findings were statistically significant, as was the case with the BSRI, the language in which the person was interviewed appeared to be the only variable significantly related to the Mirandé traditionalism component (Factor 1). Differences in Factor 2 (toughness) and Factor 3 (sensitivity) of the MSRI were small. In fact, none of the background variables (place of birth, language preference and usage, and language of the interview) were statistically significant.

A revised analysis was computed for the Mirandé traditionalism items (see Appendix A, Table 4), using place of birth, language of the interview, education, occupation, and income. Findings for education and income were statistically significant on the Mirandé traditionalism component, and those for the language of the interview approached significance. But unlike the BSRI, men with more education, higher incomes, and those who were interviewed in Spanish were less likely to endorse traditional views of gender.

Household Chores, Power, Interaction with Children, and Marital Happiness Differences in the MSRI and BSRI

This section looks at whether factors such as the distribution of household chores, marital power or decisionmaking, marital happiness, and interaction with children are related to the Bem masculinity and femininity components and the Mirandé sex role traditionalism scale. Whereas in the previous analyses factors such as income, education, and language preference were entered as independent variables, here distribution of household chores, marital decisionmaking, marital happiness, and interaction with children were treated as dependent since they appeared to be a result rather than a cause of gender role orientation.

The first step was to carry out the analysis using these three variables as dependent and the three MSRI factors as well as a number of background variables (place of birth, education, and income) as explanatory, or independent variables. With regard to distribution of household chores, the results revealed that although none of the background variables was a very good predictor of the mean number of chores performed by the husband or wife, each of the three MSRI factors was a fairly good predictor (see, Appendix A, Table 5). Factor 3 on the MSRI (sensitivity) was significant and Factors 1 (traditionalism) and 2 (toughness) approached statistical significance. As expected, men who were more traditional on the MSRI (Factor 1) performed fewer household chores, but those who scored high on "toughness" were actually *more* likely to perform household tasks than those who scored low. Perhaps even more surprising, men who scored high on the "sensitivity" dimension (Factor 3) were less likely to share in the performing of chores.

The various background variables were significantly related to marital decisions (see Appendix A, Table 5). More specifically, traditionalism as measured in the MSRI is significantly related to the number of decisions made by the man or woman, as men who are more traditional are more apt to be in marriages in which fewer decisions are made by the wife. But surprisingly, as with household tasks, men who scored high on "sensitivity" were more likely to be in marriages in which fewer decisions are made by the wife than those who were low on sensitivity. This difference approached statistical significance.[12]

The other independent variables (place of birth, language of the interview, education, occupation, and income) were also generally not good predictors of interaction with children or marital happiness, with the exception of income, which was significantly related to marital happiness (see Appendix A, Table 5). People with higher incomes were more likely to report that they felt that their marriage was "happy" or "very happy."

Traditionalism and toughness components of the MSRI were related to interaction with children, but, contrary to what was expected, men who were more traditional and those who scored higher on toughness were more likely to be involved in significant interaction with their children. Though not statistically significant, sensitivity was inversely related to interaction with children. Men who were judged to be more "sensitive" and less stereotypically macho, in other words, actually spent less time in activities such as helping children with homework or taking them on outings. Also interesting was the finding that men who were rated as tough or "super-macho" were significantly less apt to evaluate their marriages as happy or very happy.[13]

In the second phase of the analysis the same variables were included, but the BSRI was added as an independent variable to see how well it predicted scores on the dependent variables (see Appendix A, Table 6). The findings revealed that with the exception of income, which is significantly related to marital happiness, the socioeconomic and background variables were not consistently or significantly related to any of the four dependent variables. The three dimensions of the Bem Scale were also not generally related to the four dependent variables. In fact, only the marital happiness findings were statistically significant. Although the masculine dimension of the BSRI was not significantly related, those high on the "super-macho" items were less likely to rate their marriage as happy. Also, those high on the BSRI femininity component more often scored high on marital happiness.

Since the socioeconomic and background variables were not generally positively related to the dependent variables, these variables were then excluded, and multiple regressions were recomputed for the three BSRI and the three MSRI factors. The results of this analysis suggested that the MSRI is generally a better predictor than the BSRI (see Appendix A, Table 7). In fact, three of the four multiple regressions computed with the MSRI were either significant or approach statistical significance, whereas none of the four dependent variables were significant and only one of them approached significance when the BSRI was used.

It appears, therefore, that men who were more traditional in the MSRI tended to perform fewer chores, make more decisions in the household, interact more with children, and were not significantly more or less happy than their less traditional counterparts. It is interesting that men who scored high on sensitivity also performed fewer chores and made more marital decisions, but they did not differ significantly with regard to interaction with children or marital happiness.

The only dependent variable that the BSRI appeared to predict successfully was marital happiness. The masculine dimension of the BSRI did not relate to marital happiness, but the feminine and super-masculine dimensions did relate. Men who scored high on the feminine dimension more often reported their marriage as being happy, whereas those who scored high on the super-masculine dimension were more likely to report their marriages as being unhappy. When the BSRI androgyny score (not presented in the table) was entered into the multiple regression equation, the results suggested that androgyny was also not a very good predictor of any of the four dependent variables. As expected, men who were more androgynous performed more household chores than those who were less androgynous, but these differences were not statistically significant.

Implications and Conclusion

The findings presented in this chapter suggest that conventional conceptions and measures of gender may have limited applicability for non-majority populations. The guiding hypotheses of the study were generally supported with the MSRI but not with the BSRI, a more conventional measure of masculinity and femininity. The MSRI demonstrated that, as predicted, professionals, those with more education, those with higher incomes, and southern Californians were generally less traditional in their ideas about gender. But on the Bem Scale professionals, those with more education, and those with higher incomes were actually more likely to score high on Factor 1 (masculinity) than on Factor 2 (femininity).

The assumption that the Bem (BSRI) and Mirandé Sex Role (MSRI) inventories are somehow equivalent or even comparable measures of gender role orientation is seriously called into question by these findings. Indeed, many of the key variables turned out to be inversely related when we used one measure instead of the other. Not only does the MSRI appear to be a more culturally relevant and valid measure, but it also appears be a better predictor of the dependent variables in the study.

Factors such as language usage, language preference, and place of birth were generally not significantly related to the Bem masculinity component. In fact, the only variable that appeared to affect the masculinity score was whether the interview was conducted in English or Spanish, and, surprisingly, men interviewed in Spanish were less likely to endorse traditional masculine items. The androgyny score on the BSRI (the difference between the mean of the masculine items and the mean of the feminine items) proved to be a better predictor than either the masculine or the feminine score, though men who had more education, who earned a higher income, and who were engaged in professional occupations were actually less androgynous.

Language usage, language preference, and place of birth were also not good predictors of the MSRI Factor 1 (traditionalism). Education and income were significantly related to traditionalism, and the language in which the person was interviewed approached significance. These findings, moreover, were generally what we had expected, so that men with more education and higher incomes were less likely to endorse traditional conceptions of gender. Surprisingly, those who were interviewed in Spanish were also less traditional than those interviewed in English.

A possible interpretation of these findings is that the Bem Sex Role Inventory is not only less valid and reliable for Latinos, but also that it contains a distinct ethnic and class bias. The fact that professionals or managers, those with more education and higher incomes, and those who preferred to be interviewed in English scored higher on "masculinity" is, in retrospect, perhaps not that surprising. Such men, after all, are bilingual, bicultural, more assimilated and integrated into Anglo-American culture, and more apt to have internalized dominant societal conceptions of masculinity and gender. But perhaps the most important implication of the findings is that they lend support to the view that certain conceptions of masculinity that have been assumed to be unvarying and universal are, in fact, variable and culture specific.

5

Masculinity and Fatherhood

One of my favorite stories that *las tías* used to tell was about their brother and my grandfather, Alfredo. One day, as my grandparents were strolling in the *Plaza* after leaving Sunday mass, a man apparently tried to pick my grandfather's pocket. Alfredo was a large, strong man, and he caught the thief in the act. Rather than beating the perpetrator or having him arrested, he grabbed tightly onto the man's hand and continued undaunted, walking through the park with my grandmother as though nothing had happened. Onlookers laughed and ridiculed the thief as they realized what had happened and as they saw him stumbling behind my grandfather.

Even as a boy I probably knew from stories such as these that my *tias* were indirectly instilling in me values about how a man should act. A man should be judged not by such external qualities as physical strength, appearance, or looks but by internal qualities. A man should be, as Alfredo liked to say, *"Feo, fuerte, y formal,"* which literally means ugly, strong, and formal, but also implies that men should be responsible and have a strong moral character.

In this chapter the focus shifts from the closed-ended questions in the BSRI and MSRI inventories to open-ended questions about manhood, qualities admired in men, and conceptions of the role of the father in the family. These topics are examined through qualitative responses to such questions as the type of man that is "most respected and admired," special attributes that are most and least respected in a man, the "worst" or "lowest" thing a man can do, and traits or characteristics valued in a son.

Another series of open-ended questions focused on the role of the father in the family and general attitudes toward child rearing, including a father's most important responsibility or duty to children, the extent to which respondents saw themselves as good or bad fathers, the characteristics respondents associated with being a good or bad father, the strengths or weaknesses of respondents in their own roles as fathers, and basic attitudes toward children and the role of the father in rearing children and child care.

To facilitate the analysis, these open-ended, qualitative responses were grouped and coded into various categories.

Man Most Respected or Admired

Respondents were first asked to identify the man or men they most respected or admired. Open-ended responses were grouped into one of three categories: immediate family (father, son, brother), non-immediate family (cousin, aunt), and nonfamily (friend, historical figure, celebrity)(see Appendix A, Table 8). Men with more education were more apt to identify nonfamily members such as friends, acquaintances, or historical figures. A college graduate from northern California, for example, listed Gandhi, Jesus, and Bolivar, while a community college instructor identified two of his college teachers because they were activist scholars who had served as important role models for him.

> What comes to mind is two of my professors when I was an undergraduate, two educators. One of the things they both have in common is that they're scholars, but they are activist scholars. They have been involved in the community way beyond the call of duty. They felt a strong obligation to become involved.

Though respondents often listed family or friends, by far the most frequently listed persons were political and historical figures like César Chávez, Mexican revolutionary leaders Emiliano Zapata and Pancho Villa, and President Kennedy. One person from northern California said, "According to my own view, Martin Luther King, César Chávez, Gandhi, and Kennedy. Rambo would be an example of the negative view." He added that there were a number of women among those persons he respected and admired; the Virgin Mary and Joan of Arc were two he really admired. He noted further that he admired people who "stand up for their rights, live by their principles to the point of almost being willing to die for them, yet have an open mind to listen to the views of others, and modify or change, if necessary, without sacrificing their basic principles."

Respondents in professional occupations and those with more education more often identified nonfamily members as being respected or admired. Income levels made less of a difference when it came to identifying family or nonfamily members as most respected or admired, but persons with very high total family incomes and those with very low incomes were slightly more likely than those with moderate incomes to identify nonfamily members. Income levels did make a difference in whether or not an immediate or non-immediate family member was mentioned, with persons with very low incomes more often listing non-immediate family members, but the differences were not significant.

Left, Francisco Villa in presidential chair; *right,* Emiliano Zapata (*Jefes, Héroes y Caudillos,* Sistema Nacional de Fototecas Del Instituto Nacional de Antropología E Historia, Fondo Casasola. México: Fondo de Cultural Económica, 1996).

Though there were occupational, educational, and income differences that approached statistical significance in the selection of the person most respected or admired, responses did not vary markedly by place of birth, language usage, or sex role orientation.[1] Men who were born in the United States were only slightly more likely to list a nonfamily member as most respected or admired.[2]

Specific Qualities Most and Least Respected or Admired in a Man

Responses to which specific qualities were most respected or admired in a man were grouped into three categories: (1) personal qualities such as warmth or kindness, (2) being respectful or respected by others, and (3) honesty, trustworthiness, or being ethical (see Appendix A, Table 9). Although the findings show that the qualities most respected or admired in a man varied only slightly by region, differences based on income, education, and occupation were substantial and statistically significant. Men with very high incomes (over $40,000) were more likely to identify being respectful rather than being honest as a quality they most respected in a man. Foreign-born men, on the other hand, were more likely than those born in the United States to see honesty as the most valued quality, but these differences were not statistically significant.

Though differences on the Bem scale were not pronounced or significant, those who were highly traditional on the Mirandé scale were less likely to see honesty as a positive trait than those who were low or moderate on traditionalism. Men low on traditionalism more often saw being respectful as a valued quality. These differences approached statistical significance.

Traits that were *least* respected in a man were grouped into: (1) injures, abuses, or uses other people (e.g., abuses wife and/or children), (2) does not respect self or others, and (3) is selfish, irresponsible, or does not take care of the family (see Appendix A, Table 10). Although regional and occupational differences were generally insignificant, men with less education and low family income were more likely to identify selfishness or *egoísmo* as a least respected trait.[3]

From Figure 5.1 it is clear that income differences among respondents who listed the traits they *least* respected were pronounced and that respon-

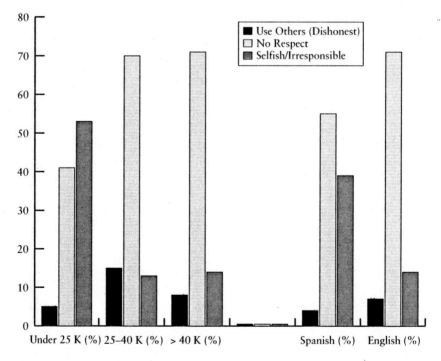

FIGURE 5.1   Qualities least respected, income (p < .02), and language (p < .01)

dents with low incomes more often identified selfishness or *egoísmo* as the least desired trait in a man.

Naming his least respected traits, one respondent said, "A man who is lazy, irresponsible. Like if he is not supportive of his own family, and one who is selfish, or just thinks of himself." Another indicated he did not respect someone who was "a liar, unreliable, egotistical, unwilling to bend, unemotional, uncaring, greedy, selfish."

Men born outside of the United States were also more likely to identify being selfish or self-centered as an undesirable trait, but the language in which the interview was conducted proved to be a better predictor of the least respected traits than place of birth. Those who were interviewed in Spanish more often identified selfishness and irresponsibility as negative traits (see Figure 5.1).

This finding may not be surprising given that *egoísmo* is a negative character trait in México and in other Latino cultures. One man, for example, reported that what he saw as the most loathsome qualities in a man were *"el no respetar a la familia. No cumplir con deberes familiares y sociales"* (lack of respect for the family. Not fulfilling familial and social obligations). And the worst or lowest thing that a man could do was *"el abandonar a la familia"* (to abandon one's family). Another respondent was more specific, noting that the trait he least respected or admired was *"un hombre realmente que tenga la familia en pobreza cuando no es necesario"* (a man who actually has his family in poverty when it is unnecessary). Another respondent similarly remarked that what he respected or admired least was *"Pues, un hombre que no toma su obligación como debe ser"* (Well, a man who does not accept his responsibilities as he should). In turn, what this man *most* respected or admired was

> *Un hombre que atiende a su familia. Que sepa el valor de la familia. Que siempre les respeta. Hay gente que piensa que un hombre debe ser valiente, pero un hombre debe ser formal con su familia. Que no los desampare* (A man who looks after the family. Who understands the value of the family. Who always respects his family. There are people who think a man should be brave, but a man should be responsible relative to his family. He should never abandon them).[4]

The Worst or "Lowest" Thing a Man Can Do

When asked what would be the worst or lowest thing a man could do, respondents provided a broad range of answers. An attorney in San Antonio jokingly said that the worst or lowest thing a man could do would be "not to pay his lawyer." Another felt that "being a homosexual" was the worst thing and still another that "giving someone AIDS" was the worst thing a man could do. Responses ranged from killing or raping someone to "bragging" or being "boastful." Because of the wide range of answers it was necessary to group them into categories. Three distinct categories emerged: (1) to physically harm or abuse someone (kill, rape, or abuse a woman or child), (2) to use others, lie, brag, or have no dignity or self-respect, and (3) to not support or to abandon one's family or to "put one's family down" (see Figure 5.2 and Appendix A, Table 11).

Language and educational differences among respondents approached significance. Respondents who were interviewed in English and those with more education were more apt to see physically harming, injuring, or abusing someone as the worst or lowest thing a man could do (see Appendix A, Table 11). Respondents interviewed in Spanish and those with less education more often saw "not supporting the family" as the worst or lowest thing a man could do.[5] Occupational and income differences were negligible.

Although men who scored high on the masculinity component of the BSRI were expected to be more inclined to see not supporting the family as the worst or lowest thing a man could do, the opposite pattern was found. Figure 5.2 shows that men who were low on the Bem masculinity component were actually most likely to identify this as the worst or lowest thing a man could do and less likely to see injuring or abusing others as the worst or lowest thing. Differences on the MSRI were also weak and insignificant.

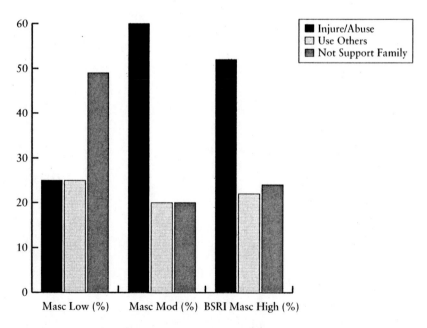

FIGURE 5.2   Worst thing a man can do and BSRI masculinity (p < .04)

Still, men who scored high on traditionalism more often listed not supporting the family or being irresponsible as the worst or lowest thing, whereas those low on traditionalism felt physically harming or injuring someone was the worst or lowest thing a man could do (see Appendix A, Table 11).

Qualities Valued in a Son

In order to tap personal values or traits that were considered important in men, respondents were asked an indirect question: "If you had (or have) a son, what kind of a man would you like him to be when he grows up?"[6] Responses ranged from "being responsible" or "working hard" to more abstract principles such as defending one's beliefs and personal qualities such as warmth or compassion. The responses were grouped into three categories: (1) a son who is responsible or hardworking, (2) a son who has integrity or defends his beliefs or principles, and (3) a son who is honest, compassionate, or warm.

The responses to this question did not vary significantly by region or socioeconomic status. Though not statistically significant (see Appendix A, Table 12), men born outside of the United States and those who were interviewed in Spanish were somewhat more apt to see being responsible or hardworking as important qualities, whereas those born in the United States and those interviewed in English more often emphasized personal attributes such as being warm or honest.

With regard to the measures of masculinity and femininity and traditionalism, men who scored low on the masculine dimension of the BSRI focused more on being responsible and hardworking and less on personal qualities such as warmth and honesty than those high or moderate on this measure. Differences in the feminine dimension of the BSRI and the MSRI were greater and statistically significant. Respondents high on femininity more often identified personal qualities rather than being responsible or hardworking as being important. Surprisingly, men ranked as highly traditional on the MSRI were significantly more likely to emphasize such personal qualities in a son as being honest or warm[7] than they emphasized being responsible or hardworking.[8]

Attitudes Toward Child Rearing and Parenting

The last section of the interview schedule focused on attitudes toward child rearing and parenting. Respondents were asked to reflect on their own values or ideology about child rearing and on how they learned about parenting. Responses were grouped according to whether they saw one of the following as the primary source of their attitudes toward raising children:

(1) their own childhood experiences or the beliefs conveyed by parents, (2) formal education or reading, and (3) friends, acquaintances, or observing others.

Regional differences among the respondents were statistically significant. Although it is not clear why this was the case, northern Californians more often identified formal reading and educational experiences as the primary source of their parental ideology or ideas toward child rearing, whereas southern Californians and Texans focused more on childhood experiences and parents as their primary source of ideas about parenting (see Appendix A, Table 15). Those interviewed in English, professionals, and men with more education and higher incomes said that education or reading had the greatest impact on their attitudes toward rearing children, although only occupational differences were statistically significant.[9] Professionals were significantly more likely to say that their ideas about raising children came from books or formal education, whereas nonprofessionals learned from parents and their own childhood experiences.

There were also statistically significant differences between persons ranked as "traditional" and "nontraditional" on the MSRI in how they viewed the origins of their ideas about child rearing.[10] Highly traditional respondents were less likely than those with moderate or low scores on traditionalism to see education or reading as influencing their attitudes toward child rearing and much more likely to identify parents and their own childhood experiences as the source of their attitudes toward parenting.

Most Important Thing About the Way a Person Is Raised

Respondents were also asked what they felt was most important about the way they were raised (see Appendix A, Table 16). Responses were grouped into three categories: being raised in a family that emphasized love and affection, in one that stressed discipline and moral values, and in one that was not intact. Figure 5.3 shows that men with more education stressed love and affection, whereas those with less education stressed discipline and moral values.

Most Important Responsibility or Duty to Children

Respondents were asked what they felt was their "most important responsibility or duty" to their children. Responses ranged from financial or physical responsibilities (e.g., taking care of their basic needs) to moral, emotional, or spiritual development (e.g., giving them moral guidance). These responses were grouped into two categories according to whether responses

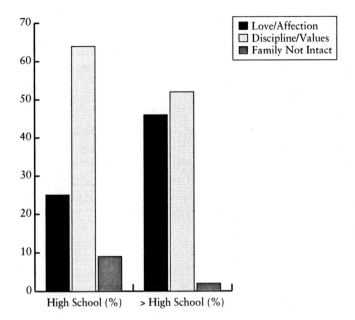

FIGURE 5.3   Importance of how raised and education (p < .05)

focused either on providing for children and taking care of their basic needs or on love, affection, and providing moral guidance. The findings generally indicated no significant differences by socioeconomic status or by region (see Appendix A, Table 17), except that individuals with less education were significantly more likely to emphasize financial responsibility and taking care of the physical needs of children more than they emphasized moral or spiritual development. Over half of the respondents with less than a high school education felt that taking care of the financial and/or physical needs of their children was their most important responsibility, as compared with only one-third of those with more education.

Views about what was considered the most important responsibility or duty to children varied by place of birth and the language of the interview. As expected, foreign-born respondents and those interviewed in Spanish more often identified providing for children or taking care of their physical needs as their most important parental responsibilities, whereas those who were born in the United States or who were interviewed in English focused more on emotional or moral development.

Differences in the BSRI and the MSRI in what was seen as the most important responsibility or duty to children were generally not significant (see Appendix A, Table 17), except that, surprisingly, respondents who ranked high on the Bem masculinity component were significantly less likely to see taking care of the physical or financial needs of children as being most important.

Two additional variables, "sensitivity" and "time spent with children," which were not included in Tables 8–16 (Appendix A), were added to the analysis because they revealed interesting and unanticipated patterns. Essentially, men who were low on sensitivity (i.e., more traditional in their gender role beliefs) were significantly less likely to stress financial or caretaker responsibilities toward children than those who were moderate or high on sensitivity (see Appendix A, Table 17). But fathers who interacted extensively with their children and who were involved in daily activities with them more often stressed financial and physical responsibilities, and the differences approached statistical significance.

Qualities of Respondents as Fathers

Respondents were asked why they considered themselves to be good fathers. Their answers were then grouped into three categories. The first category included those who felt they were good fathers because they provided for the needs of their children; the second, those who made time for and listened to their children; and the third, those who placed a high value on loving, being affectionate with, and otherwise nurturing their children.

There were regional and socioeconomic differences in the distribution of responses and, except for income, the differences approached statistical significance (see Appendix A, Table 18). Texans and those in nonprofessional occupations were more likely to stress their loving and nurturing qualities, while northern Californians and professionals focused more on making time for and listening to their children.

Men born outside of the United States and those who opted to be interviewed in Spanish were more likely to say they were good fathers because they provided for the needs of their children, whereas those born in the United States and those interviewed in English said that they were good fathers because they were loving and affectionate. Only place of birth approached statistical significance.

One U.S.-born respondent said that he felt he was a good father "because I put my love and affection for them above everything else. I like to think that I'm their friend." Another man from Texas felt he was a good father "because I spend a lot of time with my wife and kids. I go to church with them. I get involved in their activities, like sports as a coach." A third respondent said,

> I think I try to be responsive to their needs and interests as much as possible. I think I'm taking very seriously their future needs . . . being sensitive and respon-

sive to the different aspects that contribute to the children's growth and development. It's much more than putting food on the table. I try to empathize with their fears and concerns. I sure as hell wish that my dad would have taken me to Little League practice or come to my defense when there was a hassle at school.

But, as previously noted, men born outside of the United States and those interviewed in Spanish were more apt to stress being responsible, being a good provider, and taking care of the basic needs of their children. One respondent felt he was a good father *"porque yo me preocupo que a ellos no les falten comida y ropa. Y si tienen un problema, que tengan confianza en mi"* (because I make sure that they are not in need of food or clothing. And if they have a problem, that they can count on me). Another respondent felt he was a good father *"porque cumplo con mis deberes de la casa. Cumplo con mis hijos"* (because I fulfill my household responsibilities. I take care of my children).[11]

Qualities Most Admired in a Father

Respondents were asked which qualities they most admired in a father. Answers were grouped according to whether the respondents stressed being a provider, listening to and spending time with children, or being affectionate and loving (see Appendix A, Table 19). Texan men linked being a good father with being a good provider, whereas northern Californians saw being affectionate and loving as most important. These differences approached statistical significance.[12]

Since the vast majority of those interviewed considered their own fathers to have been good fathers or, at a minimum, to have done "the best job they could," respondents were asked to indicate the "good" and "bad" qualities of their own fathers (see Appendix A, Table 20). Those who felt their fathers fell short of being "good" noted that their fathers had particular vices, such as predilections for women or alcohol, or that they acted irresponsibly toward their families. Men born outside of the United States more often reported that their fathers had vices or were irresponsible.

Respondents who felt their father was a good father pointed to such qualities as being loving, affectionate, teaching moral values, and doing the best job possible under difficult circumstances.[13] One Mexican-born respondent, who switched freely from Spanish to English, had this to say about his father:

My father was married with a woman and wanted to produce *varones* [male children], so he went to this little town. He sold her a story and married my mother. When she got to this place another woman was already there. He wanted to make my mother the caretaker, so my mother split. My mother came to Baja when I was one and a half to two years, and went back for us when I was six or seven. I didn't even know her.

Soldier saying good-bye to daughter, 1924 (*Jefes, Héroes y Caudillos*, Sistema Nacional de Fototecas Del Instituto Nacional de Antropología E Historia, Fondo Casasola. México: Fondo de Cultural Económica, 1996).

Another felt his father was not a good father because *"no tenía responsabilidad a sus deberes familiares"* (he neglected his familial obligations).

Strengths and Weaknesses in a Father

The men were asked to isolate any "weaknesses" they felt they might have as fathers. Weaknesses were grouped as: (1) does not provide adequately, (2) neglects, does not spend enough time with, or does not listen to children, (3) is not as affectionate or loving as would like to be, and (4) does not have any weaknesses.

Regional, socioeconomic, and cultural differences on this question yielded some very interesting results (see Appendix A, Table 21). With regard to region, northern Californians were somewhat more inclined to emphasize a deficiency in the provider role, Texans saw the problem of neglect or not spending enough time with children as a weakness, and southern Californians typically felt that they did not have significant weaknesses. Although those with less education and lower incomes and nonprofessionals were also more likely to identify not being able to provide adequately as a weakness or to claim that they had no weaknesses at all, these differences were not statistically significant.[14]

There were important differences on this question in the BSRI and the MSRI. High or low scores in the masculine component of the BSRI appeared unrelated to the various paternal weaknesses a respondent identified. The feminine component was related, however, and these differences approached statistical significance. Differences in the MSRI traditionalism component were significantly related to what were viewed as weaknesses in a father. Interestingly, those who were very traditional in the MSRI were less likely to see any weaknesses in themselves as fathers and least apt to mention that they were not affectionate or loving fathers. Those who were low on traditionalism focused more on "neglecting or not listening" to and not being affectionate enough with children as their weaknesses as fathers.

With regard to what respondents saw as their "strengths" as fathers, four distinct categories were isolated: (1) being a good provider, (2) being a good listener, (3) being heavily involved with their children and their activities, and (4) being affectionate and loving (see Appendix A, Table 22). Nonprofessional respondents, those with less education, those interviewed in Spanish, and those born outside of the United States were more likely to list being a "good provider" as a primary reason for considering themselves to be good fathers. Professionals and men with more education, however, more often said that they were good fathers because they listened to their children and were very involved in their children's activities.

Who Is a "Really Good Father"?

Finally, respondents were asked whether they knew anyone who was a "really good father" and what characteristics qualified this person as such. Qualities identified included being a good provider, being loving and affectionate, and spending a lot of time with children (see Appendix A, Table 23).

Region, income, education, and occupation did not significantly affect the qualities identified as important in being a good father, although men with lower incomes and less education were somewhat more likely to emphasize being loving and affectionate and less likely to stress spending time with children as important. Place of birth and language influenced responses. Men born outside of the United States and those interviewed in Spanish saw being loving and affectionate toward their children as a more important indicator of good fatherhood than spending time with them.

Deconstructing Assumptions:
A Conclusion

These findings are not conclusive, but they have important implications for understanding masculinity and the role of the father within Latino culture and society in general. Perhaps the overriding implication is that the patterns observed are complex and cannot be understood by utilizing conventional or unidimensional conceptions of Latino men. A second, related implication is that as a group, Latino men are internally diverse, so that intra-ethnic differences are perhaps as great or greater than interethnic differences. Third, although social class is generally regarded as a key determinant of gender attitudes and behaviors, in this study socioeconomic differences among Latino men were often negligible or simply did not move in the predicted direction. Finally, the assumption that acculturation and greater exposure to the dominant culture leads to rejection of traditional conceptions of gender and the male role was not supported by the findings.

Contrary to what social science research and prevailing societal conceptions of Latino culture might indicate, men who were born in México or Latin America and who were interviewed in Spanish were not generally more traditional or stereotypically "macho." They were, in fact, less likely than those born in the United States and those interviewed in English to have a favorable view of the word "macho," to associate machismo with positive behaviors such as being honorable or respectful of others, or to consider themselves to be macho. Foreign-born men were also less likely to feel that love and affection were most important in how they were raised or to see providing moral or emotional guidance as their most important responsibility or duty to their children. Those with greater ties to Mexican or Latino culture stressed being selfless as a positive quality and being self-centered, or *egoísta*, as a negative one. Many of them, in fact, identified this as the attribute they least respected or admired in a man. Men with less education and a lower income similarly were more likely to identify *egoísmo* as a negative trait. In addition, those with closer ties to Mexican or Latino culture and a lower socioeconomic status more often stressed being responsible and being a good provider over "spending time" or "being a friend" to children in their evaluations of the important components of the father role.

The findings suggest that there is a distinct Latino cultural ethic surrounding masculinity and fatherhood that is radically different from dominant American conceptions. According to this ethic, whether a person is considered to be a successful man or a good father is determined not so much by such external qualities as success, fame, or wealth but by such internal qualities as responsibility, selflessness, and moral character. From this standpoint the worst or "lowest" thing a man can do is to be irresponsible, to put his interests and welfare above those of his family, or not to take care of his family. The phrase "not taking care of business"—in Spanish, not being *formal* (responsible)—is often used to describe a situation in which a man is criticized for failing to fulfill his responsibilities or duties as a man or as a father.

6

"And Ar'n't I a Man?": Toward a Chicano/Latino Men's Studies

Though most of my uncles were *matones* (tough guys), one uncle was different from the rest. Uncle Pepe was not really my *tío*. I guess he was actually my father's first cousin, or my first cousin once removed. He was much younger than my father and only about five years older than my oldest brother, Alex. I don't know exactly why, but we called him *tío*, and we nicknamed him *"Quintos"* (Nickels) because he worked and gave us nickels and dimes to buy ice cream, candy, and cards for our *albums* (pictorial histories). My two older brothers and I were very close to him. *Quintos* always took us on outings to the movies, plays, parks, or museums. Mostly, though, he took us to Chapultepec Park, where we spent many hours playing and hiking.

Quintos was very warm and affectionate. He hugged us, kissed us, and held our hands, but there was never anything sexual about this intimacy. He was simply a warm and affectionate person who cared for us a great deal, I think. In retrospect, aside from my immediate family, his was probably the most important male influence of my childhood. He didn't go to college but was self-educated and seemed more "cultured and worldly" than anyone in the family. He worked as an airline steward, spoke English and French, dressed in the latest fashions, and was well-read. In fact, one of our favorite haunts was the Benjamin Franklin Library in México City. My father was very athletic and liked to take us to soccer matches and baseball games but not to museums and certainly not to libraries.

Quintos was also my *padrino* (godfather) for my first communion. He gave me my Sunday missal and wrote in it a very nice inscription, and he provided moral guidance for me as a child. What is amazing is that I didn't realize that *Quintos* was gay until I was fifteen or sixteen years old. As I was the youngest in the family, it seemed that I was always the last one to find

117

out about a lot of things, especially family secrets. I remember that family members would occasionally make veiled references suggesting that Uncle *Quintos* was "different." I finally confronted my father about it and he said, *"Tu sabes, es uno de los otros"* (You know, he is one of the other kind). I was naive at the time, and when I probed further for an explanation, my father replied, "He doesn't like women." My father wasn't angry or disdainful when he said this. He was matter of fact about it, shrugging his shoulders and saying, *"pobrecito"* (poor guy). The way he said it made it sound like it was an affliction or disease that could not be controlled, a quirk of nature.

As I reflected on *Quintos* and his impact on my upbringing, I came to the realization that many of the values and ideals that I learned about manhood and masculinity were learned not only from men like my father and my grandfather, Alfredo, but also from women and Tío *Quintos*. I also realized that Chicano/Latino homosexuals have been grossly neglected both by the gay community and by Latinos themselves. Though I did not directly address the issue of homosexuality in the study, in this chapter I discuss Chicano/Latino gays within the context of both "The New Men's Studies" (TNMS) and Chicano/Latino men's studies.

Neglected Masculinities and Chicano/Latino Scholarship

In the past twenty years or so a rich body of feminist research and scholarship has emerged. Because this scholarship all too often mirrored the values, orientation, and concerns of upper-middle-class white women, parallel movements have developed among Chicanas/Latinas and other women of color. More recently "The New Men's Studies" has emerged, focusing on men not as apologists for the status quo but as feminist men in solidarity with feminist scholarship.

Despite increased interest in men's studies, the topic of Chicano/Latino masculinity remains neglected and virtually unexplored both within the so-called new men's studies and feminist scholarship. No less surprising, I think, is the fact that the study of Latino men and masculinity has been equally neglected within Chicana/Chicano scholarship. During the past two decades or so there has been a heightened awareness of Latino women and Chicanas, evident in the publication of several significant works on the topic (see Mora and del Castillo 1980; Sánchez and Martínez Cruz 1977; Melville 1980; Mirandé and Enríquez 1981). Though there has been a proliferation of writing by and about Chicanas and other Latinas (Córdova et al. 1984; Garcia 1989; de la Torre and Pesquera 1993; Acosta-Belén and Bose 1993; and Bose and Acosta-Belén 1995) addressing patriarchy, male oppression, and other important issues, there has been little effort to examine Chicano/Latino men as men or to assess the range and variety of Latino masculinities. Cherríe Moraga (1993), for example, contemplates the idea of a "Queer Aztlán" or a "queer nation," incorporating Mexican nationalism and grounded in our Indian heritage, without directly addressing the issue of masculinity.

Ironically, the Chicano movement and Chicano/Latino scholarship have been gender stratified and have emphasized men as the dominant figures, but there have been few serious attempts to examine either masculinity and machismo or the extent to which Chicano/Latino scholarship reflects particular masculinities.

In this chapter I propose the development of a new Chicano/Latino men's studies and begin with an overview and critique of TNMS. This is followed by a synthesis of relevant research on machismo and masculinity programmatic suggestions for studying Latino men and masculinity. Although the call for a separate and autonomous field of Chicano/Latino men's studies may be premature at this point, it is time that we begin to address the extent to which Chicano/Latino men and the varieties of masculinities among them have been ignored both by the new men's studies and Chicano(a)/Latino(a) scholarship.

The "Good Ol' Boys" and Latino Masculinity

Much of the early research on men was based on a static and stereotypical view of men and served to perpetuate traditional conceptions of masculinity and gender (Pleck 1981, 1). According to Joseph Pleck, the problem with this early research and with the term "sex role" is not only that there is arguably no such thing as a uniform, unvarying sex role but also that such terminology "tends to mask questions of power and inequality" (Lopata and Thorne 1978, 719). The new men's studies rejects the tendency of this early research to normalize and justify gender inequality by focusing on men in a way ostensibly designed to augment and support feminist scholarship.

Although TNMS has filled an important void, it has had some serious shortcomings. I propose that the new men's studies is not really new at all. Upon closer analysis it is clear that TNMS is not the study of men qua men but the study of white men. It would thus be more accurate to term it the new white men's studies.[1] When TNMS scholars discuss "men of color," the discussion is usually limited to African-American men. These authors apparently have no conception of race beyond the traditional black/white dichotomy. In *The Myth of Masculinity*, a pioneering work in the field, Joseph Pleck, for example, gave only token attention to African-American men and said nothing at all about Latino men. Thus, when Pleck mentioned "our culture," he was clearly not referring to Mexicans or Latinos.

After surveying the main currents of recent social science research on masculinity, R. W. Connell, one of the leading figures in the new men's studies, concluded that a coherent science of masculinity has not yet been produced (1995, 67). Connell identified three main projects, or theoretical attempts, to develop a science of masculinity (1995, 7). The first effort was derived from clinical knowledge obtained by therapists and was based on Freudian theory. The second, which Pleck termed the Sex Role Identity Paradigm, was a heavily social psychological approach and was based on the popular notion that there were distinct female and male sex roles. The third has been termed "the new social science," or new men's studies, and was stimulated by men's liberation and by sex role psychology but extended well beyond traditional role theory, incorporating recent research in anthropology, sociology, and history (1995, 27).

Connell characterized Pleck's comprehensive evaluation of the male role literature, or the Male Sex Role Identity paradigm, as essentially a critique of functionalist sex role theory (1995, 25). Because the functionalist sex role theory was static and failed to engender a distinct "politics of masculinity," it inhibited social change by "normalizing" male and female sex roles and making them normative (1995, 27). Although Connell presented an insightful critique of the conservative class bias in sex role theory, at the same time he failed to consider the possibility of racial bias within the new men's studies. Like other TNMS scholars, he gives only token attention to Black masculinity under the rubric of "marginalization" (1995, 80) and ignores Chicano/Latino masculinity altogether.[2]

In an exhaustive work entitled *Manhood in America*, Michael Kimmel attempted to present a cultural history of men, noting that American men have no history of themselves as men (1996, 1–2). Kimmel traced the history of American manhood from 1776 to the present and chronicled the emergence of the "self-made" man between 1776 and 1865, the unmaking of the self-made man from 1900–1920, the "new man" of the twentieth century, and the contemporary crises of masculinity. Although this is an important book, and a cultural history of American manhood is important and long overdue, Chicano/Latino men are conspicuously absent from this history, leading one to conclude either that we are invisible and have no history or that we are somehow not part of American manhood.

"Reservoir Dogs": Overview and Critique of the New Men's Studies

Because most academic research and theory has been the work of men and reflects male concerns, orientations, values, and worldviews, many critics fail to understand the need for a new men's studies. Critics of the new men's studies have noted that the existing scientific and academic world could be characterized as "The Old Men's Studies" (TOMS). Proponents of TNMS such as Connell, Brod, and Kimmel counter that most research and writing has been carried out by men but that there has been an absence of critical, reflective analyses not only of manhood but also of how masculinity affects the conduct of scientific inquiry. According to Carrigan, Connell, and Lee (1985, 551), "Though most social science is indeed about men, good-quality research that brings masculinity into focus is rare." Moreover, with the exception of work on the history of homosexual masculinity, most recent studies are below the standard set by early researchers in the 1950s (Carrigan, Connell, and Lee 1985, 551). Harry Brod observed that "while seemingly about men, traditional scholarship's treatment of generic man as the human norm in fact systematically excludes from consideration what is unique to men qua men" (Brod 1987, 2). Ironically, generalizing from the male to the generic human experience "precludes the study of masculinity as a specific male experience" (1987, 2). According to Brod,

> The most general definition of men's studies is that it is the study of masculinities and male experiences as specific and varying social-historical-cultural formations. Such studies situate masculinities as objects of study on a par with femininities, instead of elevating them to universal norms. (1987, 2)

Despite the growing literature on men and masculinity, men's studies has proved to be controversial and problematic. Clyde W. Franklin II (1988, 15–19) identified several important controversies within the field. First, what perspectives should characterize TNMS? There have been two opposing ideological perspectives within the men's movement: profeminist and nonfeminist. While the former recognizes that men have gained privilege from patriarchy and the oppression of women, the latter contends that women benefit from the institutionalization of traditional gender roles and that such roles place men at a disadvantage relative to women. Although most advocates of men's studies have assumed a profeminist stance, a substantial antifeminist strand exists within the larger so-called men's movement. This antifeminist ideology appears to be especially prevalent within the "men's rights" branch of the men's movement.

The second and perhaps most serious and recurrent controversy has centered around the assertion that TNMS and the call for more generic gender studies programs are simply insidious tactics designed to weaken and co-opt feminist studies. After a turbulent conference on "Men, Masculinity, and Social Theory" held under the auspices of the Sociological Theory Group of the British Sociological Association, two feminist critics of TNMS, Joyce E. Canaan and Christine Griffin, admitted they were reluctant to participate in the conference. They also declined to contribute to the ensuing conference volume, *Men, Masculinities, and Social Theory*, edited by Hearn and Morgan (1990), because there were fundamental problems and limitations with TNMS (1990, 2060). One problem they identified is what Connell has termed a "crisis in hegemonic masculinity," which has emerged partly as a response to the gains of the women's movement and feminism. According to Canaan and Griffin,

> The problem with the name, "men's studies," is that it suggests that studies of men are complementary with those of women. As we know very well, so-called complementary all too often results in power being wrested from the less powerful and the powerless. We recognize that "men's studies" can literally take women's jobs in teaching and research at a time of financial cutbacks. (Canaan and Griffin 1990, 211)

A third controversy surrounds sexual preference. Critics of men's studies have argued that the field has reflected the needs and concerns of heterosexual men and neglected those of homosexual men. The parent organization for men's studies, the National Organization for Changing Men (N.O.C.M.), now the National Organization for Men Against Sexism (N.O.M.A.S.), however, has taken a strong gay affirmative and anti-homophobic stance. This pro-gay position is said to have led some heterosexual men to question their allegiance to the organization and even to drop out (Franklin 1988, 17). The final controversy and the one most directly relevant to this book revolves around the issue of race. Like its feminist counterpart, the new men's studies has been almost exclusively an elite white men's movement. As has already been noted, Chicanos and Latinos, whether gay or straight, have been conspicuously absent from both the old and the new men's studies.

Folklore, Machismo, and Modernization: Toward a Profeminist Chicano/ Latino Men's Studies

There is a growing body of literature that is beginning to focus on the extent to which much of the research and theory that has been assumed to be universal is not only culturally bound but also gender specific. Victor J. Seidler proposed that many forms of masculinity are implicated in the traditions of social theory that have emerged since the Enlightenment. One of the basic tenets of the Enlightenment that has shaped our conception of "modernity" is the notion that only through reason could we guide and control our lives (Seidler 1994, 1). Thus, "within a rationalist intellectual culture we have to learn to control our emotions, for they can only be recognized as interference in a life of reason" (1994, xii).

In an insightful essay David Morgan similarly observes that there is an inherent contradiction in our understanding of masculinity, as claims to academic rationality that are gender specific have been institutionalized as universal. Morgan examines a number of sociological texts from a gender perspective and concludes that such research is replete with masculine assumptions. Weber's *Protestant Ethic and the Spirit of Capitalism,* for example, ultimately is not universal, but "a study of masculinity. . . . The main character traits of ideal-typical puritan self-control, discipline, rationality, methodicalness are traits which would probably be defined as 'masculine' by many people" (Morgan 1981, 93).

Morgan asserted, moreover, that a male culture of academic rationality—what he terms "academic machismo"—has been institutionalized in the universities. Despite the fact that academics are often depicted as "sexless" intellectuals who could not succeed in the "real world," there is intense rivalry and competition within the male world of academia.

> The arenas of the practice of academic rationality—the seminars, the conferences, the exchange in scholarly journals—are also arenas for the competitive display of masculine skills (within, to be sure, a capitalist culture). . . . Consider the phrases which are often used to describe academic exchanges— "wiped the floor with him," "tore him into little pieces," and so on—phrases more redolent of gladiatorial combat than scholarly debate. The symbolic leaders of academic folk heroes are sharp, quick on the draw, masters of the deadly put-down, and the subject of admiring gossip. (Morgan 1981, 101)

Rather than resorting to physical violence, the academic macho turns to written attacks, verbal barbs, and intellectual dueling. It is, in a sense, a ritualized, institutionalized, and highly rewarded form of male aggression. The academic macho is reminiscent of the *pelado* who is so filled with insecurities that he is determined to excel and to be the best at everything he undertakes. But for academics the most macho is not the one with the most balls but the one with the longest resume.

Despite the value in Morgan's analysis of academic culture, it should be emphasized that his conclusions cannot be generalized to all men. Morgan is describing white male culture and white academic machismo, not universal male culture. Thus, although Morgan is gender sensitive, he is culturally myopic and appears oblivious to the fact that masculinities are themselves culturally bound.

In an article titled "Class, Gender, and Machismo," anthropologist Manuel Peña reexamined the "treacherous-woman" folklore found among undocumented Mexican male agricultural workers in California. Peña contended that "the treacherous woman is a key element in the ideology of machismo and that both are intimately tied to Mexican–working class male culture" (1991, 31).

Peña did fieldwork among Mexican immigrant men who worked for a large agribusiness firm near Fresno, logging more than four hundred hours picking fruit alongside the men who collaborated in the study. The *charritas coloradas* ("off-color" jokes and stories), a style of folklore which is said to be characteristic of working-class men, form the core of the folklore of machismo. Quoting Paredes, he noted that the unvarying message is one of "sadism toward women and symbolic threats of sodomy toward men" and the complete degradation of women (Paredes 1966, 31–32).

Using a historical-materialist perspective, Peña attempted to link folklore and the ideology of machismo to the oppressed economic condition of Mexican workers. The power of this ideology is derived not from the trauma of the conquest of México, as has been argued by Ramos, Paz, Goldwert and others, but from extreme economic exploitation and the ensuing deprivation and alienation (1991, 31). The *charrita* is, thus, a sort of symbolic alibi, an ideological displacement of class exploitation and alienation onto women.

> The persistent class inequality that Mexican working-class men face, immune as it is from cultural penetration, deflects the political unconscious (Jameson 1981) toward a more overt, less mystified (though no less ideological) source of conflict and inequality—the relationship between men and women. Fully cognizant of his supremacy in the latter relationship, the working-class man wrings every bit of compensation out to his advantage, which he enhances by symbolically conflating two distinct relationships—class and gender. (Peña 1991, 41–42)

The conceptions of machismo held by the Latino men in our study failed to support the assumption that the ideology of machismo is somehow characteristic of the Mexican working class. There was not only tremendous variation in conceptions of machismo held by Latino men, but middle-class men generally had a more positive view of machismo. The vast majority of respondents saw it as a negative or synthetic form of masculinity characterized by male dominance and self-centeredness, or *egoísmo,* and did not identify themselves as being macho. Without denying the existence of male dominance and patriarchal beliefs, these findings challenge the assumption that machismo, at least as traditionally defined, is somehow a positive trait or desired cultural value.

One of the most obvious but seldom discussed factors that has shaped generalizations concerning Chicano/Latino society and gender is that such generalizations were based on the observations of white male ethnographers and were, therefore, subject to both a racial/ethnic and a gender bias. Most of the early ethnographies of Mexicans on both sides of the border were carried out by Anglo males such as William Madsen, Arthur Rubel, and Oscar Lewis. Clinical psychiatric accounts of Mexican culture were similarly largely the work of white men (see G. M. Gilbert, 1959 and Goldwert 1980, 1983, and 1985). Even the work of the noted Mexican scholar Samuel Ramos was heavily pathological and modeled on Alfred Adler's theory of masculine protest. The point simply is that these scholars interpreted Mexican culture and masculinity from their own limited cultural/class/gender perspective. Not surprisingly, with this as a yardstick Mexicans were often found wanting, and depictions tended to paint a negative caricature of both Mexican men and women. Perhaps the major flaw in conventional scholarship, then, is that it failed to grasp the nuance and complexity of Mexican/Chicano culture.

América Paredes, as previously mentioned, has been critical of Anglo ethnographers, noting that their ignorance and lack of sensitivity to Mexican and Chicano cultural and linguistic patterns have led them to numerous erroneous interpretations and distorted views. Arthur Rubel, for example, came to the following conclusion based on his observation of workers in the campaign of a Chicano political candidate:

> Sometimes the conversation of the campaigners focused on strategy. At such times there was much talk of *hacienda* [landed estate] *movida, hay mucha movida*, and "moving the people". Such phrases implied that the Mexican-American electorate—the *chicanazgo* (sic)—was a dormant mass, which had to be stirred into activity. (Paredes 1977, 4)

Paredes correctly pointed out that not only does Rubel mistake *hacienda* for *haciendo* (doing or making) and *chicanazgo* for *Chicanada* (the people), but, more importantly, he also completely misinterprets the meaning of *movida* by concluding that the Mexican-American community is a dormant mass that "needs to be moved." What the workers were saying, in fact, was the opposite—that they had to "pull a move" or "pull a fast one" on the Anglos.

Paredes noted, moreover, that Mexicans and Chicanos are experts in verbal art and that they love to put strangers on. Unfortunately, many remarks that respondents made in a kidding or flippant manner were taken very literally by these ethnographers and, therefore, were misunderstood. According to Paredes, "the use of indirect language has been refined in the word-play of the *albur* to double or triple levels of meaning" (1977, 9). The naive and untrained ethnographer, however, is incapable of either appreciating such verbal art or understanding the true meaning of these exchanges. Paredes offered the example of a young Mexican male who asks his friend in a polite voice, "How is your sister this morning?" Despite his apparent concern, he is not likely to be inquiring about her health but is instead asking euphemistically, "What is your sister's condition this morning after the rough riding I gave her last night?" (1977, 10). Although Paredes presented an important corrective for culturally insensitive ethnographers, many of the examples he used, such as the previous one, reflect a male, sexist perspective. Although Paredes is undoubtedly correct in noting that such sexual joking is common among young men, he appears impervious to the sexist and offensive nature of many of the jokes and folktales that he relates. A Chicana folklorist would undoubtedly have provided a very different treatment and interpretation of such material.

Ironically, then, though Paredes is culturally sensitive, he does not appear to be very gender sensitive. In refuting many Anglo stereotypes, he unwittingly reinforced the prevailing belief that sexism and male dominance are deeply ingrained within Chicano/Latino culture. Such joking may go on among those who subscribe to the double standard and have internalized the negative conception of machismo, but it would be wrong to infer that most Mexicans engage in this type of ritual joking behavior, especially with intimate friends.

It could be argued, in fact, that by focusing exclusively on male joking patterns and neglecting joking patterns and folklore among women and cross-gender joking, Paredes presented a very limited and unidimensional depiction of Mexican/Latino culture. He noted, for instance, that both Chicanos and Mexicans are familiar with the story of the two *compadres* (co-parents) from Alvaro Veracruz who say upon parting:

"No se olvide, compadrito" (Don't forget, my dear *compadre*)
"Ni usted tampoco, compadrito" (You either, my dear *compadre*)

Despite the appearance of civility and politeness, each *compadre* is ostensibly telling the other, "Don't forget to fuck your mother" (1977, 10). He discusses "Visiting the Widow," "The Absent Anglo Farmer's Wife," and other capers that are part of Mexican South Texas folklore. Paredes noted further that "one of the recurrent criticisms of the Anglo in Mexican folklore centers around the 'shamelessness' of Anglo women who 'go about half-naked or wearing pants, paint their faces and go out with men all by themselves'" (1977, 23). Although this discussion may be reflective of cultural conflict along the border, it is difficult not to notice that women, whether Mexican or Anglo, are the butt of most of the jokes and stories in the folklore presented. In short, though insightful, Paredes's critique of Anglo ethnographers is replete with sexist stories and jokes.

Given Paredes's critique of ethnographic studies of Mexican communities, it might be appropriate at this point to reexamine Peña's study of Mexican folklore and machismo among working-class Mexican men. Though Peña is Chicano and fluent in Spanish, Paredes cautioned that having research conducted by "insiders," especially by those who have received the same training as their mentors, does not necessarily exempt it from criticism (1977, 2).

Peña may be an "insider" but as an educated ethnographer and researcher he is an "insider-outsider" relative to working-class Mexican agricultural workers. Regardless of how astute an ethnographer Peña might be, he is not a poor, undocumented agricultural worker. More significantly, we are not told exactly how the men responded to Peña, except that "they knew the patrón had given me permission to collect 'stories and jokes' from them, which made it easier for me to intervene in their work routine" (1991, 32). Though the men were initially reluctant to share their *charritas coloradas,* they began to "open up" and eventually "this type of humor surged to the forefront" (1991, 32).

Peña began to bring a tape recorder with him to the fields, which he carefully hid in his shirt pocket. The idea that Peña could pick fruit alongside the men with a microphone "discretely concealed" in his shirt appears innocuous enough on the surface, but it raises a number of important questions. First, is it physically possible to pick fruit, carry on conversations with the men, and record the *charritas?* Second, did the men know about the microphone and consent to having their conversations recorded? Third, since the men were extremely alienated and subordinated along class lines, how would they have responded to a professional anthropologist who had been authorized by the *patrón* to study them? Would they have been distrustful? Would they have been honest? Is it possible that they might have been putting on the ethnographer, as Paredes suggested, or that they participated in a performance, essentially telling Peña what they thought he wanted to know?

Peña acknowledged that the men were hesitant to talk to him and that it was only after "the workers convinced themselves that I was especially interested in *charritas coloradas,* these became the dominant genre performed" (1991, 32). At another point Peña noted, "I asked for some charritas about women" (1991, 34). What is perhaps most amazing, given that Peña is a proponent of reflexive anthropology, is that he did not consider the possibility that the men were telling him what they thought he expected to hear.

Even if one accepts Peña's basic thesis that *charritas* are prevalent among working-class undocumented agricultural workers and that these folkloric performances are extremely sexist and degrading to women, one need not accept the conclusion that *charritas* and the degradation of women in folklore are peculiar either to the working-class or to Mexicans.

Anthropologist Renato Rosaldo (1989) extended the critique of traditional ethnography and applied it to the Chicano experience. Rosaldo contended that all too often ethnographers have treated cultures as static, objective, and impersonal entities rather than as fluid, changing, and subjective processes used by humans to understand their lives. Using the metaphor of the border, Rosaldo focused on the borderlands, or fringes, between groups, noting that these are not empty transitional zones but important sources of cultural production and change. "Social borders frequently become salient around such lines as sexual orientation, gender, class, race, ethnicity, nationality, age, politics" (Rosaldo 1989, 208).

Rosaldo believed that ethnographers can gain important insights into cultural creation by looking critically at narratives. He then turned to a case study examination of three very different Chicano narratives. The first, *"With His Pistol in His Hand": A Border Ballad and Its Hero*, compiled in 1958 by Américo Paredes, is a classic work in Chicano folklore that looks at how the story of Mexican social bandit Gregorio Cortez is recounted in the border ballads (*corridos*) of south Texas. The second, *Barrio Boy*, published in 1971, is the autobiography of Chicano scholar Ernesto Galarza, tracing his migration as a boy from a small village in Nayarit, México, to a barrio in Sacramento, California. The final work consists of a series of essays and short stories compiled by Sandra Cisneros in *The House on Mango Street*, published in 1985. This last work depicts life in a multiracial neighborhood in Chicago as seen through the eyes of a young woman.

Although the three narratives address the Chicano warrior hero, or macho patriarch, they do so from very different perspectives. According to Rosaldo, whereas Paredes saw the warrior hero in a very positive light, Galarza begins to question and to mock him, and Cisneros completely rejects him. Paredes depicted Gregorio Cortez as larger than life, a hero of mythic proportions who, as a symbol of the eroding traditional, patriarchal, Mexican feudal order, stands up to the Anglo Texan and boldly shouts his name in battle— "Yo soy Gregorio Cortez" (I am Gregorio Cortez). The young boy in Galarza's autobiography, on the other hand, begins to question patriarchal authority by identifying the diminutive Aunt Tel as the matriarch, or *jefe de familia*, and by mocking the household rooster, Coronel, who loses a fight against a turkey buzzard even though he is said to be *muy gallo* (very manly). Finally, according to Rosaldo, Cisneros is completely irreverent, rejecting patriarchal authority and the warrior hero. Referring to her name, the protagonist in *The House on Mango Street*, Esperanza, notes,

> In English my name means hope. In Spanish it means too many letters. It means sadness, it means waiting. It is like the number nine. A muddy color. It is the Mexican records my father plays on Sunday mornings when he is shaving, songs like sobbing. (Cisneros 1985, 12)

Despite their differences, these three narratives represent an evolution of culture. In a sense, they tell us "how we got to be the way we are" (Rosaldo

1989, 148). The tales are said to "follow an Edenic mythic pattern of an idealized initial condition, a fall, and subsequent struggles to survive, and perhaps thrive, into the present" (1989, 148–149). As such, they represent shifting and emergent conceptions of culture. "The trajectory of the three narrative analyses moves Chicano identity from bounded cultural purity through the mockery of patriarchs to encounters at the border zone of everyday life" (1989, 149).

Although Rosaldo is to be commended for introducing a fluid, insightful, innovative, and gender-sensitive conception of Chicano culture, there are problems with his analysis. One area of concern is that under the rubric of Chicano narratives he compared three very distinct genres: folklore, biography, and fiction. In addition, Rosaldo compared individuals who represent different generations, regions, and genders. Although his analysis is powerful and refreshing, a number of questions remain unresolved. Can we assume that Chicano culture has followed a direct trajectory from Paredes to Cisneros, or are there cultural borders that have not yet been tapped? How did women of Paredes's generation and of earlier generations, for example, address the issue of patriarchy? Is Aunt Tel an anomaly, or are there many women in our cultural heritage who wear the *calzones* (pants) and are in fact the head of the family? Is it necessary to reject Mexican culture in order to subscribe to a feminist perspective? How do contemporary Chicano/Latino men deal with their patriarchal heritage? Finally, is the mythic warrior hero found in the border ballad of Gregorio Cortez necessarily a patriarchal image? Can one identify with Cortez as a heroic figure without endorsing the oppression of women? Do the heroines of the Mexican Revolution such as La Valentina and *Las Soldaderas* and other political and literary figures such as Sara Estela Ramirez[3] represent female counterparts to the mythic warrior?

In the passage "My Name" the protagonist in *The House on Mango Street* comments on her name:

> It was my great-grandmother's name and now it is mine. She was a horse woman too, born like me in the Chinese year of the horse—which is supposed to be bad luck if you're born female—but I think this is a Chinese lie because the Chinese, like the Mexicans, don't like their women strong.
>
> My great-grandmother. I would've liked to have known her, a wild horse of a woman, so wild she wouldn't marry until my great-grandfather threw a sack over her head and carried her off just like that, as if she were a fancy chandelier. That's the way he did it. And the story goes she never forgave him. (Cisneros 1985, 12)

Cisneros's statements contain some interesting contradictions. In asserting that neither the Mexican nor the Chinese like their women strong, she reinforces the view in Mexican culture of the patriarchal, dominant male and the submissive female, but in the next breath she notes that her great-grandmother was "a wild horse of a woman, so wild she wouldn't marry" her great-grandfather until he abducted her by force. If Mexicans do not, in fact, like their women strong, the question that remains unanswered is why her great-grandfather married her at all. Why do we have ballads extolling the brave and heroic acts of women like the tough Texan drug dealer, Camelia, La Tejana?

Although Rosaldo imputes a feminine voice to Esperanza's rejection of her father's patriarchal culture and music, one could also see the devaluing of traditional culture and language as resulting from the process of assimilation that cuts across gender. In *Hunger of Memory,* for example, Richard Rodriguez is similarly alienated from his Mexican cultural and linguistic heritage. Rodriguez, disturbed by his father's "accent" in English, recalls a childhood incident where the father is talking to a gas station attendant.

> At one point his words slid together to form one word— sounds as confused as the threads of blue and green oil in the puddle next to my shoes. His voice rushed through what he had left to say. And toward the end, reached falsetto notes, appealing to his listener's understanding. Shortly afterward, walking toward home with my father, I shivered when he put his hand on my shoulder. (Rodriguez 1983, 15)

A recurrent issue faced by feminists of color is whether their gender or racial liberation would occur within or outside the Chicano/Latino community. Many Chicanas, particularly lesbians, found that they were permitted more sexual liberation outside their racial or ethnic group. Cherríe Moraga, for example, noted that initially at least, her wish to pursue a lesbian lifestyle led her to a series of choices that alienated her from her racial and cultural group. At the height of the Chicano movement she noted that she was "a closeted, light-skinned, mixed blood Mexican-American, disguised in my father's English last name" (Moraga 1993, 145). Because of her last name and her light skin and features, *La Güera,* as she was called, was able to pass in white society (1983, 85). Three years after graduating from an elite private school, she realized why it had been difficult for her to fit in.

> All along I had felt the difference, but not until I had put the words "class" and "race" to the experience, did my feelings make any sense. For years, I had berated myself for not being as "free" as my classmates. . . . But I knew nothing about "privilege" then. White was right. Period. I could pass. If I got educated enough, there would never be no telling. (1983, 55)

More recently, Aída Hurtado has attempted to develop a feminist perspective that addresses the sociopolitical, racial, and gender experiences of women of color. Drawing an analogy between domesticated animals and beasts of burden, she noted that metaphorically the white woman has been treated like a domesticated animal (1989, 854), whereas the Chicana and the African-American woman have been treated like beasts of burden. A seventy-three-year-old Black woman reflected on her experience as a former slave:

> My mother used to say that the Black woman is the white man's mule and the white woman is his dog. . . . we do the heavy work and get beat whether we do it well or not. But the white woman is closer to the master and he pats them on the head and lets them sleep in the house, but he ain't gon' treat neither one like he was dealing with a person. (Collins 1986, 17)

Although both white women and women of color are oppressed, they suffer a different type of oppression. According to Hurtado,

> Gender subordination is differentially enforced by white men on white women and women of Color. White women are subordinated through seduction: accepting middle-class standards of femininity in exchange for sharing white men's privileges. Women of Color are subordinated through rejection and treated primarily as workers as are their male counterparts. (1988, 1)

Because men of color lack economic and political power in society, they cannot utilize the same mechanisms to subordinate women. Men and women of color are economically, politically, and culturally oppressed. This common oppression creates a bond between men and women and, according to Hurtado, "increases the solidarity with men of Color" (1988, 1). Given that Chicanas belong to and identify with a particular racial or ethnic group, their subordination and oppression have been enforced primarily by control of sexuality and the threat of rejection or exclusion from the group. Hurtado related that when the female members of *El Teatro Campesino* (a theater group founded and directed by Luis Valdez), including his sister Socorro Valdez, complained that the female parts were limiting and stereotypical, they were told to establish their own theater group.[4] Being forced to set up their own company proved to be a painful experience. According to Hurtado, "Chicano feminism does not advocate separatism from Chicano men or from the Chicano community" (1988, 16). Chicanas want liberation, but they want it on their own terms.

My intent in advocating a profeminist, anti-homophobic Chicano/Latino male studies, as noted earlier, is not to supplant or in any way minimize the importance of Chicana/Latina feminism. On the contrary, my intent is simply to support and augment feminist scholarship. Although white feminists can relate as women to the oppression of the Chicana, they remain the wives, lovers, mothers, and daughters of white men. Chicano males, on the other hand, can understand racial and ethnic oppression but not gender oppression. In the end, only women of color have felt the full impact of their triple oppression as women and as persons of color and the internal oppression that occurs within the culture itself. Lesbian women of color (and to a lesser extent, gay men of color) face an added layer of oppression. Cherríe Moraga related an interesting exchange she had with a gay white male who was incapable of understanding her racial/ethnic or gender oppression. To help him see her situation more clearly, Moraga asked him to imagine for a moment that he was a woman for a day. The friend "confessed that the thought terrified him because, to him, being a woman meant being raped by men" (Moraga 1983, 53). In order to really understand her, it was necessary for him to experience the victimization directly and to come to terms emotionally with "what it feels like to be a victim" (1983, 53). White women, similarly, must be held accountable for their own racism (1983, 58).

The Latino Gay Voice and the Cult of Masculinity

Perhaps the most glaring omission in research and writing on gender and masculinities is the absence either of research and writing on Latino gay men or of attempts to articulate a Latino male gay voice. The absence of a Latino gay voice is paradoxical given the persistence of male dominance and the cult of masculinity in Latino culture. Some Chicano writers have hinted at or strongly implied the existence of a same-sex preference, but male Latino writers have remained largely in the academic closet.[5] There simply is no male counterpart to the powerful and moving portrayals of such gay Chicana writers as Cherríe Moraga, Gloria Anzaldúa, and Ana Castillo.[6]

Writings on Chicano/Latino male homosexuality have focused mostly on the issue of identity. How are Chicano/Latino men able to forge and to maintain a gay identity, particularly within a culture that is said to be fixated on masculinity and heterosexual machismo? Bernie Sue Newman and Peter Gerard Muzzonigro looked at the effects of race and traditional family values on the "coming out" process of twenty-seven gay male adolescents and found that although race as such did not have an independent effect on how "coming out" was experienced, traditional family values were seen by respondents as obstacles to the process (1993, 219). Families were categorized as traditional based on (1) the importance of religion in the family, (2) emphasis on marriage, (3) emphasis on having children, and (4) whether a language other than English was spoken in the home. Across racial groups, families with a strong emphasis on traditional values were perceived as being less accepting of homosexuality. For those who had disclosed their homosexuality to family members, the more traditional families were perceived as being less accepting and as reacting with more disapproval (Newman and Muzzonigro 1993, 224). Ironically, adolescents from more traditional families also reported an earlier age of first crush on another boy than did adolescents from less traditional families (1993, 224).

A study of childhood sexual abuse among 1,001 homosexual and bisexual men found that 37 percent reported sexual contact before the age of nineteen with an older male whom they perceived to be more powerful (Doll et al. 1992). The vast majority (94 percent) had contact with an older male, and more than half of the male partners were nineteen years of age or older. The median age of first contact with a male partner was ten years, and the median age difference between the two partners was eleven years. (1992, 858). The age gap was significantly greater for boys under six and those over fifteen.

Race was a factor, as Black and Latino participants were significantly more likely to report sexual contact with an older or more powerful partner (1992, 859). Fifty-two percent of Black, 50 percent of Latino, and 36 percent of white respondents reported contact with a more powerful partner. Latino participants were also younger (eight years) than Black (ten years) or white respondents (ten years) and were more likely to report an age difference of five years or more.

These findings suggest that sexual abuse of children may be much greater than we have been led to believe and that childhood sexual abuse of homosexual and bisexual men may be especially prevalent. The fact that first sexual contact was reported with males who were significantly older and more powerful indicates a pattern of sexual abuse. Fifty-three percent of the partners were adults nineteen years of age or older, and 43 percent were family members (1992, 858).

A study of 175 adult male sex offenders found that 76 percent of incarcerated male sexual offenders identified themselves as heterosexuals, despite the fact that they had been convicted of molesting boys (Doll et al. 1992, 861). Previous research has suggested that in comparison with sexually abused girls, sexually abused boys are more likely to come from lower socioeconomic backgrounds. The higher prevalence of reported sexual abuse among Black and Latino youth in this study may reflect actual racial or ethnic differences in the prevalence of abuse, or they may simply reflect the fact that minorities are likely to be overrepresented among clients receiving treatment at large sexually transmitted disease (STD) clinics (1992, 62).

Robert Richmond Ellis noted that although autobiography is a genre practiced by older men who are reflecting on the totality of their lives, gay writers who are attempting to come to grips with their identities have often become autobiographers at a young age (1995, 320). Focusing on Luis Antonio de Villena's *Ante el Espejo*, Ellis noted:

Villena's self-representation as a non-heterosexual and non-bourgeois within the framework of Francoist Spain (executed in the past and reaffirmed through the writing of the autobiographical text itself), reveals a camp aesthetic that current queer theory can help to inform. (1995, 321)

Ellis noted that Moe Meyer, in a groundbreaking collection of essays on "camp," defined it as "the act of being queer in an explicitly social context" (Ellis 1995, 321). But the essence of camp does not reside in the actor but in the act (Ellis 1995, 321–322). In short, for Meyer "camp" is a form of parody consistent with Anthony Giddens's assertion that "power and dominance rest on the ability to produce codes of signification" (Ellis 1995, 322).

According to Ellis, the autobiography of Villena serves as a parody or a "camp eye" that "destabilizes dominant bourgeois configurations of gender and social class and turns homosexual and aristocratic posturing into acts of defiance" (1995, 322). The dandy, like the aristocrat, "trivializes bourgeois notions of productivity and utilitarianism" (1995, 323). Although the dandy is associated with homosexuals, he is not necessarily homosexual himself. The dandy is ultimately a rebel, flaunting conventional codes of social behavior and rejecting the values of all social classes (Ellis 1995, 323).

To the extent that he is classified in sexual categories at all, he is a narcissist and exhibitionist, who uses the other as a means of asserting his own difference.... There is also ... a fundamental contradiction: the dandy refuses bourgeois essentialization that precludes queer solidarity or the recognition of a queer affinity. (Ellis 1995, 323)

By contrasting portrayals of his homosexual uncle and his heterosexual father, Villena sought to characterize male sexuality in both the pre-war and Francoist generations (Ellis 1995, 325). Whereas Villena's father was an exaggerated virile figure who "rejected the monarchism of his aristocratic family and joined the Falangists," his uncle retained close ties to the family, took on the characteristics of a dandy, and never worked (1995, 325).[7] Villena's gay uncle was mysteriously killed at the beginning of the Spanish civil war as he went to rendezvous with a lover, though Villena's father survived and was said to have "thrived under fascism" (1995, 325). Despite his uncle's tragic death, "Villena expressly revived the memory of his uncle," depicting him as a decadent and nostalgic guardian angel pitted against an alien heterosexual world (1995, 325).

Villena's linking of the dandy with narcissism and homoerotic behavior is interesting because the *pachuco*, or Chicano version of the dandy, is a positive symbol of cultural identity, heterosexuality, and machismo. Yet if one looks more closely, there are striking parallels between Villena's dandy

Xavier Mirandé strolling in México City.

and the 1940s *pachuco*, or Zoot-Suiter. Like the dandy, the *pachuco's* exaggerated ducktail haircut and clothing flaunted conventional norms of all social classes and served to antagonize American servicemen. During the so-called Zoot-Suit riots hundreds of American servicemen attacked defenseless Chicano youths and stripped them of their "drapes," or clothing.

There is a close parallel between Villena's description of the dandy and Octavio Paz's characterization of the *pachuco*. The *pachuco*, like the dandy, is an instinctive rebel who struggles against the wrath vented toward Mexicans by American society. Rather than attempting to vindicate the race or nationality of their forebears, however, the *pachucos* respond with an obstinate attitude and a will and determination to "not be like those around them" (Paz 1961, 14). According to Paz,

> Since the *pachuco* cannot adapt himself to a civilization which, for its part, rejects him, he finds no answer to the hostility surrounding him except this angry affirmation of his personality. . . . the *pachuco* actually flaunts his differences. The purpose of his grotesque dandyism and anarchic behavior is not so much to point out the injustice and incapacity of a society that has failed to assimilate him as it is to demonstrate his personal will to remain different. (1961, 14–15)

The novelty of the *pachuco* style is found in its exaggeration. The *pachuco* turns ordinary fashion into art and aesthetics by carrying the fashion to its ultimate consequence (1961, 15). Given that American fashion stresses the importance of comfort , the *pachuco* fashion, with its emphasis on the impractical, "negates the very principles of the model that inspired it. Hence its aggressiveness" (1961, 15). Paz ultimately viewed the *pachuco* as the prey of society.

> Instead of hiding he adorns himself to attract the hunter's attention. Persecution redeems him and breaks his solitude: his salvation depends on his becoming part of the very society he appears to deny. (1961, 17)

One of the few Latinos who has begun to broach the sensitive and important topic of Chicano/Latino homosexuality is the Chicano sociologist Tomás Almaguer. Noting the paucity of research on Mexican and Latino men, Almaguer observed that Chicano men must negotiate a modern American gay identity with Mexican-Latino configurations of homosexual identity and behavior (1995, 418). With no ethnographic research to draw from, Almaguer developed a theoretical perspective on Latino gay men by combining "perceptive anthropological research on homosexuality in México and Latin America" (1995, 419) with the writings of Chicana lesbians, which provide excellent insights on sexual behavior and identity.

Zoot Suit at Mark Taper Forum. *Left to right:* Rose Portillo, Danny Váldez, Evelina Fernández, Edward James Olmos, Rachel Levario, Mike Gomez. Photographer Jay Thompson. Courtesy of Center Theatre Group/Mark Taper Forum.

Almaguer's thesis is deceptively simple. In the contemporary United States sexual categories and personages are "defined in terms of sexual preference or object choice: same sex (homosexual), opposite sex (heterosexual), or both sexes (bisexual)" (1995, 419). This definition historically has led to a categorical "condemnation of all same-sex behavior" (1995, 419). In the Mexican/Latino sexual system, on the other hand, homosexuality is defined not by object choice but by the distribution of power. Mexican men, then, are able to engage in homosexual acts without impugning their masculinity or heterosexual persona as long as they assume the active inserter role. A person is considered a *maricón* (homosexual) or a *joto* (queer) only if he assumes the passive, insertee role.

> Although stigma accompanies homosexual practices in Latin culture, it does not equally adhere to both partners. It is primarily the anal-passive individual (the *cochón* or *pasivo*)[8] who is stigmatized for playing the subservient, feminine role. (1995, 420).

Not only is the *activo* or *machista* partner not stigmatized, but there is no clear linguistic category or label to classify him and, according to Almaguer, he is considered to be a normal male (1995, 420). Based on this analysis Almaguer comes to the incredible conclusion that "there is no cultural equivalent to the modern 'gay man' in the Mexican/Latin-American sexual system" (1995, 418).

Reading Almaguer's piece brought back many memories of my childhood, my dear Uncle Pepe, and my father. My father was undoubtedly macho in the positive Mexican sense of the word, but he never ridiculed or denigrated *Quintos* or gays. In fact, everyone in the family treated him with warmth, respect, and affection. After reflecting on Almaguer's thesis, I started to wonder whether my family was weird or pathological or whether there was something missing in his analysis.

To this day I don't know whether Uncle *Quintos* was the inserter or the insertee or both, but I do know that whether dominant or passive, he was unquestionably gay and his identity as a gay man transcended his sexual encounters. Although there may be some truth to Almaguer's assertion that "homosexuality in México is typically shrouded in silence" (1995, 421), it strikes me as a gross oversimplification to say that only passive participants in homosexual encounters assume a gay identity. I know that my uncle had gay friends and that he participated in the gay world, that there are gay bars and clubs in *La Zona Rosa* and in other parts of México City, and that certain cities like Guadalajara are reputed to have a large concentration of homosexuals.

Several years ago my adult nephew and I were visiting the city of Morelia in the state of Michoacan. It was evening, and we were sitting at an outdoor restaurant in the *portales*, or main downtown plaza, when we began to notice an abundance of male couples strolling by, holding hands or walking arm-in-arm. We were shocked not only by the number of visibly gay couples but by their open display of affection. We later learned that an international gay conference was being held in the city.

I, therefore, respectfully disagree with Almaguer's conclusion that there is no Mexican equivalent of the modern gay man. Although homosexual activities may be somewhat more clandestine, there is growing acceptance of gays in large metropolitan areas. Almaguer is correct in asserting that by retaining an active, inserter position, Latino men can engage in homosexual activity without impugning their heterosexual, macho identity, but he is wrong in calling this a distinctive Mexican/Latino cultural pattern. As we have seen in films such as *Deliverance* and, more recently, *Pulp Fiction*, working-class white men also sodomize other men without defining themselves as homosexual. The same pattern is repeated daily in American prisons, where the strongest, most violent, and most "macho" men attack weaker effeminate victims.

In an insightful article written more than thirty years ago, "The Social Integration of Queers and Peers" (1961), sociologist Albert Reiss made the same observation about working-class delinquent boys that Almaguer has made about Mexican/Latino men. Reiss reported that working-class youths are able to engage in homosexual relations with adult gay men without defining themselves as homosexuals as long as they assume the dominant role in the sexual exchange and get paid for sex. But if a boy were to assume the insertee role and perform oral sex on the adult homosexual or grant sexual favors without charge, he would be ostracized and termed "queer" by his peers. Thus what is essential in retaining a heterosexual identity for these young men is that they assume a traditionally dominant male role.

Though I disagree with Almaguer's characterization of homosexuality among Mexican and Latino men, he is to be commended for addressing the Chicano male gay experience and for opening up a dialogue and discussion on an important and neglected subject. If we are to gain a full understanding of men and gender in the Latino community, it is essential that we begin to examine not only conventional manifestations of machismo and heterosexuality but also the full range and variety of masculinities.

The proposed new field of Chicano/Latino men's studies lies at the intersection of Chicana feminism, Chicano studies, and men's studies. However, because Chicanas and Chicanos share a common historical, sociopolitical, cultural, linguistic, and racial bond as members of an oppressed and exploited racial and ethnic group, we cannot look to Anglo men—and their new men's studies—for direction. They are, after all, the source of our oppression. We must first come to grips with our own oppression as men and women of color before we can begin to generate and articulate paradigms that will have liberating, rather than oppressive, consequences. We must develop a flexible and transcendent view of our history and culture that enables us to gain a better understanding of racial, cultural, class, and gender oppression and to create an emancipatory vision of our past, present, and future. In the end, we must first look within ourselves and then to each other for liberation.

7

Epilogue

I was raised by strong and powerful women. My great-grandmother on my father's side, Mamá Mela, possessed an inner strength and dignity that was uncommon, and my Grandfather Alfredo's sisters, Concha and Lupe, were also strong and independent. But the woman that stands out most in my mind is Tía Márgara.

My mother's oldest sister, Tía Márgara was a large, imposing figure and probably weighed well over two hundred pounds. In her youth Márgara was a tall, attractive woman, and she had a wonderful sense of humor and an incredible singing voice. But *la tía* also had a foul mouth and seemed always to be complaining about some *desgraciados* (bastards) or *hijos de la chingada* (sons of bitches). Ironically, she embodied many stereotypically macho traits. She swore, was a chain smoker, gambled, drank tequila, and loved to sing *rancheras* (Mexican country ballads) and "belt out" the *gritos* (yells) with the songs.

What I remember most about *la tía* is the numerous confrontations and fistfights she had with both women and men. Tía Márgara liked to knit, and she usually carried long, sharp knitting needles, which served as weapons in a pinch. I recall one incident, in particular, in which she got out of the car during a traffic dispute, pulled a cab driver from his vehicle, and proceeded to pummel him with her fists. Everyone said, *"Era muy brava"* ("she was very tough"). Her physical assaults were always accompanied with verbal abuses and denunciations, so that in the end, her adversaries were both physically and spiritually subdued and humiliated.

My own biography, then, is at odds with the images of men and women that have been prevalent in social science literature and in public conceptions of Latino cultures. Latinos in general, and Mexicans in particular, have often been characterized as heirs to a cultural heritage that is said to be driven by the simultaneous veneration of the male and denigration of the female, a heritage in which men are powerful and controlling and women weak and submissive. *The Complete Dictionary of Sexology* (Francoeur et al. 1995), for example, provides the following definition of machismo:

> *machismo (adj. macho)* (Sp.) The concept and cultural imperatives associated with masculinity in Latin American cultures; the Latin American word for the mystique of manliness. Machismo stresses male physical aggressiveness, high risk taking, breaking the rules, casual and uninvolved sexual relations with women, and elective penile insertion in other men. Though useful to describe an extreme male chauvinism, the term as used by non-Latinos to some extent represents a stereotype with deep-rooted value judgments and cultural assumptions. The term is said to be derived from *macho* in the classical Aztecan language, meaning "image," "reflection of myself."

The historical and cross-cultural materials reviewed in Chapter 2 and the findings presented in subsequent chapters call into question the negative and monolithic view of machismo and Latino masculinity. Even if one acknowledges a cultural concern with outward displays of masculinity and *hombría*, such a concern is certainly not peculiar to Latino cultures. There are many societies that have focused on manhood, that have ritualized masculine rights of passage, and that value outward masculine displays. Rather than uncritically accepting the monolithic and all-encompassing view of machismo and male dominance, I have sought to present a more complete analysis that examines the origins, roots, and manifestations of Latino masculinity and the diversity and variety of masculinities.

I concluded that negative machismo, or exaggerated masculinity, was neither a response to the Conquest, as is commonly asserted by Paz, Ramos, and others, or an extension of pre-Columbian warring Aztec society. Like Catholicism and like many deadly diseases, it appears to have been imposed via the Conquest. In retrospect, the small band of *conquistadores* who conquered and subjugated millions of indigenous people under the leadership of Hernán Cortés appears to be the historical prototype of negative machismo. Though the Conquest was said to have been "divinely ordained" or willed in order to convert the "heathen natives," the *conquistadores* proved to be cruel, violent men of action who committed numerous atrocities and *chingaderas* in the name of God, crown, and king. In fact, they appear to have embodied Stevens's (1973, 58) "Seven Deadly Sins of Machismo," which include an extreme form of pride (*dignidad*), wrath, lust, anxiety, callousness toward women, an obsession with the number of conquests, and belief in male hypersexuality.

Aztec society was hierarchical, militaristic, and characterized by a clearly delineated sexual division of labor, but war and violence were not ends in themselves. War and the sacrifices of enemy prisoners were justified as necessary in order to satisfy the gods and continue the cycle of life. Across social classes, moreover, the masculine ideal included such attributes as being humble, modest, contrite, selfless, and not giving in to impetuousness or self-indulgence.

Two polar and conflicting images of machismo emerged from this study that correspond roughly to Spanish and Aztec conceptions of masculinity. A majority of respondents did not identify with being macho because they saw machismo as a negative or synthetic form of masculinity, characterized by profound feelings of inferiority or inadequacy in men, male dominance, and the subordination and denigration of women. This finding calls into question the idea that machismo, at least as it has been traditionally conceived, is somehow a positive or desired cultural trait or value.

The minority of respondents who did identify with being macho had a positive conception of the term. For them, there was an important distinction between being macho (male) and being *machista* (sexist). Rather than linking being macho with pathology, violence, or the denigration of women, for these men it meant adherence to a code of ethics—similar to the Aztec code—that guided behavior and included attributes such as being honest, respectful, modest, sincere, loyal, and, perhaps most importantly, the expectation that one "should stand up for one's rights and beliefs." The worth of a man, according to this view, is not measured by external attributes, such as physical strength, sexual prowess, fighting ability, or drinking behavior, but rather by internal qualities and especially the strength of one's character. A man who claims to be *muy macho*, who thinks he is *chingón*, who goes around holding his genitals and committing numerous *chingaderas*, or who is otherwise fixated on proving his manhood is not macho. In a manner reminiscent of the pre-Columbian ideal of masculinity, a real macho, according to this view, is honest, respectful, modest, self-effacing, and selfless. He is confident in his sense of self and in his masculinity and does not feel a need to prove himself to anyone (Ramirez 1979, 162).

Another important, and paradoxical, conclusion is that the positive sense of being macho is essentially an androgynous quality, as *la hembra* (the female) is the feminine counterpart of *el macho*. *Hembrismo* (femaleness) similarly is not demonstrated by external attributes, such as toughness, physical beauty, large breasts, sexuality, or excessive femininity, but by internal qualities such as pride, dignity, courage, perseverance in the face of adversity, and selflessness.

Looking back on my childhood and adolescent sex role socialization and experiences, I now realize that I was provided with a wealth of positive and negative images of masculinity and femininity. As I reflected on the family folklore surrounding Tía Márgara and the many stories extolling her strong character and toughness and on the incident related in the introduction to this book, where my father confronted Tío Roberto as he was beating up his wife, I realized it took a lot of courage, or "balls," for my father to get involved in a family squabble and to stand up to his brother-in-law. But I also came to the realization that it probably took even more courage for my mother to intervene. She was, after all, the youngest of seven children, a young woman who grew up in Sayula, a small village in Jalisco, in an era when women ostensibly occupied traditional subordinate roles and did not intervene in the affairs of men. It was often said in traditional depictions that a distinguishing characteristic of Mexican culture is that "the older order the younger, and the men the women" (Rubel 1959). By intervening in the physical confrontation between two grown men, my mother was not only challenging her older brother but also, indirectly, symbolically challenging her husband and the traditional, subordinate role of women.

From conversations with African-Americans, I have learned that Blacks reserve the word "woman" for a female that has an inner strength of character, respects herself and the people around her, and is relentless in her support of her children and her community. The power and inner strength of the Black woman is symbolized by Sojourner Truth. Her real name was Isabella, and she was born a slave on a Dutch estate in New York in 1797 and was eventually freed in 1828. Her powerful "And Ar'n't I a Woman" declaration was made in 1851 at a women's rights convention in Akron, Ohio. She took the floor and exclaimed:

> But what's all dis here talkin' 'bout? Dat man ober dar say dat women needs to be helped into carriages, and lifted ober ditches, and to have de best place every whar. Nobody eber helped me into carriages, or ober mud puddles, or gives me any best place (and raising herself to her full height and her voice to a pitch like rolling thunder, she asked), and ar'n't I a woman? Look at me! Look at my arm! (And she bared her right arm to the shoulder, showing her tremendous muscular power.) I have plowed, and planted, and gathered into barns, and no man could head me—and ar'n't I a woman? . . . I have borne thirteen chilern and seen 'em mos' all sold off into slavery, and when I cried out with a mother's grief, none but Jesus heard—and ar'n't I a woman? (Olive 1968, 134)

Sojourner Truth attended a number of antislavery meetings in northern Indiana. At the meeting house of the United Brethren, a large number of slavery supporters were in attendance. Responding to the persistent rumor that she was actually a man, Sojourner Truth rose to speak to the gathering, asking why they suspected her to be a man. Dr. Strain's call for a vote on whether the audience believed her to be a man was met with a boisterous, "Aye." But she held her ground, responding that her breasts had suckled many a white baby even while she had to neglect her own children. She added that though these white men had sucked her colored breasts, "they were far more manly than they (her persecutors) appeared to be" (Olive 1968, 139). Finally, as she turned to expose her bosom to the entire congregation, she quietly asked "if they, too, wished to suck!" (1968, 139).

Machismo and conventional conceptions of masculinity and gender roles have typically been associated in the literature with backward rural Chicano/Latino culture. It was, therefore, assumed that modernization and assimilation to American culture would lead to the eventual rejection of traditional values, including machismo and adherence to traditional conceptions of gender roles. Maxine Baca Zinn (1990, 71) has noted that an implicit assumption underlying this view is that industrialization and urbanization will automatically lead to modernization and concomitant changes in family structure.

In the conventional social science model and in popular thought, patriarchal family ideology and structure were considered to be part of the "cultural baggage" that would eventually be replaced by a modern sex role ideology. With increased exposure to American culture, immigrant Mexican families would inevitably take on "modern" values, and family structure would move from being traditional to modern (Baca Zinn 1990, 71).

My findings are consistent with a growing body of evidence that has begun to challenge the modernization/acculturation hypothesis. Men with greater ties to Latino culture, as indicated by being born outside of the United States or preferring to be interviewed in Spanish, were generally found to be more negative in their views of machismo and less traditional in their conceptions of gender. Although most respondents were negative in their views of machismo, those who were interviewed in Spanish were overwhelmingly negative in these views. Men who were not born in the United States and who opted to be interviewed in Spanish were less likely to have a positive view of the word "macho" or to associate it with positive behaviors, to see "love and affection" as the most important thing about the way they were raised, or to say that providing love or moral guidance was the most important responsibility that they had toward their children. Those with greater ties to Mexican/Latino culture and those of a lower socioeconomic status, moreover, were more apt to identify being self-centered, or *egoísta,* as a negative quality in a man.

The findings point to the presence of a distinctive Mexican cultural ethic surrounding manhood, masculinity, and the father role, an ethic that appears especially strong among poor and working-class men. This ethic dictates that the success of a man or father is measured not so much by external qualities, such as wealth, education, or power, but by internal ones such as being honest, responsible, and hardworking, sacrificing for one's children, and, most of all, not being selfish. A man who has an honest job, who works hard to provide for his family, and who is responsible and puts the interests of the family above his own is considered a success and a good man and father. One who does not look after his family is not considered successful as a man, regardless of how much money he has or how important his job is. One of the worst or lowest things that a man can do, according to this ethic, is to be selfish and irresponsible or to succumb to such personal vices as drinking, drugs, gambling, or women, and, most of all, to not take care of the family.

These polar and contradictory views of machismo and masculinity can be reconciled if one begins to see masculinity in Chicano/Latino cultures not as conforming to either the positive or negative conception of machismo, but rather as representing horns of a dilemma or choices faced by men. There is not one but various masculinities, so that a man is evaluated according to the extent that he is seen as being responsible or irresponsible, honest or dishonest, *egoísta* or selfless. Marital transgressions, although not accepted, may be tolerated if a man is perceived to be responsible and as taking care of the needs of his family.

The findings also call into question an assumption that is indirectly linked to the modernization/acculturation hypothesis, the assumption that social class is a key determinant of masculine attitudes and behavior and that traditional, patriarchal values are much more prevalent in the lower classes. Just as it has been assumed that modernization and acculturation will automatically lead to rejection of traditional, patriarchal values, so too is it assumed that traditional gender roles will be discarded as individuals acquire more education and better-paying jobs. Unfortunately, since racial oppression and class oppression go hand in hand, it is often difficult, if not impossible, to separate the relative influence of race and class. Mexican and Chicano communities that have been the objects of ethnographic research have typically been poor rural communities, and many of the observed characteristics have been attributed to culture rather than to class or rural residence. Though "the assumption that family structure is a consequence of cultural values is pervasive in Mexican family research," such research has seldom taken structural factors into account or focused on the internal diversity found among Mexican and Chicano families (Baca Zinn 1979b, 62).

My findings did not generally support the assumption that socioeconomic status is a critical determinant of gender role attitudes and behavior or the related assumption that traditional masculinity is somehow more prevalent in the working class. In fact, working-class respondents were often found to be more egalitarian and less traditional.

The Bem Sex Role Inventory (BSRI) is a measure of masculinity and femininity that has been widely utilized in social science research. Contrary to what I expected, men who had more education or higher incomes and those engaged in professional occupations scored higher on the masculine component of the BSRI and were found to be less, rather than more, androgynous. Those who opted to be interviewed in English similarly scored higher on the masculine component and were less androgynous.

Whereas the BSRI conceives of masculinity and femininity as individual attributes, a new measure was introduced, the Mirandé Sex Role Inventory

(MSRI), which looks at masculinity and femininity within a cultural and situational context. The MSRI produced findings that were more consistent with the hypotheses, as respondents with more education and higher incomes and professionals were generally less traditional.

The findings suggest that much of what is assumed to be universal in the study of gender roles and masculinity and femininity is, in fact, particular and culture specific. The dominant sex role paradigm that has prevailed in the social sciences, for example, assumes that aggression and assertiveness are masculine traits, whereas being emotional, affectionate, and showing one's feelings are feminine qualities. Ironically, the prototypical view of the macho as cold, insensitive, and lacking in emotion appears more consistent with Anglo than with Latino conceptions of masculinity. Superheroes such as Rambo, Superman, and Batman, perhaps, best epitomize this image of white masculinity. In Chicano/Latino culture it is both permissible and desirable for men to be emotional, to show their feelings, and to kiss, hug, and be affectionate with male children. Latino men can at once be warm, loving, and tender, and self-reliant, self-sufficient, and willing to take a stand.

R. W. Connell (1995), one of the leading voices in the new feminist scholarship by men, pointed to the complicated nature of what he terms "masculinities" and calls for the rejection of hegemonic masculinities. Ironically, Connell and other leading new feminist scholars have engaged in their own brand of hegemonic discourse by ignoring masculinity among Latinos and other subordinated communities and assuming that an understanding of other masculinities can be attained by subsuming them under Euro-American theoretical models. Connell talked about working-class masculinities and mentioned in passing Robert Staples's pioneering work on Black men. He largely ignored other people of color, except when observing that "for those native peoples, in turn, the history of gender was violently made obvious by conquests, and by the colonial systems under which they had to deal with the gender regiments of the colonizer" (1995, 227). I fully endorse the call for ending hegemonic masculinities and believe that perhaps the most important conclusion that can drawn from this study is that there is not a single Chicano/Latino masculine mode but a variety of masculinities that are not only different, but often contradictory. We should remember that these masculinities are not a subpart of the dominant masculinities and that they are as complex and varied as Euro-American masculinities.

Glossary

Cacique. Indian noble, lord, or local chief.

Calzones. Literally means shorts or underwear but is used to connote strength or power. A person who "has the *calzones*," whether male or female, is believed to "wear the pants" or to be the dominant person in a relationship or family.

Chicana. Designates women of Mexican descent who are living in the United States.

Chingada. In Mexican folklore this refers to the "Great Whore," or mythical Indian mother, who was violated or raped by the Spaniards during and subsequent to the Conquest. The term is often linked to *"La Malinche,"* or Doña Marina (see *"La Malinche"*).

Chingar. An aggressive form of sexual intercourse with numerous connotations revolving around power and the idea of being controlled, subjugated, or "fucked over" by someone in power.

Compadre/Comadre. Literally co-parent. Term used to designate the relationship between a parent and the godparent of one's children.

Conquista. The conquest of México by Spain. For Mexicans the term is generally capitalized because it is considered to have been the ultimate Conquest.

Corridos. Mexican songs or ballads that generally serve as an oral history or chronicle of important social and historical events, experiences, or personalities.

Hembra. Refers to women or more generally to the female of the species. Unlike a term such as "feminine," *hembra* and *hembrismo* have very positive connotations, implying a strong woman, a strong-willed woman, and a woman with internal strength or character.

Joto/a. Somewhat pejorative term for a homosexual. It can be roughly translated as "queer."

Macho. Literally denotes a male animal like a "he-goat" or "he-mule." Also used to distinguish the male (*macho*) from the female (*hembra*). For example, it can refer to the *macho* (male) part of an instrument that is inserted into the *hembra* (female) or "open" part. The variety of connotations are discussed more fully throughout the text.

Machismo. This term has numerous and diverse connotations in México and in the United States and is often associated with exaggerated masculinity, male chauvinism, or an extreme male supremacist ideology.

Machista. One who subscribes to the ideology of machismo.

Malinche/malinchista. Used by the Indians to refer to Hernán Cortés. Today it is a negative term connoting a traitor/traitress or "sell-out." It is associated in Mexican folklore with Doña Marina, or Malinalli Tenepal (her Aztec name), a young Indian woman of noble lineage sold into slavery as a child by her mother and stepfather and given to Cortés as a gift shortly after his arrival on the Mexican coast. She served as Cortés's translator and was apparently respected by both the Indians and the Spaniards. The Spaniards addressed her as "Doña," a term of great deference and respect (see Mirandé and Enríquez 1981, 24–31, 182, 241).

Maricón. Literally means "sissy" or effeminate and is used as a synonym for homosexual. There is no Spanish equivalent to the word "gay." *Joto* and *puto* (male whore) are more pejorative and offensive terms for homosexuals.

Mestizaje. The process of interbreeding of Spaniards and the indigenous population of the Americas producing a mixed race of people. Mexican philosopher José Vasconcelos referred to the product of this mixing as *La Raza Cósmica*, or the cosmic race.

Motecuhzoma. A line of Aztec kings or rulers. Motecuhzoma was the last of the Motecuhzomas, and when the Spaniards arrived he believed that "the white men must be Quetzalcoatl and other gods returning from across the waters." (León-Portilla 1962, vii). The name was spelled Montezuma by the Spaniards, but in México today it is spelled Moctezuma (León-Portilla 1962, xxxi). **Motecuhzoma** is more consistent with the original indigenous or Nahua name.

Nepantla/Nepantlism. The Indian conception of "being in the middle" or being neutral, particularly with regard to culture.

Padrino. Godfather.

El Pipila. One of the primary heroes in the Mexican War of Independence who carried a large concrete slab on his back to deflect bullets as he single-handedly led the attack on the enemy munitions depot in Guanajuato. After *El Pipila* burned down the entrance, Mexican troops stormed the fortress. He is considered to be a national hero for his bravery and for risking his life for his *patria*, or homeland.

Parable. A simple story illustrating a moral or religious lesson.

Pulque. An alcoholic drink made from the fermented sap of the maguey (a cactus-like plant), which was used by the Aztecs and continues to be consumed in contemporary México.

Puto. Literally means a male whore. It is an extremely pejorative and denigrating term used to describe homosexuals. The word can be used to insult or demean any man and is offensive whether applied to homosexual or heterosexual men.

Rancheras. Traditional Mexican songs and music that often embody societal ideals and values.

Soldaderas. Women who fought during the Mexican Revolution and traveled with the men on top of railroad cars. Although this term is often used to romanticize the women who accompanied, cooked for, nurtured, and otherwise supported the men during battle, many were involved in actual combat. Others served as military officers and commanded large regiments. There is support for a view of women as warriors or soldiers dating back to pre-Columbian times (see Salas 1990).

Tenochtitlán. The capital of the Aztec empire located in what is today México City.

Tío/Tía. Uncle/Aunt.

Valentina. Mexican woman who is idealized in *corridos* and recognized for her heroic deeds during the Mexican Revolution. She is a prototype of the strong Mexican woman.

Notes

Introduction

1. There was undoubtedly an immediate physical attraction between us, but I believe we were ultimately attracted to one another's intellect. I, at least, was dazzled by her intelligence, her command of language, and the depth of her observations. We also brought different skills to the project. She was a woman, a humanist, and a literary person, whereas I was a man, a social scientist, and a researcher. There was a dynamic tension, a creative synergy that produced a special work that neither one of us could have created alone.

2. The book within the book is a story unto itself that is well beyond the scope of this manuscript. Suffice it to say that our work on the book coincided with the development of a close, intimate, and incredibly romantic personal relationship. We began as colleagues and became much more. What is significant here is that our intensely personal and emotional involvement, rather than making for a smoother working relationship, appeared to intensify our differences and to exacerbate the conflict. We soon learned that we were two stubborn and strong-willed individuals, neither of whom was willing to readily yield a point of view or perspective without an intense battle.

3. These themes are developed more fully in Chapter 2.

4. "Rovier" is a name my parents created by combining their two names, Rosa and Xavier.

5. This is a paraphrase rather than a verbatim quote, since I obviously cannot recall her exact words. I have interviewed my mother on tape recently and inquired about numerous childhood memories. She has reluctantly talked about and elaborated on this incident. I suppose she is embarrassed by her brother's behavior. She also says that it is not right to talk negatively about people who are dead. She is particularly reluctant to say anything bad about my father, though she has been known to be very critical of him. She said that despite all of his faults and all of the grief that he caused, he was unquestionably the best-looking man that she ever saw and was *"muy hombre."*

Chapter One

1. There is ample evidence to suggest that "we are not invariably rational maximizers of our utility in either the cognitive or motivational sense" (West 1989, 870). Neither do we always know what is best for us, nor do we always seek it.

2. The fifty questions included in the study were pared down from an initial list of over one hundred items. Seventy-nine of these items were included in a pretest administered to ninety male and female high school students in southern California. The items were also pretested on several adult men and women.

3. In a snowball sample, rather than attempting to draw a random or representative sample, after the interview respondents are asked to suggest names of possible respondents. In this manner the sample grows like a snowball as new names are added to the base of the study.

4. See Mirandé (1985) for a critique of this view.

5. For an excellent critique of conventional social science, see Paredes (1977).

6. Gerald López (1992, 23–24) characterizes the tendency in law for lawyers to establish a hierarchical relationship with the attorney at the top and clients at the bottom as "regnant" law practice.

7. Per the agreement with the Human Subjects Committee and the protocol, the names of the respondents have been changed to protect their anonymity and privacy.

8. I think the women were right. In retrospect, I wish that my resources had been sufficient to interview both spouses and to compare their responses.

Chapter Two

1. Throughout this book I have opted to capitalize certain words like *El Castillo* because for a Mexican there is only one Castle, one *Conquista,* and one *Revolución.*

2. My father worked as a movie extra during the golden age of Mexican cinema in the 1940s and 1950s. In an American film about the Conquest, *Captain from Castille,* he played one of Cortés's captains and appeared bearded and on horseback next to Tyrone Power and Cesar Romero. The movie was filmed in the city of Morelia in the state of Michoacan. I should add that the movie presents a very distorted and positive, or pro-Spanish, view of the Conquest.

3. There is a pathetic irony in Ramos's analysis. The irony is that Ramos sees the Mexican as inauthentic and is critical of the Mexican's tendency to "imitate," but he then proceeds to imitate Euro-American theorists like Adler and to see the salvation of the Mexican as lying in the potential for self-discovery through psychoanalysis.

4. My father had a role in at least one Cantinflas film. In *Un Día con el Diablo* Cantinflas portrays an inept private in the Mexican army who ends up endearing himself to the general's daughter and recording incredibly moving patriotic messages for the troops. Cantinflas's character climbs into a war tank and blows up a building with a number of soldiers. My father played one of the soldiers in the bombed building. In another scene in the general's residence, he played one of the soldiers who comes to the general's residence to inform him that Cantinflas inadvertently recorded an emotional, gripping, and patriotic radio speech that was a great success with the troops.

5. This criticism is very similar to Américo Paredes's (1977) critique of Anglo ethnographers who fail to understand the nuance of Chicano language and culture.

Chapter Three

1. I won't go into the reasons for the separation and eventual divorce at this time, except to note that there was a tragic element to the whole thing. My parents were both very strong-willed, intelligent, beautiful, charismatic people. Like Evangelina and I, they appeared on the surface, at least, to be an ideal couple, but they somehow did not mesh as a unit. Part of the problem, I think, is that my mother was sixteen when she married my father, and he was twenty-six. She told me that her parents were very strict and they would not let her see him. My mother believes that if she had had an open courtship and had gotten to know my father, she would not have married him. But it wasn't that she did not love him or that she wasn't attracted to him.

2. Educational and occupational differences were statistically significant and income differences approached significance. The conventional measure of statistical significance defines a probability of .05 or less as "significant" and a probability of .01 as highly significant.

3. The one exception to this pattern that we found was that moderate income-earners more often associated macho with negative behaviors than did those with low or high incomes.

Chapter Four

1. Scores on each item range from "1" ("Never or almost never true") to "7" ("Always or almost always true").

2. The eigen value measures the strength of the factor and how much of the "total variation" is explained by it. Factor 1 (masculinity), for example, had an eigen value of 6.3 and explained 15.9 percent of the total variance, whereas Factor 2 (femininity) had an eigen value of 4.6 and explained 11.5 percent of the variance.

3. The eigen value for the condensed Bem scale was 5.7 for Factor 1 (masculinity); this explained 20.4 percent of the variance and had a reliability coefficient of .83. Factor 2 (femininity) had an eigen value of 4, explained 15.6 percent of the variance, and had a reliability coefficient of .S7.

4. The fourteen masculine items remained virtually the same, with factor loadings increasing slightly by one or two points. Only one factor loading, "sensitive to the needs of others," increased by as many as four points, from .37 to .41 on the revised three-factor analysis.

5. The BSRI three-factor scale for all items with a factor loading of .40 or greater yielded an eigen value of 6.1 for Factor 1, which explained 18.4 percent of the variance, and 4.4 for Factor 2, which explained 13.3 percent of the variance. The coefficient of reliability was .83 for Factor 1 and .81 for Factor 2. Factor 3, however, had a low eigen value of 1.9 percent, explained only 7.9 percent of the variance, and had a coefficient of reliability of .57.

6. When only items with factor loadings of .50 or greater were included in the analysis, the reliability of each factor increased, as did the proportion of variance explained by the factor. When the four items with the weakest loading were dropped, Factor 1 (masculinity) was reduced to ten items with factor loadings of .50

or greater, had an eigen value of 4.8, and explained 21.7 percent of the variance, whereas Factor 2 (femininity) retained the same eight items, had an eigen value of 4.0, and explained 18.0 percent of the variance. Factor 3 was reduced to five items, had an eigen value of 2.0, and explained 9.2 percent of the variance. The total variance explained by the revised factors was 48.9 percent. The reliability or Alpha value for the BSRI was .84 for Factor 1, .82 for Factor 2, and .57 for Factor 3.

7. Since I believed the various components would be correlated, I decided to perform what is termed an oblique rotation. Factor 1 had an eigen value of 7.4, explaining 29 percent of the variance in traditionalism, and had a reliability coefficient of .91. Factor 2 had an Alpha Value of .75, an eigen value of 3.4, and explained 13.4 percent of the variance. The correlation between Factor 1 and Factor 2 was –.08.

8. I say "imply" because endorsing the items does not necessarily mean that one believes that women occupy a subordinate status in the family. The fact that a man should have "complete respect and authority" in the family or that he should assume "all of the financial responsibilities of marriage" does not necessarily mean that a woman should not also have complete respect and authority and assume the financial responsibilities of marriage.

There may be a cultural difference here in that the Anglo cultural model seems more exclusive than the Mexican/Latino model. In the dominant culture it is more likely to be assumed, in other words, that one gender is somehow granted "respect and authority" or "responsibility" to the exclusion, or at the expense, of the other.

9. Factor 1 had a reliability of .92, whereas the reliability of Factor 2 was .76 and Factor 3 was .67.

10. Table 1 in Appendix A contains a detailed breakdown of regional, occupational, educational, and income differences on the BSRI. So as not to overwhelm the reader with data and statistics, I have omitted the table from the text. The reader interested in a more detailed analysis is referred to Appendix A.

11. Income and occupation were significantly related. Education was not significantly related but approached statistical significance.

12. The multiple regressions for the third factor, interaction with children, and the fourth factor, marital happiness, were not statistically significant (see Appendix A, Table 5).

13. The other factors (traditionalism and sensitivity) were not related to marital satisfaction.

Chapter Five

1. There were substantial differences by region. For a reason that is not readily apparent, northern Californians were more likely than either Texans or southern Californians to list someone other than a family member as most respected or admired (see Appendix A, Table 8). More than one out of two northern Californians identified someone other than a family member as the person they most respected or admired, whereas only one of five southern Californians and one of four Texans listed nonfamily members.

2. A person's score on the Bem (BSRI) and Mirandé (MSRI) sex role scales also did not appear to have a significant impact on the type of person listed as most

respected, although individuals with moderate scores on the masculine component of the BSRI were somewhat more apt to list a nonfamily member than those low or high on this scale. But on the MSRI, those who subscribed to more traditional attitudes toward gender roles more often listed nonfamily members.

3. Education differences approached statistical significance and income differences were significant. See Table 10, Appendix A.

4. The qualities least respected did not appear to vary substantially according to sex-role orientation, particularly as measured by the BSRI, although those who scored high on the feminine component of the BSRI were slightly more apt to see not respecting oneself or others as the least respected trait. Similarly, those who were not highly traditional on the MSRI were much more likely to see the "lack of respect" in himself and others as a negative quality in a man. These differences were statistically significant.

5. Regional differences were not significant, although southern Californians more often identified not supporting the family as the worst or lowest thing and focused less on physically harming or injuring someone (killing or raping) as a devalued trait.

6. This was clearly a hypothetical question tapping an ideal dimension, and it was asked irrespective of whether the respondent actually had male children.

7. Although Tables 13 and 14 (Appendix A) are not discussed in the text, they contain interesting findings on the qualitative meaning of "macho" and examples of "macho behavior."

8. Differences in the toughness dimension of the MSRI were less clear and not significant, although those who were moderate on toughness saw honesty or warmth as important qualities in a son and were less likely to see being responsible or hardworking as important.

9. Where respondents were born and whether the interview was conducted in English or Spanish did not significantly affect the response to this question. Those interviewed in English were somewhat more likely to see reading and education as a significant influence on their views of child rearing.

10. Differences in the Bem Sex Role Inventory were not significant.

11. The BSRI and MSRI were not significantly related to the reasons respondents gave to explain why they considered themselves to be good fathers, except that individuals who scored high on the BSRI femininity dimension were more likely to say that they were good fathers because they spent time with their children and because they were loving and nurturing, but the difference was not significant.

12. Neither place of birth, language of the interview, nor sex role orientation influenced responses significantly, but those interviewed in English were somewhat more likely to stress being loving and affectionate. Education, occupation, and income did not differentiate on this factor. See Appendix A, Table 19.

13. Though socioeconomic and regional differences did not affect answers to this question, northern Californian men more often indicated that their fathers had vices or were irresponsible (see Appendix A, Table 20). These differences approached statistical significance. The language in which the interview was conducted did not affect responses.

14. Differences in place of birth and language were also not significant, but U.S.-born persons and those interviewed in English felt they neglected their children,

were not as affectionate or loving as they would like to be, or that they did not spend enough time with their children. See Appendix A, Table 21.

Chapter Six

1. A few works have focused on African-American men, but these works were written by African-Americans and emerged largely outside of the TNMS (Wilkinson and Taylor 1977; Staples 1978 and 1982; Wallace 1978).

2. Other works within men's studies have also failed to address Latino men. See Clatterbaugh (1990) and Easthope (1990).

3. Sara Estela Ramirez was an important Texan leader in the early twentieth century (Mirandé and Enríquez 1981, 206–207, 222).

4. For a discussion of the struggle of the *mujeres* of *El Teatro Campesino*, see Broyles-González (1993).

5. See, for example, Richard Rodriguez's (1992) *Days of Obligation: An Argument with My Mexican Father,* and "'Sissy' Warriors Vs. 'Real' Men: A Perspective on Gays in the Military" (1995). For a discussion of homosexuality in Chicano literature, see Juan Bruce-Novoa (1992).

6. Argentinean writer Manuel Puig (1994) provides an insightful analysis of the relationship between a gay male and a revolutionary who share a cell in prison in *El Beso de la Mujer Araña* (The Kiss of the Spider Woman).

7. My father was definitely a "dandy," and he didn't work a whole lot, but he was neither effeminate nor an "exaggerated virile figure." I had a strong sense that he was very secure in his masculinity and heterosexuality.

8. "*Cochón*" is a term used in Nicaragua to refer to passive homosexuals. It is derived from the word "*colchon,*" or mattress, and refers to the fact that the active party gets on top of the passive one, as on a mattress. There is obviously a contradiction here in that Almaguer is implying that there are active, inserter homosexuals, whereas in the next breath he notes that only the passive one is defined as a *maricón*.

References

Acosta-Belén, Edna, and Christine E. Bose. 1993. *Researching Women in Latin America and the Caribbean*. Boulder, Colo.: Westview Press.

Acosta-Belén, Edna, and Christine E. Bose. 1990. "From Structural Subordination to Empowerment: Women and Development in Third World Contexts." *Gender & Society* 4:299–320.

Alarcón, Norma, Ana Castillo, and Cherríe Moraga, eds. 1989. *Third Woman: The Sexuality of Latinas*. Volume 4. Berkeley: Third Woman Press.

Almaguer, Tomás. 1995. "Chicano Men: A Cartography of Homosexual Identity and Behavior." In *Men's Lives*, ed. Michael S. Kimmel and Michael A. Messner, 418–431. Boston: Allyn and Bacon.

Anzaldúa, Gloria, and Cherríe Moraga. 1981. *This Bridge Called My Back: Writings by Radical Women of Color*. Boston: Persephone Press.

Aramoni, Aniceto. 1965. *Psicoanalisis de la dinamica de un pueblo*. México, D.F.: B. Costa-Amic.

———. 1972. "Machismo." *Psychology Today* (January): 69–72.

Baca Zinn, Maxine. 1979a. "Field Research in Minority Communities: Ethical, Methodological and Political Observations by an Insider." *Social Problems* 27 (December): 209–219.

———. 1979b. "Chicano Family Research: Conceptual Distortions and Alternative Directions." *The Journal of Ethnic Studies* 7 (fall): 59–71.

———. 1982. "Chicano Men and Masculinity." *The Journal of Ethnic Studies* 10 (summer): 29–44.

———. 1990. "Family, Feminism, and Race in America." *Gender & Society* 4 (March): 68–82.

Becker, Howard S. 1967. "Whose Side Are We on?" *Social Problems* 14 (winter): 239–247.

Bem, Sandra L. 1974. "The Measurement of Psychological Androgyny." *Journal of Consulting and Clinical Psychology* 42 (April): 155–162.

Bermudez, Maria Elvira. 1955. *La vida familiar del mexicano*. México City: Robredo.

Blacker, Irwin R., and Harry M. Rosen. 1962. *Conquest: Dispatches of Cortez from the New World*. New York: Grosset & Dunlap.

Bonilla García, Luis. 1959. *La mujer a traves de los siglos*. Madrid: Aguilar.

Bose, Christine E., and Edna Acosta-Belén. 1995. *Women in the Latin American Development Process*. Philadelphia: Temple University Press.

Brandes, Stanley. 1980. *Metaphors of Masculinity: Sex and Status in Andalusian Folklore*. Philadelphia: University of Pennsylvania Press.

Brod, Harry, ed. 1987. *The Making of Masculinities: The New Men's Studies.* Boston: Allen & Unwin.

Brod, Harry, and Michael Kaufman. 1994. *Theorizing Masculinities.* Thousand Oaks, Calif.: Sage.

Broyles-González, Yolanda. 1994. *El Teatro Campesino: Theater in the Chicano Movement.* Austin: University of Texas Press.

Bruce-Novoa, Juan. 1992. "Homosexuality and the Chicano Novel." In *Homosexuality in Literary Studies,* ed. Wayne R. Dynes and Stephen Donaldson. New York: Garland Press.

Burkhart, Louise M. 1988. "Doctrinal Aspects of Sahagún's *Colloquios.*" In *The Work of Bernardino de Sahagún: Pioneer Ethnographer of Sixteenth-Century Aztec Mexico,* ed. J. Klor de Alva, H. B. Nicholson, and Eloise Quiñones Keber. Albany: State University of New York.

Canaan, Joyce E., and Christine Griffin. 1990. "The New Men's Studies: Part of the Problem or Part of the Solution?" In *Men, Masculinities & Social Theory,* ed. Jeff Hearn and David Morgan. London: Unwin Hyman.

Carrigan, Tim, Bob Connell, and John Lee. 1985. "Toward a New Sociology of Masculinity." *Theory and Society* 14, no. 5:551–604.

Caso, Alfonso. 1958. *The Aztecs: People of the Sun.* Translated by Lowell Dunham. Norman: University of Oklahoma Press.

Castillo, Ana. 1994. *So Far from God.* New York: Plume.

Cisneros, Sandra. 1985. *The House on Mango Street.* Houston: Arte Publico Press.

Clatterbaugh, Kenneth. 1990. *Contemporary Perspectives on Masculinity.* Boulder, Colo.: Westview Press.

Clendinnen, Inga. 1985. "The Cost of Courage in Aztec Society." *Past and Present: A Journal of Historical Studies,* no. 107:44–89.

———. 1991. *Aztecs.* Cambridge: Cambridge University Press.

Collins, Patricia Hill. 1986. "Learning from the Outsider Within: The Sociological Significance of Black Feminist Thought." *Social Problems* 33 (October/December): 14–32.

Coltrane, Scott. 1992. "The Micropolitics of Gender in Nonindustrial Societies." *Gender & Society* 6:86–107.

Coltrane, Scott, and Elsa O. Valdez. 1993. "Reluctant Compliance: Work-Family Role Allocation in Dual-Earner Chicano Families." In *Men, Work, and Family,* ed. Jane C. Hood, 151–175. Thousand Oaks, Calif.: Sage.

Connell, R. W. 1995. *Masculinity.* Berkeley: University of California Press.

Córdova, Teresa, Norma Cantú, Gilberto Cárdenas, and Juan Garcia, eds. 1984. *Chicana Voices: Intersections of Class, Race, and Gender.* Colorado Springs: National Association for Chicano Studies.

Cromwell, Vicky L., and Ronald E. Cromwell. 1978. "Perceived Dominance in Decision-Making and Conflict Resolution Among Anglo, Black and Chicano Couples." *Journal of Marriage and the Family* 40 (November): 749–759.

Cromwell, Ronald E., and Rene A. Ruiz. 1979. "The Myth of Macho Dominance in Decision Making Within Mexican and Chicano Families." *Hispanic Journal of Behavioral Sciences* 1 (December): 355–373.

de la Torre, Adela, and Beatriz M. Pesquera. 1993. *Building with Our Hands: New Directions in Chicana Studies.* Berkeley: University of California Press.

Delgado, Abelardo. 1974–1975. "Machismo." *La Luz* 3, no. 9:6 (December); 3, no. 10:7 (January); 3, no. 11:7 (February).

Díaz del Castillo, Bernal. 1963. *The Conquest of New Spain.* Translated by J. M. Cohen. Baltimore: Penguin.

_____. 1908. *The Conquest of New Spain.* Translated by Alfred Percival Maudslay. London: Hakluyt Society.

Doll, Lynda S., Dan Joy, Brad N. Barthow, Janet S. Harrison, Gail Bolan, John M. Douglas, Linda E. Saltzman, Patricia M. Moss, and Wanda Delgado. 1992. "Self-Reported Childhood and Adolescent Sexual Abuse Among Adult Homosexual and Bisexual Men." *Child Abuse & Neglect* 16:855–864.

Easthope, Antony. 1990. *What a Man's Gotta Do: The Masculine Myth in Popular Culture.* Boston: Unwin.

Ellis, Robert Richmond. 1995. "Camping It Up in the Francoist Camp: Reflections on and in *Ante el espejo* of Luis Antonio de Villena." *MLN* 110 (March): 320–334.

Franklin, Clyde W., II. 1988. *Men and Society.* Chicago: Nelson-Hall.

Galarza, Ernesto. 1971. *Barrio Boy.* Notre Dame: Notre Dame University Press.

Garcia, Alma. 1989. "The Development of Chicana Feminist Discourse, 1970–1980." *Gender & Society* 3 (June): 217–238.

Gilbert, G. M. 1959. "Sex Differences in Mental Health in a Mexican Village." *International Journal of Social Psychiatry* 3 (winter): 208–213.

Gilligan, Carol. 1982. *In a Different Voice: Essays on Psychological Theory and Women's Development.* Cambridge: Harvard University Press.

Gilmore, David D. 1990. *Manhood in the Making: Cultural Concepts of Masculinity.* New Haven: Yale University Press.

Goldwert, Marvin. 1980. *History as Neurosis: Paternalism and Machismo in Spanish America.* Lanham, MD: University Press of America.

_____. 1983. *Machismo and Conquest: The Case of Mexico.* Lanham, Md.: University Press of America.

_____. 1985. "Mexican Machismo: The Flight from Femininity." *The Psychoanalytic Review* 72 (spring): 161–169.

Gutmann, Matthew C. 1994. "The Meaning of Macho: Changing Mexican Male Identities." *Masculinities: Interdisciplinary Studies on Gender* 2, no. 1 (spring): 21–33.

_____. 1996. *The Meaning of Macho: Being a Man in México City.* Berkeley: University of California Press.

Hartzler, Kaye, and Juan N. Franco. 1985. "Ethnicity, Division of Household Tasks and Equity in Marital Roles: A Comparison of Anglo and Mexican American Couples." *Hispanic Journal of Behavioral Sciences* 7 (December): 333–344.

Hawkes, Glenn R., and Minna Taylor. 1975. "Power Structure in Mexican and Mexican-American Farm Labor Families." *Journal of Marriage and the Family* 37 (November): 807–811.

Hearn, Jeff, and David Morgan. 1990. *Men, Masculinities, and Social Theory.* London: Unwin Hyman.

Hondagneu-Sotelo, Pierrette. 1992. "Overcoming Patriarchal Constraints: The Re-construction of Gender Relations Among Mexican Immigrant Women and Men. *Gender & Society* 6:393–415.

Hondagneu-Sotelo, Pierrette, and Michael A. Messner. 1994. "Gender Displays and Men's Power: The 'New Man' and the Mexican Immigrant Man." In *Theorizing Masculinities*, ed. Harry A. Brod and Michael Kaufman, 200–218. Thousand Oaks, Calif.: Sage.

Hurtado, Aída. 1988. "The Politics of Sexuality in the Gender Subordination of Chicanas." Revision of a paper presented at the Third International Conference on the Hispanic Cultures of America in Barcelona, Spain.

_____. 1989. "Relating to Privilege: Seduction and Rejection in the Subordination of White Women and Women of Color." *Signs: Journal of Women in Culture and Society* 14 (summer): 833–855.

Kantorowski Davis, Sharon, and Virginia Chavez. 1985. "Hispanic Househus-bands." *Hispanic Journal of Behavioral Sciences* 7 (December): 317–332.

Kimmel, Michael. 1996. *Manhood in America*. New York: The Free Press.

Klor de Alva, J. 1988. "Sahagún and the Birth of Modern Ethnography: Represent-ing, Confessing, and Inscribing the Native Other." In *The Work of Bernardino de Sahagún: Pioneer Ethnographer of Sixteenth-Century Aztec Mexico*, ed. J. Klor de Alva, H. B. Nicholson, and Eloise Quiñones Keber, 31–52. Albany: State University of New York.

León-Portilla, Miguel. 1962. *The Broken Spears: The Aztec Account of the Conquest of Mexico*. Boston: Beacon.

_____. 1990. *Endangered Cultures*. Translated by Julie Goodson-Lawes. Dallas: Southern Methodist University Press.

Lewis, Oscar. 1960. *Tepoztlan*. New York: Holt, Rinehart & Winston.

_____. 1961. *The Children of Sanchez*. New York: Random House.

Lopata, Helena Z., and Barrie Thorne. "On the Term 'Sex roles.'" 1978. *Signs: Journal of Women in Culture and Society* 3:718–721.

López, Gerald P. 1992. *Rebellious Lawyering: One Chicano's Vision of Progressive Law Practice*. Boulder, Colo.: Westview Press.

Luzod, Jimmy A., and Carlos H. Arce. 1979. "An Exploration of the Father Role in the Chicano Family." Paper presented at the National Symposium on the Mexican American Child in Santa Barbara, California.

Madsen, William. 1973. *The Mexican-Americans of South Texas*. 2d ed. New York: Holt, Rinehart & Winston.

Mejia, Daniel P. 1975. "Cross-Ethnic Father Role: Perceptions of Middle Class Anglo American and Mexican American Parents." Ph.D. dissertation, University of California, Irvine.

Melville, Margarita B., ed. 1980. *Twice a Minority: Mexican American Women*. St. Louis: C. V. Mosby.

Mendoza, Vicente T. 1962. *"El machismo en Mexico a traves de las canciones, cor-ridos, y cantares."* In *Cuadernos del instituto nacional de antropologia III*, 75–86. Buenos Aires: Ministerio de Educación y Justicia.

Merton, Robert K. 1972. "Insiders and Outsiders: A Chapter in the Sociology of Knowledge." *American Journal of Sociology* 78 (July): 9–48.

Mirandé, Alfredo. 1978. "Chicano Sociology: A New Paradigm for Social Science." *Pacific Sociological Review* 21 (July): 293–312.

_____. 1982. "Sociology of Chicanos or Chicano Sociology?: A Critical Assessment of Emergent Paradigms." *Pacific Sociological Review* 25 (October): 495–508.

_____. 1985. *The Chicano Experience: An Alternative Perspective.* Notre Dame: University of Notre Dame Press.

Mirandé, Alfredo, and Evangelina Enríquez. 1981. *La Chicana: The Mexican-American Woman.* Chicago: University of Chicago Press.

Montiel, Miguel. 1970. "The Social Science Myth of the Mexican American Family." *El Grito: A Journal of Contemporary Mexican American Thought* 3 (summer): 56–63.

Mora, Magdalena, and Adelaide R. del Castillo, eds. 1980. *Mexican Women in the United States: Struggles Past and Present.* Los Angeles: Chicano Studies Research Center Publications, University of California, Los Angeles.

Moraga, Cherríe. 1983. *Loving in the War Years.* Boston: South End Press.

_____. 1993. *The Last Generation.* Boston: South End Press.

Morgan, David. 1981. "Men, Masculinity and the Process of Sociological Enquiry." In *Doing Feminist Research*, ed. Helen Roberts, 83–113. London: Routledge & Kegan Paul.

Nash, June. 1978. "The Aztecs and the Ideology of Male Dominance." *Signs: Journal of Women in Culture and Society* 4 (winter): 349–362.

Newman, Bernie Sue, and Peter Gerard Muzzonigro. 1993. "The Effects of Traditional Family Values on the Coming Out Process of Gay Male Adolescents." *Adolescence* 28 (spring): 213–226.

Nieto, Daniel S. 1983. "Hispanic Fathers: The Growing Phenomenon of Single Fathers Keeping Their Children." *The National Hispanic Journal* 1 (spring): 14–19.

Norušis, Marija J. 1990. *SPSS: Introductory Statistics.* Chicago: SPSS, Inc.

Olive, Gilbert. 1968. *Narrative of Sojourner Truth.* New York: Arno Press.

Paredes, Américo. 1958. *"With His Pistol in His Hand": A Border Ballad and Its Hero.* Austin: University of Texas Press.

_____. 1966. "The Anglo-American in Mexican Folklore." In *New Voices in American Studies*, ed. Ray B. Browne and Donald H. Wenkelman. Lafayette, Ind.: Purdue University Press.

_____. 1967. *"Estados Unidos, Mexico y el Machismo." Journal of Inter-American Studies* 9 (January): 65–84.

_____. 1977. "On Ethnographic Work Among Minority Groups: A Folklorist's Perspective." *New Scholar* 6 (fall and spring): 1–33.

Paz, Octavio. 1961. *The Labyrinth of Solitude.* Translated by Lysander Kemp. New York: Grove.

Peña, Manuel. 1991. "Class, Gender, and Machismo: The 'Treacherous-Woman' Folklore of Mexican Male Workers." *Gender and Society* 5, no. 1 (March): 30–46.

Pleck, Joseph H. 1981. *The Myth of Masculinity.* Cambridge: The MIT Press.

Pleck, Joseph H. and Robert Brannon. 1978. "Male Roles and the Male Experience: Introduction." *Journal of Social Issues* 34 (winter): 1–4.

Proceso Inquisitorial del Cacique de Tetzcoco. 1910. *Archivo General y Publico de la Nación.* México: Eusebio Gómez De La Puente.

Procesos de Indios Idolatras y Hechiceros. 1912. *Archivo General de la Nación.* México: Tip. Guerrero Hnos.

Puig, Manuel. 1994. *El beso de la mujer araña.* New York: Vintage.

Ramirez, Raul. 1979. "Machismo: A Bridge Rather than a Barrier to Family and Marital Counseling." In *La Frontera Perspective,* ed. Patricia Preciado Martin, 61–62. Tucson: La Frontera Center.

Ramirez, Santiago, and Ramon Parres. 1957. "Some Dynamic Patterns in the Organization of the Mexican Family." *The International Journal of Social Psychiatry* 3 (summer): 18–21.

Ramos, Samuel. 1962. *Profile of Man and Culture in Mexico.* Translated by Peter G. Earle. Austin: University of Texas Press.

Reiss, Albert J., Jr. 1961. "The Social Integration of Queers and Peers." *Social Problems* 9:102–120.

Rodriguez, Richard. 1983. *Hunger of Memory: The Education of Richard Rodriguez.* New York: Bantam.

_____. 1992. *Days of Obligation: An Argument with My Mexican Father.* New York: Penguin.

_____. 1995. "'Sissy' Warriors Vs. 'Real' Men: A Perspective on Gays in the Military." In *Men's Lives,* ed. Michael S. Kimmel and Michael A. Messner. Boston: Allyn and Bacon.

Rosaldo, Renato. 1989. *Culture and Truth: The Remaking of Social Analysis.* Boston: Beacon.

Rubel, Arthur J. 1966. *Across the Tracks: Mexican Americans in a Texas City.* Austin: University of Texas Press.

Sahagún, Fray Bernardino de. 1946. Vols. 1–3 of *Historia general de las cosas de Nueva España.* México City: Nueva España.

_____. 1969. *Florentine Codex: General History of the Things of New Spain.* 13 pts. Translated by Charles E. Dibble and Arthur J. O. Anderson. Santa Fe: School of American Research and the University of Utah.

Salas, Elizabeth. 1990. *The Soldaderas in the Mexican Revolution: Myth and History.* Austin: University of Texas Press.

Sanchez, Alejandro F. 1979. "History and Culture of the Tecato (Chicano "Junkie"): Implications for Prevention and Treatment." In *La Frontera Perspective,* ed. Patricia Preciado Martin, 51–57. Tucson: La Frontera Center.

Sánchez, Rosaura, and Rosa Martínez Cruz, eds. 1977. *Essays on la Mujer.* Los Angeles: Chicano Studies Research Center Publications, University of California, Los Angeles.

Seidler, Victor J. 1994. *Unreasonable Men: Masculinity and Social Theory.* London: Routledge.

Shelton, Beth Anne, and Daphne John. 1993. "Ethnicity, Race, and Difference: A Comparison of White, Black, and Hispanic Men's Household Time." In *Men, Work, and Family,* ed. Jane C. Hood, 131–150. Thousand Oaks, Calif.: Sage.

Soustelle, Jacques. 1968. *Daily Life of the Aztecs.* Translated by Patrick O'Brian. New York: Macmillan.

Staples, Robert. 1978. "Masculinity and Race: The Dual Dilemma of Black Men." *Journal of Social Issues* 34 (winter): 169–183.

_____. 1982. *Black Masculinity: The Black Male's Role in American Society.* San Francisco: Black Scholar Press.

Stevens, Evelyn P. 1965. "Mexican Machismo: Politics and Value Orientations." *The Western Political Quarterly* 18 (December): 848-857.

_____. 1973. "Machismo and Marianismo." *Society* 10 (September/October): 57–63.

Valdez, Luis. 1972. Introduction to *Aztlan: An Anthology of Mexican American Literature,* ed. Luis Valdez and Stan Steiner. New York: Knopf.

Villa, Francisco (Pancho). 1913. "Letter From Pancho Villa to President Madero." January 20, 1913. Department of Historical Research, *Instituto Nacional de Antropología e Historia,* Document no. 429336.

Wallace, Michele. 1978. *Black Macho and the Myth of the Superwoman.* New York: Warner Books.

West, Robin. 1989. "Economic Man and Literary Woman: One Contrast." *Mercer Law Review* 39:867.

Wilkinson, Doris. 1987. "Ethnicity." In *Handbook of Marriage and the Family,* ed. Marvin B. Sussman and Suzanne K. Steinmetz, 183–210. New York: Plenum.

Wilkinson, Doris Y., and Ronald I. Taylor, eds. 1977. *The Black Male in America: Perspectives on His Status in American Society.* Chicago: Nelson-Hall.

Womack, John. 1969. *Zapata and the Mexican Revolution.* New York: Vintage.

Ybarra, Leonarda. 1982. "When Wives Work: The Impact on the Chicano Family." *Journal of Marriage and the Family* 44 (February): 169–178.

Zavella, Patricia. 1987. *Women's Work and Chicano Families: Cannery Workers of the Santa Clara Valley.* Ithaca: Cornell University Press.

Zorita, Alonso de. 1963. *Life and Labor in Ancient Mexico: The Brief and Summary Relations of the Lords of New Spain.* Translated by Benjamin Keen. New Brunswick, N.J.: Rutgers University Press.

Appendix A

TABLE 1   Region, Occupation, Education, Income, and the BSRI (BEM Sex Role Inventory)

	BSRI 1— Masculine			BSRI 2— Feminine			BSRI 3— Super Masculine		
	Mean	Eta	Sig.	Mean	Eta	Sig.	Mean	Eta	Sig.
Region									
N. California	49.5	.17	.25	45.3	.09	.69	23.3	.21	.13
S. California	51.6			45.6			22.2		
Texas	53.4			44.4			22.0		
Education									
Less than High School	42.2	.53	.25	46.4	.14	.39	22.8	.21	.12
High School	54.9			43.9			24.4		
Some College	54.2			44.7			22.2		
Occupation									
Nonprofessional	48.4	.30	.00	44.5	.09	.40	22.5	.01	.89
Professional	54.2			45.5			22.5		
Income		.53	.00		.27	.74		.28	.69

	Multiple Regression								
	BSRI 1— Masculine			BSRI 2— Feminine			BSRI 3— Super Masculine		
Variable	Beta	T	Sig.	Beta	T	Sig.	Beta	T	Sig.
TEXAS	.26	2.20	.03	−.10	−.78	.44	−.04	−.33	.75
EDUCATION	.31	2.28	.03	−.13	−.88	.38	.11	.68	.50
SOUTH	.16	1.42	.16	−.01	−.10	.92	−.04	−.28	.78
OCCUPATION	−.05	−.42	.66	−.29	−2.13	.04	.05	.36	.72
INCOME	.16	1.20	.23	−.28	−1.93	.04	.01	.06	.95
(Constant)		1.38	.17		5.64	.00		2.43	.02

Multiple R = .50	Multiple R = .32	Multiple R = .11
R Square = .25	R Square = .10	R Square = .02
Adj. R Sq. = .19	Adj. R Sq. = .04	Adj. R Sq. = .06
F = 4.80, Sig. = .00	F = 1.68, Sig. = .15	F = .17, Sig. = .97

NOTE: The variable NORTH had a T value of .00 and Sig. of 1.00 and was not included in the equation.

TABLE 2   Region, Occupation, Education, Income, and the MSRI (Mirandé Sex Role Inventory)

	MSRI 1—Traditional			MSRI 2—Tough			MSRI 3—Sensitive		
	Mean	Eta	Sig.	Mean	Eta	Sig.	Mean	Eta	Sig.
Region									
N. California	49.49	.30	.01	7.80	.08	.68	7.94	.22	.05
S. California	55.89			7.34			8.57		
Texas	51.57			7.63			9.23		
Education									
Less than High School	58.64	.43	.00	7.79	.10	.63	7.93	.18	.20
High School	52.42			8.14			9.29		
Some College	49.77			7.46			8.77		
Occupation									
Nonprofessional	56.16	.40	.00	7.76	.08	.43	8.54	.03	.73
Professional	49.11			7.42			8.40		
Income		.46	.01		.41	.05		.22	.89

	Multiple Regression								
	MSRI 1—Traditional			MSRI 2—Tough			MSRI 3—Sensitive		
Variable	Beta	T	Sig.	Beta	T	Sig.	Beta	T	Sig.
TEXAS	.01	.09	.03	.20	1.56	.12	.34	2.70	.01
EDUCATION	-.26	-1.86	.07	.06	.38	.70	.15	1.03	.31
SOUTH	.23	1.97	.05	-0.8	-.67	.51	.23	1.85	.07
OCCUPATION	.09	.71	.48	.17	1.20	.23	.27	2.02	.05
INCOME	-.12	-.87	.39	.03	.18	.86	.18	1.30	.20
(Constant)		4.01	.00		2.67	.01		.34	.73

	Multiple R = .47			Multiple R = .28			Multiple R = .36		
	R Square = .23			R Square = .08			R Square = .13		
	Adj. R Sq. = .17			Adj. R Sq. = .02			Adj. R Sq. = .07		
	F = 4.30, Sig. = .00			F = 1.24, Sig. = .30			F = 2.17, Sig. = .07		

NOTE: The variable NORTH had a T value of .00 and Sig. of 1.00 and was not included in the equation.

TABLE 3 Nativity, Language Usage and Preference, Socioeconomic Status, and the BSRI (BEM Sex Role Inventory)

Variable	BSRI 1— Masculine			BSRI 2— Feminine			BSRI 3— Super Masculine		
	Beta	T	Sig.	Beta	T	Sig.	Beta	T	Sig.
Place of Birth	.07	.70	.49	.01	.13	.90	−.12	−1.09	.28
Language Preference	−.04	−.36	.72	.02	.16	.88	.04	.38	.70
Language Usage	−.14	−1.24	.22	.09	.77	.45	−.01	−.11	.92
Language of Interview	.31	2.78	.00	−0.6	−.51	.61	.08	.68	.50
(Constant)		7.46	.00		11.56	.00		15.88	.00

	Multiple R = .43 R Square = .19 Adj. R Sq. = .15 F = 5.47, Sig. = .00			Multiple R = .14 R Square = .02 Adj. R Sq. = −.02 F = .47, Sig. = .76			Multiple R = .13 R Square = .02 Adj. R Sq. = −.03 F = .38, Sig. = .82		

Variable	BSRI 1— Masculine			BSRI 2— Feminine			BSRI 3— Super Masculine		
	Beta	T	Sig.	Beta	T	Sig.	Beta	T	Sig.
Place of Birth	−.11	−1.04	.30	−.16	−1.35	.18	.11	.90	.37
Language of Interview	.17	1.50	.49	−.09	−.70	.49	.13	.95	.35
Education	.29	2.27	.03	−.34	−2.30	.02	.01	.04	.97
Occupation	.02	.15	.89	−.34	−2.72	.01	−.06	−.43	.67
Income	.22	2.06	.04	−.16	−1.35	.18	−.09	−.68	.50
(Constant)		4.74	.00		12.13	.00		11.51	.00

	Multiple R = .60 R Square = .36 Adj. R Sq. = .32 F = 10.00, Sig. = .00			Multiple R = .35 R Square = .12 Adj. R Sq. = .07 F = 2.50, Sig. = .04			Multiple R = .13 R Square = .02 Adj. R Sq. = −.04 F = .33, Sig. = .89		

TABLE 4   Nativity, Language Usage and Preference, Socioeconomic Status, and the MSRI (Mirandé Sex Role Inventory)

Variable	MSRI 1— Traditional			MSRI 2— Tough			MSRI 3— Sensitive		
	Beta	T	Sig.	Beta	T	Sig.	Beta	T	Sig.
Place of Birth	.08	.76	.45	.10	.93	.36	.15	1.43	.16
Language Preference	.06	−.59	.56	−.26	−.23	.82	−0.9	−.87	.39
Language Usage	−.09	−.80	.43	.01	.07	.94	−.10	−.82	.41
Language of Interview	−3.8	−3.30	.00	−.08	−.66	.51	−.01	−.08	.94
(Constant)		11.57	.00		5.25	.00		5.73	.00

Multiple R = .33	Multiple R = .11	Multiple R = .22
R Square = .11	R Square = .01	R Square = .05
Adj. R Sq. = .07	Adj. R Sq. = −.03	Adj. R Sq. = −.01
F = 2.93, Sig. = .02	F = .30, Sig. = .88	F = 1.16, Sig. = .33

Variable	MSRI 1— Traditional			MSRI 2— Tough			MSRI 3— Sensitive		
	Beta	T	Sig.	Beta	T	Sig.	Beta	T	Sig.
Place of Birth	−.11	−1.04	.30	.16	−1.35	.18	.11	.90	.37
Language of Interview	.17	1.49	.14	−.09	−.70	.49	.13	.95	.35
Education	.29	2.27	.03	−.34	−2.30	.02	.01	.04	.97
Occupation	.02	.15	.89	−.34	−2.72	.01	−.06	−.43	.67
Income	.22	2.06	.04	−.10	−.80	.43	−.09	−.68	.50
(Constant)									

Multiple R = .60	Multiple R = .35	Multiple R = .13
R Square = .36	R Square = .12	R Square = .02
Adj. R Sq. = .32	Adj. R Sq. = .07	Adj. R Sq. = −.04
F = 10.01, Sig. = .00	F = 2.50, Sig. = .04	F = .33, Sig. = .89

TABLE 5   The MSRI, Household Chores, Marital Decisions, Interaction with Children, and Marital Happiness

Variable	Mean Chores Performed			Mean Marital Decisions			Mean Interaction with Children			Mean Marital Happiness		
	Beta	T	Sig.	Beta	T	Sig.	Beta	T	Sig.	Beta	T	Sig.
Place of Birth	.00	.01	.99	-.12	-1.07	.29	-.06	-.51	.61	-.08	.65	.52
Language of Interview	-.03	-.28	.78	-.16	-1.27	.21	-.13	-.93	.36	.08	.56	.58
Education	.07	.46	.65	-.21	-1.54	.13	-.16	-1.04	.30	.07	.44	.66
Occupation	.06	.47	.64	.18	1.47	.15	.02	.18	.86	-.02	-.12	.90
Income	.18	1.44	.15	.04	.38	.70	.14	1.14	.26	-.33	-2.60	.01
MSRI 1—Traditional	.19	1.67	.10	-.50	-4.80	.00	-.26	-2.25	.03	-.09	-.76	.45
MSRI 2—Toughness	-.19	-1.70	.09	-.11	-1.09	.28	-.20	-1.74	.09	.26	2.29	.02
MSRI 3—Sensitive	.26	2.25	.03	-.19	-1.85	.07	.12	1.04	.30	-.08	-.65	.52
(Constant)		3.47	.00		9.98	.00		5.99	.00		1.92	.06
	Multiple R = .35 R Square = .12 Adj. R Sq. = .04 F = 1.47, Sig. = .18			Multiple R = .54 R Square = .29 Adj. R Sq. = .23 F = 4.49, Sig. = .00			Multiple R = .33 R Square = .11 Adj. R Sq. = .03 F = 1.31, Sig. = .25			Multiple R = .34 R Square = .12 Adj. R Sq. = .04 F = 1.46, Sig. = .18		

TABLE 6 The BSRI, Household Chores, Marital Decisions, Interaction with Children, and Marital Happiness

Variable	Mean Chores Performed			Mean Marital Decisions			Mean Interaction with Children			Mean Marital Happiness		
	Beta	T	Sig.	Beta	T	Sig.	Beta	T	Sig.	Beta	T	Sig.
Place of Birth	-.00	-.04	.97	.01	-.11	.91	-.00	-.06	.95	.08	.65	.52
Language of Interview	-.06	-.41	.69	-.01	-.09	.93	-.01	-.10	.92	-.02	-.14	.89
Education	.03	.16	.88	-.11	-.65	.52	-.11	-.64	.53	-.04	-.31	.76
Occupation	.14	.98	.33	.06	.41	.69	-.02	-.13	.90	-.14	-1.04	.30
Income	.11	.83	.41	.11	.80	.43	.15	1.08	.28	-.34	-2.69	.01
BSRI 1—Masculine	.08	.61	.54	-.03	-.18	.86	-.01	-.07	.94	.17	1.33	.19
BSRI 2—Feminine	-.13	-1.06	.29	.14	1.14	.26	-.06	-.50	.62	-.30	-2.64	.01
BSRI 3—Super Masculine	-.01	-.06	.95	-.02	-.15	.88	-.10	-.84	.40	.21	1.96	.05
(Constant)		4.03	.00		3.36	.00		4.12	.00		1.93	.06

Mean Chores Performed:
Multiple R = .21
R Square = .05
Adj. R Sq. = -.04
F = .52, Sig. = .84

Mean Marital Decisions:
Multiple R = .19
R Square = .04
Adj. R Sq. = -.05
F = .41, Sig. = .91

Mean Interaction with Children:
Multiple R = .18
R Square = .03
Adj. R Sq. = -.05
F = .39, Sig. = .92

Mean Marital Happiness:
Multiple R = .40
R Square = .16
Adj. R Sq. = .08
F = 2.03, Sig. = .05

TABLE 7   The MSRI, BSRI, Household Chores, Marital Decisions, Interaction with Children, and Marital Happiness

Variable	Mean Chores Performed			Mean Marital Decisions			Mean Interaction with Children			Mean Marital Happiness		
	Beta	T	Sig.	Beta	T	Sig.	Beta	T	Sig.	Beta	T	Sig.
MSRI 1—Traditional	.18	1.83	.07	-.32	-3.39	.01	-.20	-1.95	.05	-.03	-.25	.80
MSRI 2—Toughness	-.15	-1.39	.17	-.08	-.83	.41	-.16	-1.51	.13	.21	1.94	.06
MSRI 3—Sensitive	.20	1.87	.06	-.25	-2.50	.01	.08	.75	.45	-.06	-.52	.61
(Constant)		6.18	.00		4.89	.00		5.63	.00		1.02	.31
	Multiple R = .26 R Square = .07 Adj. R Sq. = -.04 F = 2.22, Sig. = .09			Multiple R = .43 R Square = .18 Adj. R Sq. = .16 F = 7.04, Sig. = .00			Multiple R = .27 R Square = .07 Adj. R Sq. = .06 F = 2.37, Sig. = .07			Multiple R = .20 R Square = .04 Adj. R Sq. = .01 F = 1.26, Sig. = .29		

Variable	Mean Chores Performed			Mean Marital Decisions			Mean Interaction with Children			Mean Marital Happiness		
	Beta	T	Sig.	Beta	T	Sig.	Beta	T	Sig.	Beta	T	Sig.
BSRI 1—Masculine	.10	.96	.34	-.04	.41	.68	-.02	-.15	.88	-.00	-.04	.97
BSRI 2—Feminine	-.16	-1.45	.15	.15	1.33	.19	-.05	-.43	.67	-.22	-2.05	.04
BSRI 3—Super Masculine	-.02	-.21	.83	-.04	-.38	.70	-.11	-1.01	.32	.24	2.29	.02
(Constant)		6.18	.00		4.89	.00		5.63	.00		1.02	.31
	Multiple R = .18 R Square = .03 Adj. R Sq. = .00 F = 1.08, Sig. = .36			Multiple R = .14 R Square = .02 Adj. R Sq. = -.01 F = .64, Sig. = .59			Multiple R = .00 R Square = .00 Adj. R Sq. = -.01 F = .00, Sig. = .99			Multiple R = .27 R Square = .07 Adj. R Sq. = .04 F = 2.39, Sig. = .07		

TABLE 8   Regional, Socioeconomic, Cultural, and Gender Role Differences in Person Most Respected/Admired

	Region			Education	
	% N. Cal.	% S. Cal.	% Tex.	% High School	% High School+
Person Respected					
Immed. Fam.	34	65	63	51	53
Non-Immed. Fam.	13	15	11	20	6
Friend/Celebrity	53	20	26	29	41
	Chi-Square = 8.64, Sig. = .07			Chi-Square = 5.32, Sig. = .07	

	Occupation		Income (Thousands of Dollars)		
	% Prof.	% Nonprof.	% Under 25	% 25–40	% 40+
Person Respected					
Immed. Fam.	53	52	43	54	55
Non-Immed. Fam.	6	16	19	13	5
Friend/Celebrity	41	32	38	32	40
	Chi-Square = 3.0, Sig. = .23		Chi-Square = 3.55, Sig. = .47		

	Place of Birth		Language of Interview	
	% U.S.	% Non-U.S.	% Spanish	% English
Person Respected				
Immed. Fam.	54	48	51	53
Non-Immed. Fam.	8	18	17	7
Friend/Celebrity	39	35	32	40
	Chi-Square = 2.42, Sig. = .30		Chi-Square = 3.12, Sig. = .21	

	BSRI 1—Masculine			BSRI 2—Feminine		
	% Low	% Moderate	% High	% Low	% Moderate	% High
Person Respected						
Immed. Fam.	57	42	58	47	43	64
Non-Immed. Fam.	17	10	3	13	13	6
Friend/Celebrity	28	48	39	13	13	11
	Chi-Square = 5.76, Sig. = .22			Chi-Square = 3.60, Sig. = .46		

	MSRI 1—Traditional			MSRI 2—Tough		
	% Low	% Moderate	% High	% Low	% Moderate	% High
Person Respected						
Immed. Fam.	49	44	65	52	49	62
Non-Immed. Fam.	9	9	15	16	11	5
Friend/Celebrity	43	47	21	32	40	33
	Chi-Square = 6.04, Sig. = .20			Chi-Square = 2.25, Sig. = .69		

NOTE: Total percentages in columns for this and remaining tables in Appendix A do not necessarily add up to 100 percent. This is because percentages have been rounded off.

TABLE 9   Regional, Socioeconomic, Cultural, and Gender Role Differences in
Qualities Respected in a Man

	Region			Education	
	% N. Cal.	% S. Cal.	% Tex.	% High School	% High School+
Qualities Respected					
Warm	6	20	18	18	11
Respectful	63	45	50	49	59
Honest	31	35	32	33	30
	Chi-Square = 3.10, Sig. = .54			Chi-Square = 1.24, Sig. = .54	

	Occupation		Income (Thousands of Dollars)		
	% Prof.	% Nonprof.	% Under 25	% 25–40	% 40+
Qualities Respected					
Warm	13	15	24	3	17
Respectful	60	50	29	56	71
Honest	26	35	48	42	12
	Chi-Square = 1.89, Sig. = .55		Chi-Square = 18.02, Sig. = .00		

	Place of Birth		Language of Interview	
	% U.S.	% Non-U.S.	% Spanish	% English
Qualities Respected				
Warm	16	9	13	14
Respectful	57	49	56	55
Honest	27	42	31	31
	Chi-Square = 2.91, Sig. = .23		Chi-Square = .04, Sig. = .97	

	BSRI 1—Masculine			BSRI 2—Feminine		
	% Low	% Moderate	% High	% Low	% Moderate	% High
Qualities Respected						
Warm	12	10	18	18	14	8
Respectful	56	52	58	55	62	50
Honest	32	39	24	27	24	42
	Chi-Square = 2.13, Sig. = .70			Chi-Square = 3.55, Sig. = .47		

	MSRI 1—Traditional			MSRI 2—Tough		
	% Low	% Moderate	% High	% Low	% Moderate	% High
Qualities Respected						
Warm	3	23	15	8	13	23
Respectful	63	57	46	48	61	50
Honest	34	20	39	44	27	27
	Chi-Square = 8.43, Sig. = .07			Chi-Square = 4.40, Sig. = .35		

TABLE 10   Regional, Socioeconomic, Cultural, and Gender Role Differences in Qualities Least Respected in a Man

	Region			Education	
	% N. Cal.	% S. Cal.	% Tex.	% High School	% High School+
Qualities Least Respected					
Uses Others	13	5	16	6	13
No Respect	75	70	63	59	69
Selfish/Irresponsible	13	25	22	35	18
	Chi-Square = 2.77, Sig. = .60			Chi-Square = 4.38, Sig. = .11	

	Occupation		Income (Thousands of Dollars)		
	% Prof.	% Nonprof.	% Under 25	% 25–40	% 40+
Qualities Least Respected					
Uses Others	12	10	5	16	7
No Respect	69	63	42	70	71
Selfish/Irresponsible	20	27	53	14	22
	Chi-Square = .77, Sig. = .68		Chi-Square = 11.96, Sig. = .02		

	Place of Birth		Language of Interview	
	% U.S.	% Non-U.S.	% Spanish	% English
Qualities Least Respected				
Uses Others	13	6	5	15
No Respect	67	59	56	71
Selfish/Irresponsible	19	34	39	15
	Chi-Square = 3.21, Sig. = .20		Chi-Square = 8.49, Sig. = .01	

	BSRI 1—Masculine			BSRI 2—Feminine		
	% Low	% Moderate	% High	% Low	% Moderate	% High
Qualities Least Respected						
Uses Others	6	17	9	16	10	6
No Respect	65	67	70	58	60	80
Selfish/Irresponsible	29	17	22	26	30	14
	Chi-Square = 3.02, Sig. = .55			Chi-Square = 5.10, Sig. = .28		

	MSRI 1—Traditional			MSRI 2—Tough		
	% Low	% Moderate	% High	% Low	% Moderate	% High
Qualities Least Respected						
Uses Others	12	9	12	12	11	10
No Respect	85	52	59	60	68	65
Selfish/Irresponsible	3	39	29	28	21	25
	Chi-Square = 13.46, Sig. = .00			Chi-Square = .53, Sig. = .97		

TABLE 11   Regional, Socioeconomic, Cultural, and Gender Role Differences in Worst or "Lowest" Thing a Man Can Do

	Region			Education	
	% N. Cal.	% S. Cal.	% Tex.	% High School	% High School+
Lowest Thing					
Injure/Abuse	49	26	52	35	47
Use Others	15	21	24	15	25
Non-Support of Family	36	53	24	50	28
	Chi-Square = 5.35, Sig. = .25			Chi-Square = 4.97, Sig. = .08	

	Occupation		Income (Thousands of Dollars)		
	% Prof.	% Nonprof.	% Under 25	% 25–40	% 40+
Lowest Thing					
Injure/Abuse	47	39	37	51	41
Use Others	22	22	32	16	21
Non-Support of Family	31	39	32	32	38
	Chi-Square = .80, Sig. = .67		Chi-Square = 2.42, Sig. = .66		

	Place of Birth		Language of Interview	
	% U.S.	% Non-U.S.	% Spanish	% English
Lowest Thing				
Injure/Abuse	45	39	30	52
Use Others	24	18	23	21
Non-Support of Family	31	42	48	27
	Chi-Square = 1.25, Sig. = .53		Chi-Square = 5.44, Sig. = .07	

	BSRI 1—Masculine			BSRI 2—Feminine		
	% Low	% Moderate	% High	% Low	% Moderate	% High
Lowest Thing						
Injure/Abuse	26	60	53	38	48	50
Use Others	26	20	22	19	23	27
Non-Support of Family	49	20	25	44	29	24
	Chi-Square = 9.92, Sig. = .04			Chi-Square = 3.32, Sig. = .55		

	MSRI 1—Traditional			MSRI 2—Tough		
	% Low	% Moderate	% High	% Low	% Moderate	% High
Lowest Thing						
Injure/Abuse	56	37	36	58	39	38
Use Others	21	26	18	21	23	19
Non-Support of Family	24	37	46	21	39	43
	Chi-Square = 4.72, Sig. = .32			Chi-Square = 3.73, Sig. = .44		

TABLE 12   Regional, Socioeconomic, Cultural, and Gender Role Differences in Qualities Valued in a Son

	Region			Education	
	% N. Cal.	% S. Cal.	% Tex.	% High School	% High School+
Valued in Son					
Responsible	40	42	37	47	38
Principled	13	16	17	19	15
Honest/Warm	47	42	46	34	49
	Chi-Square = .29, Sig. = .99			Chi-Square = 1.61, Sig. = .45	

	Occupation		Income (Thousands of Dollars)		
	% Prof.	% Nonprof.	% Under 25	% 25–40	% 40+
Valued in Son					
Responsible	37	45	52	34	42
Principled	21	11	19	14	15
Honest/Warm	42	45	29	51	44
	Chi-Square = 2.13, Sig. = .35		Chi-Square = 2.06, Sig. = .58		

	Place of Birth		Language of Interview	
	% U.S.	% Non-U.S.	% Spanish	% English
Valued in Son				
Responsible	36	52	46	37
Principled	15	19	21	13
Honest/Warm	49	29	33	50
	Chi-Square = 3.59, Sig. = .17		Chi-Square = 2.89, Sig. = .24	

	BSRI 1—Masculine			BSRI 2—Feminine		
	% Low	% Moderate	% High	% Low	% Moderate	% High
Valued in Son						
Responsible	52	36	38	41	66	23
Principled	21	16	13	22	14	14
Honest/Warm	27	48	50	38	21	63
	Chi-Square = 4.44, Sig. = .44			Chi-Square = 14.69, Sig. = .01		

	MSRI 1—Traditional			MSRI 2—Tough		
	% Low	% Moderate	% High	% Low	% Moderate	% High
Valued in Son						
Responsible	32	59	30	46	35	50
Principled	27	6	15	21	13	18
Honest/Warm	41	35	55	33	53	32
	Chi-Square = 10.27, Sig. = .04			Chi-Square = 4.26, Sig. = .37		

TABLE 13　Regional, Socioeconomic, Cultural, and Gender Role Differences in the Meaning of "Macho"

	Region			Education	
	% N. Cal.	% S. Cal.	% Tex.	% High School	% High School+
Macho Meaning					
Synthetic/Dominant	49	69	56	78	43
Male/*Varonil*	15	13	9	13	13
Principled/Ethical	36	19	34	9	44
	Chi-Square = 2.37, Sig. = .67			Chi-Square = 12.82, Sig. = .00	

	Occupation		Income (Thousands of Dollars)		
	% Prof.	% Nonprof.	% Under 25	% 25–40	% 40+
Macho Meaning					
Synthetic/Dominant	40	70	56	71	43
Male/*Varonil*	18	7	11	9	18
Principled/Ethical	42	23	33	21	40
	Chi-Square = 8.42, Sig. = .01		Chi-Square = 5.96, Sig. = .20		

	Place of Birth		Language of Interview	
	% U.S.	% Non-U.S.	% Spanish	% English
Macho Meaning				
Synthetic/Dominant	48	69	64	48
Male/*Varonil*	9	21	21	7
Principled/Ethical	42	10	15	45
	Chi-Square = 9.79, Sig. = .01		Chi-Square = 10.34, Sig. = .01	

	BSRI 1—Masculine			BSRI 2—Feminine		
	% Low	% Moderate	% High	% Low	% Moderate	% High
Macho Meaning						
Synthetic/Dominant	69	46	42	62	57	41
Male/*Varonil*	16	14	10	14	4	21
Principled/Ethical	16	39	48	24	39	38
	Chi-Square = 8.20, Sig. = .08			Chi-Square = 6.06, Sig. = .19		

	MSRI 1—Traditional			MSRI 2—Tough		
	% Low	% Moderate	% High	% Low	% Moderate	% High
Macho Meaning						
Synthetic/Dominant	52	50	63	59	64	22
Male/*Varonil*	15	9	13	14	9	22
Principled/Ethical	33	41	23	27	27	56
	Chi-Square = 2.47, Sig. = .65			Chi-Square = 9.80, Sig. = .04		

TABLE 14   Regional, Socioeconomic, Cultural, and Gender Role Differences in
Examples of Macho Behavior

	Region			Education	
	% N. Cal.	% S. Cal.	% Tex.	% High School	% High School+
Macho Behavior					
Drink/Fight	56	77	59	81	51
Honorable/Responsible	44	24	41	19	49
	Chi-Square = 2.08, Sig. = .35			Chi-Square = 8.44, Sig. = .00	

	Occupation			Income (Thousands of Dollars)		
	% Prof.	% Nonprof.		% Under 25	% 25–40	% 40+
Macho Behavior						
Drink/Fight	50	70		56	76	53
Honorable/Responsible	50	30		44	24	48
	Chi-Square = 4.12, Sig. = .04			Chi-Square = 4.79, Sig. = .09		

	Place of Birth		Language of Interview	
	% U.S.	% Non-U.S.	% Spanish	% English
Macho Behavior				
Drink/Fight	54	76	76	51
Honorable/Responsible	46	24	24	49
	Chi-Square = 3.93, Sig. = .05		Chi-Square = 6.36, Sig. = .01	

	BSRI 1—Masculine			BSRI 2—Feminine		
	% Low	% Moderate	% High	% Low	% Moderate	% High
Macho Behavior						
Drink/Fight	71	56	49	65	61	51
Honorable/Responsible	29	44	51	36	39	49
	Chi-Square = 3.51, Sig. = .17			Chi-Square = 1.24, Sig. = .54		

	MSRI 1—Traditional			MSRI 2—Tough		
	% Low	% Moderate	% High	% Low	% Moderate	% High
Macho Behavior						
Drink/Fight	52	59	72	73	67	30
Honorable/Responsible	49	41	28	27	33	70
	Chi-Square = 2.89, Sig. = .23			Chi-Square = 10.08, Sig. = .01		

TABLE 15   Regional, Socioeconomic, Cultural, and Gender Role Differences in Source of Ideas on Child Rearing

	Region			Education	
	% N. Cal.	% S. Cal.	% Tex.	% High School	% High School+
Ideas on Child Rearing					
Childhood/Parents	32	72	71	63	47
Education/Reading	65	22	29	33	51
Friends/Observation	3	6	0	3	1
	Chi-Square = 13.69, Sig. = .01			Chi-Square = 2.93, Sig. = .23	

	Occupation		Income (Thousands of Dollars)		
	% Prof.	% Nonprof.	% Under 25	% 25–40	% 40+
Ideas on Child Rearing					
Childhood/Parents	42	65	61	58	45
Education/Reading	58	30	33	39	55
Friends/Observation	0	4	6	3	0
	Chi-Square = 8.71, Sig. = .01		Chi-Square = 4.63, Sig. = .33		

	Place of Birth		Language of Interview	
	% U.S.	% Non-U.S.	% Spanish	% English
Ideas on Child Rearing				
Childhood/Parents	54	50	58	48
Education/Reading	44	47	39	50
Friends/Observation	2	3	3	2
	Chi-Square = .46, Sig. = .79		Chi-Square = 1.22, Sig. = .54	

	BSRI 1—Masculine			BSRI 2—Feminine		
	% Low	% Moderate	% High	% Low	% Moderate	% High
Ideas on Child Rearing						
Childhood/Parents	52	52	49	59	46	46
Education/Reading	48	45	52	41	50	54
Friends/Observation						
	Chi-Square = 2.24, Sig. = .69			Chi-Square = 3.80, Sig. = .21		

	MSRI 1—Traditional			MSRI 2—Tough		
	% Low	% Moderate	% High	% Low	% Moderate	% High
Ideas on Child Rearing						
Childhood/Parents	38	47	72	48	53	12
Education/Reading	62	50	25	52	44	46
Friends/Observation	0	0	3	0	4	0
	Chi-Square = 9.89, Sig. = .04			Chi-Square = 2.00, Sig. = .73		

TABLE 16   Regional, Socioeconomic, Cultural, and Gender Role Differences in
What Was Important in How Raised

	Region			Education	
	% N. Cal.	% S. Cal.	% Tex.	% High School	% High School+
Importance of How Raised					
Love/Affection	39	30	42	26	46
Discipline/Values	58	60	58	66	52
Family Not Intact	3	10	0	9	2
	Chi-Square = 4.02, Sig. = .40			Chi-Square = 5.97, Sig. = .05	

	Occupation		Income (Thousands of Dollars)		
	% Prof.	% Nonprof.	% Under 25	% 25–40	% 40+
Importance of How Raised					
Love/Affection	44	33	29	46	39
Discipline/Values	52	63	62	54	56
Family Not Intact	4	4	10	0	5
	Chi-Square = 1.93, Sig. = .55		Chi-Square = 4.29, Sig. = .37		

	Place of Birth		Language of Interview	
	% U.S.	% Non-U.S.	% Spanish	% English
Importance of How Raised				
Love/Affection	44	31	33	43
Discipline/Values	55	58	60	55
Family Not Intact	2	9	8	2
	Chi-Square = 4.22, Sig. = .12		Chi-Square = 2.87, Sig. = .24	

	BSRI 1—Masculine			BSRI 2—Feminine		
	% Low	% Moderate	% High	% Low	% Moderate	% High
Importance of How Raised						
Love/Affection	31	46	39	40	32	41
Discipline/Values	64	50	58	57	65	53
Family Not Intact	6	4	3	3	3	6
	Chi-Square = 1.83, Sig. = .77			Chi-Square = 1.13, Sig. = .89		

	MSRI 1—Traditional			MSRI 2—Tough		
	% Low	% Moderate	% High	% Low	% Moderate	% High
Importance of How Raised						
Love/Affection	53	31	33	28	47	32
Discipline/Values	44	66	61	68	49	64
Family Not Intact	3	3	6	4	4	5
	Chi-Square = 4.48, Sig. = .35			Chi-Square = 3.28, Sig. = .51		

TABLE 17   Regional, Socioeconomic, Cultural, and Gender Role Differences in Most Important Responsibility to Children

	Region			Education	
	% N. Cal.	% S. Cal.	% Tex.	% High School	% High School+
Responsibility to Children					
Financial/Physical	46	39	32	54	33
Emotional/Moral	54	61	68	46	67
	Chi-Square = 1.17, Sig. = .56			Chi-Square = 4.46, Sig. = .03	

	Occupation		Income (Thousands of Dollars)		
	% Prof.	% Nonprof.	% Under 25	% 25–40	% 40+
Responsibility to Children					
Financial/Physical	34	46	33	45	43
Emotional/Moral	66	54	67	55	57
	Chi-Square = 1.56, Sig. = .21		Chi-Square = .77, Sig. = .68		

	Place of Birth		Language of Interview	
	% U.S.	% Non-U.S.	% Spanish	% English
Responsibility to Children				
Financial/Physical	33	56	51	33
Emotional/Moral	67	44	49	67
	Chi-Square = 4.80, Sig. = .03		Chi-Square = 3.53, Sig. = .06	

	BSRI 1—Masculine			BSRI 2—Feminine		
	% Low	% Moderate	% High	% Low	% Moderate	% High
Responsibility to Children						
Financial/Physical	47	48	21	36	48	33
Emotional/Moral	53	52	79	64	52	67
	Chi-Square = 6.56, Sig. = .03			Chi-Square = 1.73, Sig. = .42		

	MSRI 1—Traditional			MSRI 2—Tough		
	% Low	% Moderate	% High	% Low	% Moderate	% High
Responsibility to Children						
Financial/Physical	37	44	38	32	38	50
Emotional/Moral	63	56	62	68	60	50
	Chi-Square = .46, Sig. = .79			Chi-Square = 1.59, Sig. = .45		

	MSRI 3—Sensitivity			Children Questioned	
	% Low	% Moderate	% High	% High Interest	% Low Interest
Responsibility to Children					
Financial/Physical	22	55	41	49	32
Emotional/Moral	78	45	59	51	69
	Chi-Square = 6.16, Sig. = .05			Chi-Square = 3.36, Sig. = .06	

TABLE 18   Regional, Socioeconomic, Cultural, and Gender Role Differences in Why Person Considers Self a Good Father

	Region			Education	
	% N. Cal.	% S. Cal.	% Tex.	% High School	% High School+
Why Good Father					
Provides for Needs	10	35	6	23	11
Makes Time/Listens	47	35	41	32	49
Loves/Nurtures	43	29	53	45	40
	Chi-Square = 9.03, Sig. = .06			Chi-Square = 3.52, Sig. = .17	

	Occupation		Income (Thousands of Dollars)		
	% Prof.	% Nonprof.	% Under 25	% 25–40	% 40+
Why Good Father					
Provides for Needs	8	21	24	15	8
Makes Time/Listens	53	33	33	47	46
Loves/Nurtures	39	47	43	38	46
	Chi-Square = 5.40, Sig. = .07		Chi-Square = 3.25, Sig. = .52		

	Place of Birth		Language of Interview	
	% U.S.	% Non-U.S.	% Spanish	% English
Why Good Father				
Provides for Needs	10	26	21	11
Makes Time/Listens	46	42	41	46
Loves/Nurtures	44	32	39	44
	Chi-Square = 4.54, Sig. = .10		Chi-Square = 1.85, Sig. = .40	

	BSRI 1—Masculine			BSRI 2—Feminine		
	% Low	% Moderate	% High	% Low	% Moderate	% High
Why Good Father						
Provides for Needs	24	7	13	20	24	3
Makes Time/Listens	36	47	47	43	38	47
Loves/Nurtures	39	47	40	37	38	50
	Chi-Square = 4.07, Sig. = .40			Chi-Square = 6.53, Sig. = .16		

	MSRI 1—Traditional			MSRI 2—Tough		
	% Low	% Moderate	% High	% Low	% Moderate	% High
Why Good Father						
Provides for Needs	9	21	13	8	19	11
Makes Time/Listens	46	36	50	54	40	42
Loves/Nurtures	46	42	37	38	42	47
	Chi-Square = 2.71, Sig. = .61			Chi-Square = 2.59, Sig. = .63		

TABLE 19   Regional, Socioeconomic, Cultural, and Gender Role Differences in Qualities Admired in a Father

	Region			Education	
	% N. Cal.	% S. Cal.	% Tex.	% High School	% High School+
What Makes a Good Father					
Provider	3	5	12	6	6
Listens/Is Consistent	72	95	79	85	79
Affectionate/Loving	25	0	9	9	15
	Chi-Square = 9.10, Sig. = .06			Chi-Square = .62, Sig. = .73	

	Occupation		Income (Thousands of Dollars)		
	% Prof.	% Nonprof.	% Under 25	% 25–40	% 40+
What Makes a Good Father					
Provider	6	7	0	6	10
Listens/Is Consistent	79	83	95	83	71
Affectionate/Loving	15	11	5	11	19
	Chi-Square = .40, Sig. = .82		Chi-Square = 5.14, Sig. = .27		

	Place of Birth		Language of Interview	
	% U.S.	% Non-U.S.	% Spanish	% English
What Makes a Good Father				
Provider	8	3	3	8
Listens/Is Consistent	81	81	90	76
Affectionate/Loving	12	16	8	16
	Chi-Square = .90, Sig. = .64		Chi-Square = 3.12, Sig. = .21	

	BSRI 1—Masculine			BSRI 2—Feminine		
	% Low	% Moderate	% High	% Low	% Moderate	% High
What Makes a Good Father						
Provider	0	10	6	13	0	3
Listens/Is Consistent	88	74	81	72	86	86
Affectionate/Loving	12	19	13	16	14	11
	Chi-Square = 3.57, Sig. = .47			Chi-Square = 5.89, Sig. = .21		

	MSRI 1—Traditional			MSRI 2—Tough		
	% Low	% Moderate	% High	% Low	% Moderate	% High
What Makes a Good Father						
Provider	6	6	6	4	4	14
Listens/Is Consistent	77	80	88	75	84	82
Affectionate/Loving	18	14	6	21	13	5
	Chi-Square = 2.01, Sig. = .73			Chi-Square = 5.33, Sig. = .25		

TABLE 20   Regional, Socioeconomic, Cultural, and Gender Role Differences in
Why Father Considered Good or Bad

	Region			Education	
	% N. Cal.	% S. Cal.	% Tex.	% High School	% High School+
Why Father Good/Bad					
Has Vices/Irresponsible	19	11	3	13	13
Loving/Affectionate	81	89	97	87	87
	Chi-Square = 4.00, Sig. = .14			Chi-Square = .01, Sig. = .94	

	Occupation		Income (Thousands of Dollars)		
	% Prof.	% Nonprof.	% Under 25	% 25–40	% 40+
Why Father Good/Bad					
Has Vices/Irresponsible	16	11	5.3	12	17
Loving/Affectionate	84	89	95	88	83
	Chi-Square = .54, Sig. = .46		Chi-Square = 1.67, Sig. = .43		

	Place of Birth		Language of Interview	
	% U.S.	% Non-U.S.	% Spanish	% English
Why Father Good/Bad				
Has Vices/Irresponsible	8	23	16	12
Loving/Affectionate	92	77	84	89
	Chi-Square = 4.25, Sig. = .04		Chi-Square = .45, Sig. = .50	

	BSRI 1—Masculine			BSRI 2—Feminine		
	% Low	% Moderate	% High	% Low	% Moderate	% High
Why Father Good/Bad						
Has Vices/Irresponsible	16	13	13	13	15	15
Loving/Affectionate	84	87	87	88	85	85
	Chi-Square = .11, Sig. = .95			Chi-Square = .09, Sig. = .96		

	MSRI 1—Traditional			MSRI 2—Tough		
	% Low	% Moderate	% High	% Low	% Moderate	% High
Why Father Good/Bad						
Has Vices/Irresponsible	13	15	12	13	15	10
Loving/Affectionate	87	85	88	87	85	91
	Chi-Square = .10, Sig. = .95			Chi-Square = .37, Sig. = .82		

TABLE 21   Regional, Socioeconomic, Cultural, and Gender Role Differences in Perceived Weaknesses as Father

	Region			Education	
	% N. Cal.	% S. Cal.	% Tex.	% High School	% High School+
Weaknesses					
Not Provider	30	18	7	10	50
Neglects/Doesn't Listen	34	24	43	23	42
Not Affectionate	34	12	23	23	30
No Weaknesses	23	47	27	47	27
	Chi-Square = 8.31, Sig. = .22			Chi-Square = 5.92, Sig. = .12	

	Occupation		Income (Thousands of Dollars)		
	% Prof.	% Nonprof.	% Under 25	% 25–40	% 40+
Weaknesses					
Not Provider	4	9	5	6	5
Neglects/Doesn't Listen	45	28	42	25	41
Not Affectionate	29	26	11	31	33
No Weaknesses	22	37	42	38	21
	Chi-Square = 4.52, Sig. = .21		Chi-Square = 6.78, Sig. = .34		

	Place of Birth		Language of Interview	
	% U.S.	% Non-U.S.	% Spanish	% English
Weaknesses				
Not provider	7	6	5	7
Neglects/Doesn't Listen	38	31	32	39
Not Affectionate	32	22	21	32
No Weaknesses	23	41	42	21
	Chi-Square = 3.13, Sig. = .37		Chi-Square = 4.75, Sig. = .19	

	BSRI 1—Masculine			BSRI 2—Feminine		
	% Low	% Moderate	% High	% Low	% Moderate	% High
Weaknesses						
Not provider	6	7	4	7	4	6
Neglects/Doesn't Listen	38	41	32	50	37	25
Not Affectionate	27	22	39	30	15	41
No Weaknesses	29	30	25	13	44	28
	Chi-Square = 2.31, Sig. = .88			Chi-Square = 11.11, Sig. = .08		

	MSRI 1—Traditional			MSRI 2—Tough		
	% Low	% Moderate	% High	% Low	% Moderate	% High
Weaknesses						
Not Provider	7	3	10	9	6	5
Neglects/Doesn't Listen	43	27	40	35	33	47
Not Affectionate	37	38	7	22	37	11
No Weaknesses	13	32	43	35	25	37
	Chi-Square = 14.37, Sig. = .03			Chi-Square = 5.80, Sig. = .45		

TABLE 22   Regional, Socioeconomic, Cultural, and Gender Role Differences in Strengths as Father

	Region			Education	
	% N. Cal.	% S. Cal.	% Tex.	% High School	% High School+
Strengths					
Provider	10	12	13	21	6
Listens	67	71	69	57	75
Loves Them/Spends Time	23	18	19	21	19
	Chi-Square = .35, Sig. = .99			Chi-Square = 5.56, Sig. = .06	

	Occupation		Income (Thousands of Dollars)		
	% Prof.	% Nonprof.	% Under 25	% 25–40	% 40+
Strengths					
Provider	6	16	18	11	8
Listens	75	65	59	74	73
Loves Them/Spends Time	20	19	24	14	20
	Chi-Square = 2.68, Sig. = .26		Chi-Square = 2.19, Sig. = .70		

	Place of Birth		Language of Interview	
	% U.S.	% Non-U.S.	% Spanish	% English
Strengths				
Provider	9	14	18	7
Listens	71	68	65	73
Loves Them/Spends Time	20	18	18	21
	Chi-Square = .56, Sig. = .73		Chi-Square = 2.96, Sig. = .22	

	BSRI 1—Masculine			BSRI 2—Feminine		
	% Low	% Moderate	% High	% Low	% Moderate	% High
Strengths						
Provider	16	3	9	13	4	12
Listens	74	69	69	66	74	73
Loves Them/Spends Time	10	28	22	22	22	15
	Chi-Square = 5.14, Sig. = .27			Chi-Square = 2.13, Sig. = .71		

	MSRI 1—Traditional			MSRI 2—Tough		
	% Low	% Moderate	% High	% Low	% Moderate	% High
Strengths						
Provider	6	12	14	0	15	11
Listens	71	71	68	83	61	79
Loves Them/Spends Time	24	18	18	17	24	11
	Chi-Square = 1.52, Sig. = .82			Chi-Square = 6.14, Sig. = .18		

TABLE 23   Regional, Socioeconomic, Cultural, and Gender Role Differences in Why Someone Is Considered Good Father

	Region			Education	
	% N. Cal.	% S. Cal.	% Tex.	% High School	% High School+
Why Good Father					
Provider	11	17	18	13	18
Loving/Affectionate	67	50	54	74	53
Spends Time	22	33	29	13	30
	Chi-Square = 1.46, Sig. = .83			Chi-Square = 3.31, Sig. = .19	

	Occupation		Income (Thousands of Dollars)		
	% Prof.	% Nonprof.	% Under 25	% 25–40	% 40+
Why Good Father					
Provider	19	14	25	13	18
Loving/Affectionate	60	56	75	55	58
Spends Time	21	31	0	32	24
	Chi-Square = .99, Sig. = .61		Chi-Square = 5.21, Sig. = .27		

	Place of Birth		Language of Interview	
	% U.S.	% Non-U.S.	% Spanish	% English
Why Good Father				
Provider	18	10	20	15
Loving/Affectionate	47	91	72	53
Spends Time	35	0	8	33
	Chi-Square = 12.85, Sig. = .00		Chi-Square = 5.60, Sig. = .06	

	BSRI 1—Masculine			BSRI 2—Feminine		
	% Low	% Moderate	% High	% Low	% Moderate	% High
Why Good Father						
Provider	9	7	30	7	18	22
Loving/Affectionate	73	61	44	68	59	48
Spends Time	18	32	26	25	23	30
	Chi-Square = 7.92, Sig. = .09			Chi-Square = 3.29, Sig. = .51		

	MSRI 1—Traditional			MSRI 2—Tough		
	% Low	% Moderate	% High	% Low	% Moderate	% High
Why Good Father						
Provider	17	15	17	6	16	26
Loving/Affectionate	53	63	61	65	57	58
Spends Time	30	22	22	29	27	16
	Chi-Square = .79, Sig. = .94			Chi-Square = 3.13, Sig. = .51		

Appendix B

TABLE 1   MSRI Item Responses

Mean Rank	Item	% Agree
1.	Man should help with chores and child-care	98 (4)
2.	Woman should always be faithful	95 (20)
3.	Not right for a man to get high, stoned, or wasted	91 (13)
4.	Man should always be faithful	90 (50)
5.	Woman who is not virgin is just as good wife/mother	89 (29)
6.	Women are equal to men	88 (5)
8.	Worst thing man can do is disgrace his family	87 (26)
8.	Man should put wife and kids above everything else	87 (18)
8.	Marriage is a fifty-fifty proposition with man/woman equal	87 (14)
10.5	Worst thing man can do is not take care of wife/children	86 (24)
10.5	Good man spends lots of time with wife/children	86 (23)
12.	Good for man to cry or show his emotions	84 (32)
13.5	Man who hits a woman is not really a man	83 (10)
13.5	Better to die on feet than to live on knees	83 (8)
15.	Woman should always honor and respect her man	81 (16)
16.	Man should stand up for beliefs, even if it means death	78 (1)
17.	Man's word is his most important possession	77 (9)
18.	Worst thing woman can do is disgrace her family	76 (49)
19.	Person has the right to question father's orders	75 (39)
20.	Not important for woman to be virgin when she marries	73 (25)
21.	Man's home is his castle	72 (48)
22.	Worst thing someone can do is insult your mother	71 (34)
23.	When a man gives his word, should not change his mind	70 (6)
24.	Son should always obey father, even if grown up	67 (28)
25.	Woman should always honor and obey husband	65 (22)
26.	Worst thing wife can do is embarrass him in front of friends	64 (44)
27.	Women are more sensitive and emotional than men	63 (40)
28.	Good for married woman to work	61 (19)
29.5	Better if married woman does not have to work	60 (27)
29.5	Real man has complete authority in the family	60 (3)
31.	Real man can withstand pain, hardship, and failure	59 (7)

(continues)

TABLE 1   (continued)

Mean Rank	Item	% Agree
32.	Woman should not dance without husband's permission	58 (21)
33.	Man should be able to handle all financial responsibilities of marriage	52 (41)
34.	Real woman does not need to be dependent on man	51 (2)
35.	Real woman is strong and independent	48 (47)
36.	One should defend family honor, even if it means death	44 (36)
37.	Man should wear the pants in the family	36 (46)
38.5	Most important thing father gives children is family name	35 (38)
38.5	Man should be boss, even if he can't provide for family	35 (15)
40.	The father is the more influential parent	30 (42)
41.	The mother is the head of the family	24 (45)
42.5	Wife should not question what husband does/where he goes	20 (43)
42.5	Women are more intelligent than men	18 (11)
44.5	Men should never cry or show feelings	11 (30)
44.5	Boys should be taught that men do not cry	11 (17)
46.5	Natural for man to fool around after marriage	10 (33)
46.5	Father should not kiss or be too emotional with sons	10 (37)
48.	To get respect have to be stronger and tougher	9 (12)
49.	Man should never back down from a fight	8 (35)
50.	Natural for woman to fool around after marriage	7 (31)

NOTE: Figure in parentheses is the original number of the item on the interview schedule.

About the Book and Author

Although patriarchy, machismo, and excessive masculine displays are assumed to be prevalent among Latinos in general and Mexicans in particular, little is known about Latino men or macho masculinity. *Hombres y Machos: Masculinity and Latino Culture* fills an important void by providing an integrated view of Latino men, masculinity, and fatherhood—in the process refuting many common myths and misconceptions.

Examining how Latino men view themselves, Alfredo Mirandé argues that prevailing conceptions of men, masculinity, and gender are inadequate because they are based not on universal norms but on limited and culturally specific conceptions. Findings are presented from in-depth personal interviews with Latino men (specifically, fathers with at least one child between the ages of four and eighteen living at home) from four geographical regions and from a broad cross-section of the Latino population: working and middle class, foreign-born and native-born. Topics range from views on machos and machismo to beliefs regarding masculinity and fatherhood. In addition to reporting research findings and placing them within a historical context, Mirandé draws important insights from his own life.

Hombres y Machos calls for the development of Chicano/Latino men's studies and will be a significant and provocative addition to the growing literature on gender, masculinity, and race. It will appeal to the general reader and is bound to be an important supplementary text for courses in ethnic studies, women's studies, men's studies, family studies, sociology, psychology, social work, and law.

Alfredo Mirandé is professor of sociology and ethnic studies at the University of California at Riverside. He is the author of *The Age of Crisis, La Chicana, The Chicano Experience,* and *Gringo Justice.*

Index

Printed in the United States
· 26576LVS00005B/151

9 780813 331973